# DIGITAL LIBRARIES and Information Networks

# Digital Libraries and Information Networks

Amjad Ali

Ess Ess Publications

4837/24, Ansari Road, Darya Ganj,
New Delhi-110002
✆ : 23260807, 41563444
Fax : 011-41563334
E-mail: info@essessreference.com
url:http://www.essessreference.com

**Ess Ess Publications**
4837/24, Ansari Road,
Darya Ganj,
New Delhi-110 002.

Tel.: 23260807, 41563444
Fax: 41563334
E-mail: info@essessreference.com
www.essessreference.com



Ess Ess
Rs.1375/-



**First Published - 2007**

ISBN: 81-7000-515-9 (10 Digit)
978-81-7000-515-5 (13 Digit)

Published By Ess Ess Publications and printed at Salasar Imaging Systems

PRINTED IN INDIA

# Preface

Problems related to the explosion of information during the last 60 years prepared ground for the development of digital libraries and information networks. It was, in fact, an appeal to the technology to help mankind meet its needs regarding scholarly communication. Vannevar Bush may be attributed to be the first to clearly describe the concept of digital library in 1945. Twenty years later, Licklider painted a more complete picture, identifying the needs for better distributed-processing human-computer interaction, document management and retrieval. But the real development of digital libraries *per se* only began in the early 1990s.

Digital libraries and information networks extend and integrate approaches adopted in traditional libraries and distributed information systems, to yield high-end information systems, services, and institutions. They facilitate us with a huge mass of information without any limitation of time and space and perform other vital functions also like the preservation of linguistic, literary, historical, and cultural heritage and making access to information simpler and cheaper. Such new devices support in education, especially, in the context of distance or lifelong learning. They allow rich media types to be included and managed effectively and encourage authors to create and share, and others to collaborate and quickly build on newly discovered knowledge.

In India, digital libraries are passing through the process of development in most of the cases. Only a few of them have attained the stage of maturity. My rigorous efforts in gathering details of them during the last three years could hardly fetch a list of 69 digital libraries through out the country, which include the digital library initiatives as well. Similarly, there are only a few information networks of repute though they are being built up over the last two decades.

In this volume, some popular digital libraries and information networks have been discussed in detail, which have been developed and operated internationally as well as within the country. India has developed some very reputed information networks, which are equally appreciated and utilized all over the world. Some digital libraries, which are ahead of the others, have also been discussed in detail.

I am really indebted to Mr. Sumit Sethi of Ess Ess Publications, New Delhi who gave me the idea to write this book and also arranged for its publication in a very short time after submission of the manuscript. I hope the book will be useful for the students of library and information studies.

**Dr. Amjad Ali**

# Contents


**1. International Digital Libraries** ........................ 9

1. Internet Public Library ........................ 9
2. Universal Digital Library ........................ 26
3. California Digital Library ........................ 53
4. Harvard University Digital Library ........................ 71
5. Digital Library of Georgia ........................ 90
6. Indiana University Digital Library ........................ 103
7. SMETE Digital Library ........................ 117
8. Digital South Asia Library ........................ 132
9. Digital Library of India ........................ 144
10. Vidyanidhi ........................ 159

**2. Indian Digital Libraries** ........................ 170

1. Archives of Indian Labour ........................ 170
2. Advaita Sharada Project ........................ 172
3. CSCS Media and Culture Archive ........................ 177
4. Dgital Library of Ayurvedic Medicine ........................ 180
5. Digital Library of Indian Institute of Management, Kozhikode ........................ 181
6. Digital library of Indigenous Knowledge ........................ 183
7. Digital Library of IIT, Kharagpur ........................ 185
8. Gyandoot ........................ 186
9. Indian National Digital Library in Engineering Science and Technology (INDEST) ........................ 188
10. Kalasampada ........................ 190
11. Muktabodha Digital Library and Archiving Project ........................ 193

12. Nalanda Digital Library ........ 195
13. National Resource Centre for Women ........ 197
14. Periyar University Digital Library ........ 199
15. Physical Research Laboratory Digital Initiatives ........ 202
16. TIFR Digital Library Initiative ........ 204
17. Traditional knowledge Digital Library ........ 205

**3. International Information Networks ........ 208**

1. Online Computer Library Center (OCLC) ........ 208
2. Consortium of University Research Libraries (CURL) ........ 220
3. Library Information Networks Research (RLG) ........ 232
4. International Nuclear Information System (INIS) ........ 243
5. International Federation for Information Processing (IFIP) ........ 260
6. The Pan African Development Information System [PADIS] ........ 266
7. INSPEC ........ 273
8. Information for All Programme (IFAP) ........ 287
9. IFLANET ........ 294
10. MEDLINE (Medical Literature Analysis and Retrieval System Online) ........ 304

**4. Indian Information Networks ........ 334**

1. Information and Library Network (INFLIBNET) ........ 334
2. INFONET ........ 351
3. Developing Library Network (DELNET) ........ 358
4. Calcutta Library Network (CALIBNET) ........ 370
5. Agricultural Resources Information System (AgRIS) ........ 378

*Bibliography* ........ 395

*Index* ........ *410*

# 1 International Digital Libraries

## 1. INTERNET PUBLIC LIBRARY

The Internet Public Library (IPL) was founded at the School of Information and Library Studies of the University of Michigan in 1995. The idea was twofold: (1) to ask some interesting and important questions about the interconnections of libraries, librarians, and librarianship with a distributed networked environment, and (2) to learn a lot about these issues by actually designing and building the Internet Public Library. A group of 35 students, led by Prof. Joseph Janes, began the work on the IPL. Besides the original reference center, a youth division was added to educate and familiarize young children to the IPL.

The Internet Public Library Project seeks to challenge and redefine the roles and significance of libraries in an increasingly distributed and digital world. Libraries have always been places of learning and excitement, opening new worlds of information, enlightenment and entertainment to all who enter. Libraries and the people who work in them are committed to democracy and equality of access, the dignity of their patrons, and the freedom to express and investigate all points of view.

Technologies have always permitted libraries to accomplish their aims more effectively. The rise of libraries as we know them today is due in large part to the explosion in volume and diversity of printed and recorded matter. Simultaneously, however, each new medium brings with it difficulties and change. The technologies of global internetworking present yet another set of challenges and opportunities to the library community.

**Mission Statement**

The Internet Public Library (IPL) is a public service organization and learning/teaching environment founded at the University of Michigan School of Information and hosted by Drexel University's College of Information Science & Technology. It is engaged in activities in the following areas:

1. Provide library services to Internet users. Activities include: finding, evaluating, selecting, organizing, describing, and creating information resources; and direct assistance to individuals.
2. Use a learn-by-doing approach to train information professionals and students to work in an increasingly digital environment.
3. Develop technology and best practices for providing library services via the Internet, including digital reference service and collection management.
4. Conduct research aimed at improving the services and increasing the body of knowledge about digital libraries and librarianship.
5. Promote services. Share the resources with the professional community. Participate in efforts to create and promote relevant standards. Disseminate technology and practices to others. Develop relationships with

organizations pursuing similar goals. Provide leadership in these activities.

6. Develop a model and plan for long-term sustainability and growth for organization and services.

It approaches the above activities via the values and principles of the profession of librarianship.

**Library Bill of Rights**

The American Library Association affirms that all libraries are forums for information and ideas, and that the following basic policies should guide their services.

1. Books and other library resources should be provided for the interest, information, and enlightenment of all people of the community the library serves. Materials should not be excluded because of the origin, background, or views of those contributing to their creation.
2. Libraries should provide materials and information presenting all points of view on current and historical issues. Materials should not be proscribed or removed because of partisan or doctrinal disapproval.
3. Libraries should challenge censorship in the fulfillment of their responsibility to provide information and enlightenment.
4. Libraries should cooperate with all persons and groups concerned with resisting abridgment of free expression and free access to ideas.
5. A person's right to use a library should not be denied or abridged because of origin, age, background, or views.
6. Libraries which make exhibit spaces and meeting rooms available to the public they serve should make such facilities available on an equitable basis, regardless of the

beliefs or affiliations of individuals or groups requesting their use.

## IPL Collection Policy

The collection policies of IPL are based on the following factors:

**The Role of the Internet Public Library :** The Internet Public Library is an educational, research, and service laboratory; two of its major roles are educating students at graduate schools of information and providing library services to Internet users.

As part of the Internet Public Library's service, Internet Public Library volunteers select (credential) and maintain links to web sites in the IPL's major areas of concentration:

- Arts & Humanities
- Business
- Computers
- Education
- Entertainment
- Health
- Government
- Regional
- Science & Tech
- Social Science
- Ready Reference
- Magazines
- Newspapers
- KidSpace
- TeenSpace
- Literary Criticism
- Blogs

* Associations on the Net
* Native American Authors
* POTUS (Presidents of the United States)

**Purpose of Policy**

* To guide the students in the Internet Public Library workshop courses and collection volunteers in the selection of web sites.
* To inform the public about the principles upon which selections are made.

**Definition of Selection :** "Selection" refers to the decision that must be made either to add materials or to retain materials already in the collection.

**Goal for Selection :** The IPL's goal for selection is to maintain a balanced and broadly representative collection of websites for information, reference and research.

**General Principles :** Materials to be added to the collections of the Internet Public Library are selected on the merits of a particular site in relation to the needs of the user community.

The user community for the Internet Public Library includes people of all ages, nationalities, occupations, and levels of education. The patrons' needs are the guiding factors when selecting materials.

Children's sites are not included in the general collections, rather they are in KidSpace. Sites specifically for teens are found in TeenSpace.

English is the primary language of the Internet Public Library. Its primacy does not preclude the selection of materials in foreign languages, especially in the BPI (the Spanish version of the IPL), foreign reference sources, German Ready Reference, Italian Ready Reference, newspaper, and magazine collections, but it is a guiding principle when selecting sites for inclusion in the general collections, Kidspace, and Teenspace.

**Principles for Selection :** The following principles are applied to sites under consideration for inclusion in the Internet Public Library:

- ★ Content is freely available and substantial
  - ★ No barrier for access to primary material on the site (Examples: preference is given to sites that require no registration or subscription required for access, or an online journal site must provide article content and not just citation info and abstract)
- ★ Authoritative
  - ★ Source of the material is trustworthy
  - ★ Affiliation with recognized authorities in a field
  - ★ Reputable credentials
  - ★ Background/history in providing authoritative information on a topic
  - ★ Credentials or reputation of sponsoring organization
  - ★ Other authoritative web sites also link to this site
- ★ Popularity
  - ★ Score from Alexa (http://www.alexa.com/), "linked to" in Advanced Google site or similar data may be considered
- ★ Uniqueness
  - ★ Different in features or content from sites on the same subject already in the IPL
- ★ Contact Info readily available
- ★ Reliable
  - ★ The site is available each time it's accessed
- ★ Load time is reasonable
- ★ Navigable

    - Site design is clear and features are obvious or directions are easy to follow
- Content of site seems not to be plagiarized and adheres to U.S. copyright law
- Site is updated as appropriate to the subject area
- Contains few or no interfering ads or pop-ups
- Reading level and writing style are appropriate to the general user community

The Internet Public Library does not include:

- Sites or material that violate U.S. copyright law
- Articles from journals or magazines
- Sites that are strictly commercial and have no informational content
- Sites with extremist views
- Sites whose audiences are intended to be exclusively academic
- Erotica
- Degree or course programs, university gateway pages, or homepages. Webpages from colleges or universities on specific subjects are welcome.
- Sites whose only author or publisher information is a web development company. Rarely, these sites provide rich content not found elsewhere.
- For-pay or subscription sites. The exceptions are:
    - The subscription is free
    - The site provides some free information to which the Internet Public Library has applied its criteria

The IPL generally does not include pages from sites that are themselves collections or directories. For example, the LII is included in the IPL, however sections such as LII's Literary and Books Page (http://www.lii.org/pub/topic/literature) are not. There are exceptions if a page has sufficient informative content on a topic, if the page is likely to be maintained, and if it deemed extremely likely that a user will search for that topic only and not broader categories in the host site for that page. For example, the BBC News Country profile on East Timor (http://news.bbc.co.uk/2/hi/asia-pacific/country_profiles/1508119.stm) is included as are certain pages from About.com.

The IPL does have a section for Web Directories and Search Engines, but these sites have been chosen by, or given express approval by, senior staff members.

**Specific Criteria for Selection in the Major Subject Areas**

**Arts & Humanities :** Arts & Humanities are defined as human artistic endeavors throughout the world. Those endeavors include: Fine and Graphic Arts, Literature, Language, History, Libraries, Philosophy, Religion & Theology, Culture, Classics, and Museum Studies.

**Business :** Business is defined as the realms of commerce and industry; the production, distribution, and consumption of goods and services and the management of economic systems, specifically including the following:

> Accounting, Agriculture, Banking, Business Administration & Management, Business Directories, Business & Economics News, Commerce & Trade, Consumer Issues & Services, E-Commerce, Economics, Employment, Entrepreneurship, Finance, History of Business & Economics, Industry, Insurance, International Business, Labor & Workplace, Marketing & Advertising, Non-Profit Organizations, Real Estate, Statistics, and Taxation.

**Computers :** The computers collection includes information technology, computing machines, their connections, and their capabilities. In particular it contains: Computers & Internet News, Computer Hardware, Computer Science, Computer Software, Cyberculture, History of Computers & Internet, Internet, Platforms, Programming, and System Administration.

**Education :** Education is defined as schooling and instruction, the provision of knowledge or training in a particular area or form a particular purpose. Sub-collections of the education collection include: Adult Education, Alternative Education, Early Childhood and Pre-school, Education News, English as a Second Language (ESL), Higher Education, K-12 Education, Literacy, International Education, Special Education, Teachers & Administrators, and Vocational Education.

**Entertainment :** Entertainment includes activities of amusement and diversion, specifically including the:

> Arts & Crafts, Books, Entertainment & Leisure News, Fashion, Food, Games, History of Entertainment & Leisure, Hobbies, Home & Garden, Movies, Music, Outdoor Recreation, Paranormal Phenomena, Pets, Radio, Sports, Television, Theater, and Travel & Tourism.

**Health :** The health collection covers all aspects of human and animal health and medicine. Particular areas of interest in this field include: Alcohol, Drugs & Tobacco, Alternative Medicine, Anatomy & Physiology, Consumer Information, Disabilities, Diseases, Disorders & Syndromes, Donors and Transplants, Exercise & Fitness, First Aid, General Medicine, Geriatrics, Health & Medical Sciences News, Health Care Management & Policy, History of Medicine, Injuries,

Medical Technology, Medications & Pharmaceuticals, Men's Health, Mental Health, Nursing, Nutrition & Diet, Occupational Health & Safety, Oral Health & Dentistry, Pain Treatment & Management, Pediatrics, Preventive Medicine, Professional Resources, Public Health, Sexuality, Specializations, Surgery, Veterinary Medicine, and Women's Health.

**Government, Politics, Law and Law Enforcement**

Government is defined as rules and principles governing a community and enforced by a political authority; matters having to do with the control and administration of public policy in a political unit; the study of the processes, principles, and structure of government and of political institutions. These include: Government, History of Law, Government & Political Science, Law, and Law Enforcement.

**Regional**

Regional resources are those related to, or about, a specific nation or region of the world. Place names are based on the Library of Congress's MARC Code List for Geographic Areas and/or the Getty Thesaurus of Geographic Names. The collection includes topics such as: Geography, Modern Day History, Current Events, Directories, Maps, National Libraries, and General Reference Sites That Include Country or Region Information.

**Science & Technology**

Science and technology are defined as the natural and physical sciences and their practical applications. This includes: the Science of Agriculture & Aqua Culture, Astronomy, Chemical Sciences (Chemistry), Communications, Controversial Topics in Science, Earth Sciences, Electronics, Energy, Engineering, Environmental Sciences & Ecology, History of Science & Technology, Horology (Time Measurement, Clocks, Calendars),

Life Sciences, Mathematics, Paleontology, Physics, Science and Technology Libraries, Science & Technology News, and Transportation.

**Social Science**

The social sciences are the studies of human society and of individual relationships in and to society. This includes: Anthropology, Archaeology, Social Customs, Traditions and Folklore, Education, Ethnicity, Culture and Race, Gender & Sexuality, Geography, History, History of Social Sciences, People by Age Group, Political Science, Psychology, Social Issues and Social Welfare, Social Sciences News, and Sociology.

**Ready Reference**

Ready reference includes the basic research tools such as almanacs, dictionaries and encyclopedias. The Ready Reference collection was created to assist IPL reference librarians in answering reference questions. Any site that could be useful in answering reference questions is a candidate for inclusion in this collection. These include:

Almanacs, Directories, Biographies, Calculation & Conversion Tools, Calendars, Census Data & Demographics, Dictionaries, Encyclopedias, Experts & How-To, Genealogy, Geography, Grammars, News & Current Events, Periodical Directories, Quotations, Search Engines, Style and Writing Guides, Telephone and Address, Time & Weather, Trivia, and Web Directories.

**Magazines**

The IPL Magazine Collection lists online versions of magazines, newsletters and professional journals, as well as similar publications that exist only in electronic form, such as e-zines and e-journals.

To be considered for inclusion, the online version must

include a significant number of articles or other information that are free to the general public, not just tables of contents and subscription information.

**Newspapers**

The Newspapers collection lists online newspapers that feature regular news coverage of a particular geographic area. In order to be considered for inclusion, the newspaper must offer some free, regularly updated news. Since this collection is global in scope, the newspaper does not have to be published in English to be included.

The Internet Public Library collects at least one national newspaper for every country in the world. A balanced representation is sought whenever possible. The names of geographic regions and countries are those established in the Library of Congress's MARC Code List for Geographic Areas.

The Online Newspapers collection lists online versions of print newspapers which feature regular news coverage of a particular geographic area. The collection currently includes representation from a total of 160 countries and 13 non-self-governing territories, as well as all 50 U.S. States and the District of Columbia . However, although the collection is continuously expanding, it makes no claim of being comprehensive.

Balance in Point of View. In order to be considered for inclusion, the newspaper should make an effort in its editorial stance to maintain objectivity. Objectivity is a subjective criterion, and the Internet Public Library attempts to avoid newspapers whose editorial stance is clearly in service of a specific political ideology or a partisan bias. For example, while the Washington Post is generally accepted as an objective news organization, the World Socialist Web Site (WSWS) would not fit that description and might instead be included in another category, such as Political Advocacy Groups. In some cases, such as countries where the official news agency is state-controlled, the objectivity criterion is necessarily somewhat elastic.

Reliability/Frequency. Another criterion for inclusion is reliability and frequency. In order to be considered for inclusion, the newspaper must offer at least some free, regularly updated news content (it should not be a completely subscription-contingent website), should be readily uploadable under normal Internet traffic conditions, and should be logically and easily navigable. Frequency can range from updating throughout the day, as many major newspapers do, or updating once a week or once a month, in the cases of less-frequently published newspapers. In general, if a newspaper's site has not been updated in over three months, its continued inclusion will be revisited.

Geographical Representation. As much as possible, the newspapers included in the collection should represent all regions of the world. If a newspaper falters in some of the other criteria for inclusion but helps give geographical balance, it may be included in the IPL.

In addition, the collection makes an effort to represent countries and/or territories that are in dispute, such as Cyprus and Taiwan . This policy will follow national boundaries as defined by the MARC Code List for Countries . For instance, occupied Palestine is not considered a separate "country" under this definition, but rather a subdivision of Israel .

Language Inclusivity. As the collection is global in scope, a newspaper does not have to be published in English to be included. However, if the foreign-language newspaper is published within the United States, other criteria are also considered such as the newspaper's having a WorldCat entry, its inclusion in ARL/CRL databases and the Librarians' Index to the Internet, and its size and the scope of the community that the newspaper serves.

**KidSpace**

The Internet Public Library provides children in grades 3-7 with information to further their interests as well as provide support for their educational needs. A very limited amount of information is included for preschool through grade 2. The Internet Public Library also provides materials to support parents and teachers in their work with children.

Links selected for KidSpace conform to criteria similar to the general collections, but there are some special considerations:

- ★ Sites should not contain material considered sexually explicit or that contain material which is considered harmful to minors by U.S. standards
- ★ Sites cannot contain inappropriate or confusing ads or numerous pop-up ads (i.e., ads in the center of a page that make it difficult for a child to distinguish the ad from the content)

**TeenSpace**

The Internet Public Library provides teens in grades 8-12 with information that supports their educational objectives, social needs and personal interests. TeenSpace provides current, authoritative information that is teen-friendly and toward teens.

Links selected for TeenSpace conform to the same criteria as the general collections.

**Literary Criticism**

The Internet Public Library Literary Criticism Collection contains critical and biographical websites about authors and their works.

## Blogs

Blogs soon will be or are already no longer a separate collection. They are still set off under the individual subject headings in which they appear. The Internet Public Library selectively collects blogs according to the following criteria. Sites must:

- ★ Provide news & information, not an opinion (though highly informed gossip and opinions are acceptable) or provide a glimpse into what it is like to be a doctor, lawyer, librarian, etc.
- ★ Are authored by someone well-known in his/her field or someone qualified to discuss the subject of the weblog
- ★ Provide a solid place to begin research in a particular area
- ★ Focus on a particular area, subject, occupation, hobby, etc.
  - ★ N.B. Sites can also be too specific, e.g., a blog devoted to a single American basketball team.
- ★ Have a high ranking on sites such as...
  - ★ **Technorati :** a search engine that lists the number of times a particular blog has been linked to
  - ★ **Google Link :** a service of Google that lists the number of sites, not just blogs, which link to a particular blog
  - ★ **Alexa :** a web site that gives statistics and the number of visitors to a particular blog and how that number of visitors ranks out of all websites
- ★ Have existed for at least a year (unless they are extraordinarily popular)
- ★ Have made the news in other media (print, TV, radio) because of their popularity
- ★ Received at least 1 or 2 comments per post

- ⋆ Are based on reputable sources; may be "Best of..." or "Most Popular..." websites or weblogs
- ⋆ Frequently mentioned or linked to from other blogs

**Associations on the Net**

This collection includes the official sites of various professional and trade associations, cultural and art organizations, political parties and advocacy groups, labor unions, and academic societies. National and international associations, as opposed to local chapters, are selected. Sites must offer more than just information on how to join or an address; rather sites should use the web environment to disseminate information.

Directories or sites that charge a fee are not included.

**Native American Authors**

Sites in this special collection provide information on Native North American authors with bibliographies of their published works, biographical information, and links to online resources including interviews, online texts, and tribal websites.

**Articles, Excerpts, Parts of Larger Works :** The database contains articles from scholarly journals that have not been indexed in commonly-available academic journal indexes. Articles that appear as book chapters are also included. Newspaper articles are excluded.

**Tribal Affiliation :** The tribal authority for this database is the Tribal Leaders Directory (http://www.doi.gov/leaders.pdf, 2006) produced by the U.S. Department of the Interior, a list of 562 federally-recognized American Indian Tribes and Alaska Natives and all the Regions, Agencies, and Offices within the Bureau of Indian Affairs.

**POTUS**

POTUS (Presidents of the United States) is a representative site about the American Presidency including biographies, speeches and writings, election results, odd facts and Presidency highlights. This site is owned and maintained by an IPL alumnus and is updated periodically by its owner and by IPL staff.

**Link Checking**

Links are generally checked and updated by students each Fall and Winter academic term. Individual students may also be assigned certain subject headings in which links are checked individually. Replacement sites are based upon the same selection principles. Senior staff may fix a smaller number of broken links throughout the year as they are reported by clients.

**User Suggestions**

User suggestions are generally evaluated by students during the academic year and added as appropriate within the IPL Collection Policy. Senior staff add some sites throughout the year and submit others as new site suggestions via the IPL's contact form.

**Current Projects**

**Accessibility :** The IPL is working with Mike Elledge, a Usability Consultant at the University of Michigan, to make all parts of our site accessible to users with disabilities.

**Blogs Collection :** New IPL blogs collection helps users navigate the blogosphere, offering general information about blogs, links to blogs on a variety of subjects, and even includes our own blog about blogs!

***Science Reference and Resources***

In response to the popularity of science resources on the site and the large number of science-related questions asked by IPL users, a group of students and staff are investigating how to improve resources and reference service in this area. The group is examining best practices for science education in libraries and other fields, science questions sent to our reference service, and the availability of science information on the Internet.

### *Redesign and Expansion*

A project is underway to update the TeenSpace section of our site. The changes, developed in consultation with Ann Arbor teens, will include a redesigned interface, additional content, and new ways for teens to engage with the IPL.

### *Congressional Research Service Report Collection*

Reports created at the request of Congress members are being collected from various sources so that they can be preserved and made available to the general public.

### *Ask-A-Question Service*

When the IPL began, online reference was a new concept. Over 50,000 questions later, it learned a lot! to continue to attract new participants and develop new policies to help serve users.

## 2. UNIVERSAL DIGITAL LIBRARY

Universal Digital Library is a project proposal under the Indo-US Science and Technology Collaboration initiatives. It is intended to develop a digital library containing on million books and to make the same available for the mankind on the World Wide Web.

The aim of the project is to digitize around a million books in the next three years. This joint initiative is planned to synergetically capitalize on the availability of the state-of-the-art of hardware and software in the US for digitizing, storing and accessing of information and the quality manpower available in India. This would act as a forerunner for many such initiatives with other countries, particularly in China and Korea and would culminate in the grandiose vision of digitizing all the formal knowledge and make available in a location and time independent way for the benefit of the mankind.

Today's scanning technology offers the possibility of digitizing an entire book in two hours. In order to take million books to the web, it is estimated that around 1000 man years would be needed. If the project is carried out in a developed country like the United States of America, it would cost at least around 40M $ besides the cost of the hardware, space and energy. It is economically feasible to try this out in developing nations like India.

As part of this project, it is planned to create 10 centres across India that would be commissioned to run three shifts with a work force of 40 in each centre. This would be adequate to meet the manpower demand of 1000 man years in 3 years. Each centre would then require around 15 scanning stations (Total 150 Scanning Stations). The cost of each scanning station including its maintenance over the three years period would be approximately US $ 30,000. Thus with a hardware and software cost of 5M $, over the three years period, it looks plausible to think in terms of the Universal Digital Library that will hold at least a million books.

It is proposed that the hardware and software costs are met from the US side while the manpower needs are met by the Indian side.

## Vision

For the first time in history, all the significant literary, artistic, and scientific works of mankind can be digitally preserved and made freely available, in every corner of the world, for our education, study, and appreciation and that of all our future generations.

Up until now, the transmission of our cultural heritage has depended on limited numbers of copies in fragile media. The fires of Alexandria irrevocably severed our access to any of the works of the ancients. In a thousand years, only a few of the paper documents we have today will survive the ravages of deterioration, loss, and outright destruction. With no more than 10 million unique book and document editions before the year 1900, and perhaps 100 million since the beginning of recorded history, the task of preservation is much larger. With new digital technology, though, this task is within the reach of a single concerted effort for the public good, and this effort can be distributed to libraries, museums, and other groups in all countries.

Existing archives of paper have many shortcomings. Many other works still in existence today are rare, and only accessible to a small population of scholars and collectors at specific geographic locations. A single wanton act of destruction can destroy an entire line of heritage. Furthermore, contrary to the popular beliefs, the libraries, museums, and publishers do not routinely maintain broadly comprehensive archives of the considered works of man. No one can afford to do this, unless the archive is digital.

Digital technology can make the works of man permanently accessible to the billions of people all over the world. Andrew Carnegie and other great philanthropists in past centuries have recognized the great potential of public libraries to improve the quality of life and provide opportunity the citizenry. A universal digital library, widely available through free access on the Internet, will improve the global society in ways beyond measurement. The Internet can house a Universal Library that is free to the people.

### Mission

The mission is to create a Universal Library which will foster creativity and free access to all human knowledge. As a first step in realizing this mission, it is proposed to create the

Universal Library with a free-to-read, searchable collection of one million books, primarily in the English language, available to everyone over the Internet. Within 10 years, it is expected that the collection will grow to 10 Million books. The result will be a unique resource accessible to anyone in the world 24 × 7, without regard to nationality or socioeconomic background.

The first major project of Universal Library is the Million Book Digital Library project. Typical large high-school libraries house fewer than 30,000 volumes. Most libraries in the world have less than a million volumes. The total number of different titles indexed in OCLC's WorldCat is about 48 million. One million books, therefore, is more than the holdings of most high-schools, and is equivalent to the libraries at many universities and represents a useful fraction of all available books.

One of the goals of the Universal Library is to provide support for full text indexing and searching based on OCR (optical character recognition) technologies where available. The availability of online search allows users to locate relevant information quickly and reliably thus enhancing student's success in their research endeavors. This 24x7 rescurce would also provide an excellent testbed for language processing research in areas such as machine translation, summarization, intelligent indexing, and information retrieval.

The Universal Library will be mirrored at several locations worldwide so as to protect the integrity and availability of the data. Several models for sustainability are being explored. Usability studies would also be conducted to ensure that the materials are easy to locate, navigate, and use. Appropriate metadata for navigation and management would also be created.

The primary long-term objective is to capture all books

in digital format. It is believed that such a task is impossible and could take hundreds of years, and never be completed. Thus, as a first step it is planned to demonstrate the feasibility by undertaking to digitize 1 million books (less than 1% of all books in all languages ever published) by 2005. Such a project has the potential to change how education is conducted in much of the world.

A secondary objective of this project will be to provide a test bed that will support other researchers who are working on improved scanning techniques, improved optical character recognition, and improved indexing. The corpus this project creates will be one to three orders of magnitude larger than any existing free resource.

## Copyright Laws

Currently, the copyright laws do not permit books published in the last 50 years in India and 100 years in the US to be digitized and distributed free. These laws are based on the earlier era wherein the life cycle of Information products was large. Currently, obsolescence is the common thing in science and technology and in many areas the obsolescence rate is so rapid that the life cycle of Information products such as books is reduced to a few years. There is a world wide awareness of this and WIPO is seriously directing its efforts towards this issue. Indo-US team could generate critical inputs to shape the copyright laws world over in general and in India and the USA in particular, that would be in tune with the aspirations of the Digital Economy. This would also ensure that the copyright laws protect the interest of the creator and consumer of information and still make economic sense.

Further, it is proposed that most of the books, in the 'million books to the web' project would come from the United States. After scanning, modality could be worked out by which the books may be retained in the respective retained Centres. The latter may be justified by the fact that the cost of the transportation back to the US after digitizing may be high.

## Research and Development

Several attendant technologies are to be developed besides the hardware and software and the identification of books for scanning in order to ensure that the books of Indian Origin are included dominantly in the digitization. First is the research and development needed to ensure that an error free character recognizer in Indian Languages is made available to the centres. Further, an appropriate software to identify various fonts and the title, heading etc and to create meta files that can be used for accessing the information has to be perfected. Most of the Indian knowledge particularly in Sanskrit etc may not be available in printed form at all and even if unavailable, the quality of the paper and the background may not be suitable for feeder based scanner and character recognizer. In such cases, appropriate speech technologies to convert speech to text in Indian Languages and / or photographic scanner technologies may have to be developed.

The technology development described above would also form the focus of the R&D efforts proposed under the Indo-US collaboration. On the Indian side, the Indian Institute of Science, Bangalore would act as a nodal agency to coordinate amongst various academic institutions and governmental agencies from the Indian side. The Carnegie Mellon University would play the same role from the US side.

## Technical Details

### *1. Database creation*

Creating a scalable database to support the Universal Library is one of the desired objectives. The resulting globally distributed database will appear to be a virtual central database from any place around the world. Mirroring the database in several countries will also ensure security and availability. The database will house both an image file and a text file at about 50-60 megabytes per book. A 100 terabytes of online storage currently costs around $150,000 and is expected to be under $5000 by year 2005 and thus making it possible to mirror the site in many countries.

### *2. Scanning*

Earlier in the project, the scanner of choice was an inexpensive duplex scanner that required the books to be disbound so that the pages could be fed through in batches. While the economy and speed of this technique were most attractive, several technical problems occurred. The pages had to be cut on all four edges for smooth feeding. The project required the purchase of a $10,000 guillotine to accomplish this. The guillotine was somewhat dangerous, required in-depth training in use and safety, slowed the process, and nullified the economy of the inexpensive scanner.

Dust, an inevitable accompaniment to older books, proved to be a formidable opponent. Dust caused frequent jamming and subsequent cleaning of the scanner. Paper fixatives were employed to counteract the dust. Spraying on the fixative slowed the project and was not entirely satisfactory.

Currently, the Universal Library project uses a Minolta PS7000 overhead scanner, which is potentially able to scan 10000 pages operating on a 3-shift basis. Although this scanner was 5 times more expensive than the conventional roll-fed double sided scanner we used earlier, it proved to be more reliable. Books did not have to be disbound. The image processing software for curvature correction, deskewing, despeckling and cropping allows for thick books to be scanned either flat or in an angled cradle that reduces wear on the spine. Careful training is required to operate the scanner, and several different employees were successfully trained in our pilot experiment.

In summary, the advantages of the Minolta scanner were:

★ Disbinding via a guillotine is not necessary.

★ Books can be reused in their original form.

★ Dust, thick paper, and long books can be easily accommodated.

★ Training requirements are reasonable.

★ Equipment is reliable

### 3. Data Production

The current approach for document scanning is to digitize the documents at the archival quality of 600 dots per inch (dpi) as a binary image (1 bit per pixel). The resulting images are stored as TIFF (Tagged Image File Format) files. (TIFF version 5.0 is acceptable. Subject to testing, version 6.0 (or later) may also be acceptable). The resolution of the images is high enough so as to permit reading of the the original pages directly on a computer screen.

### 4. Optical Character Recognition (OCR)

We do not plan to correct the OCR output as part of this project. The primary function of OCR is to allow searching inside the text. Unlike in other efforts, the output of the OCR text will not be used for direct viewing by the public. It will only be used for creating a searchable index (where errors tend to have limited impact).

Because words are often repeated, the 98% success rate will allow students and scholars to find relevant passage. In the pilot projects, the OCR program Abby Fine Reader was run after the scanning was completed.

Chinese and Japanese OCR programs are also available and will be used whenever needed. This project has also stimulated efforts towards the development of OCRs in Indian Languages. Providing a testbed that will allow for the creation of even better OCR programs is one of the goals of this project. Scholars will be able to run newer OCR programs over the scans and possibly correct the output manually.

### *5. Metadata*

Digital Library Federation standards and metadata best practices will be used throughout this project. Bibliographic metadata for the pilot project will be derived from existing library catalog records. Carnegie Mellon libraries developed software that uses the standard Z39.50 protocol to search and retrieve relevant metadata from catalog records fields. Thus, author, title, and publication data do not have to be rekeyed.

Entering metadata information manually is time-consuming. One of the current research projects is the creation of software for "automatic discovery of document structure". This will permit users to create hyperlinks which are not present in the original printed version of the book and navigate through the chapters.

Administrative metadata supports the maintenance and archiving of the paper or digital objects and ensures their long-term availability by providing information about how the files were created and stored. Administrative metadata will be maintained internally as file descriptions in the project databases and externally as part of the copyright permission database.

The Digital Library Federation, a supporter of this project, has several initiatives underway that will allow commercial browsers to harvest metadata more aggressively. The results of DLF's metadata harvesting project will be explored for possible application to the resources produced in this project (www.diglib.org).

### 6. Quality control

The standards established for quality control are those currently endorsed by the Digital Library Federation, whose missions include the establishment of best practices and the development of standards. The project must maintain a 98% accuracy rate for the quality of images and the inclusion of all pages.

The process of scanning a book involves finding a library that owns the book, pulling the book, transporting the book to the scanning site, scan the pages, and returning the book to the original library. This process will be expensive. Maintaining high quality the first time the book is scanned will be essential. A demonstration of high quality, reliable work done on materials currently in China and India will give U.S. libraries confidence that their collections should be shared.

## Benefits

The principal benefit of the Universal Library will be to supplement the formal education system by making knowledge available to anyone who can read and has access. Libraries have played a vital role in the advancement of human society. Societal advance depends on young people having access to books via libraries and other means. Making this unique web resource available free to everyone around the world will enhance the learning process.

Libraries are unevenly distributed around the world and within each country. In the U.S., the NCES Survey noted that in 1996, 3,408 of 3,792 institutions of higher education had libraries holding 806.7 million volumes. The 112 largest university libraries in the United States and Canada each have at least 1.8 million books. They are members of the Association for Research Libraries. Massachusetts has about 25 million volumes; New York has about 31 million volumes, and California has about 40 million volumes in their ARL Libraries (Association for Research Libraries, 1999/2000). Other states, such as North and South Dakota, have no large libraries. A few large public libraries have several million volumes. However, most junior colleges, high schools, and public libraries have much smaller collections. Making this large knowledge repository can revolutionize research at all levels of education and give a much-needed boost at minimal cost to our national educational infrastructure. This impact will be further enhanced given the convenience of online access, and the benefit of full text searching at word and phrase levels.

A secondary benefit of online search is to make locating the relevant information inside of books far more reliable and much easier. Student success in finding exactly what they seek will increase and increased success will enhance student willingness to perform research using this large resource. NCES reports that 84 percent of libraries around the country are open between 60 and 80 hours a week. This digital library would be open all the 168 hours the week on a 24x7x365 basis. More than one individual will be able to use the same book at the same time. Thus, popular works will not be checked out and thus unavailable to others.

This million-book project will produce an extensive and rich testbed for use in further textual language processing research. It is hoped that at least 10,000 books among the million will be available in more than one language, providing a unique resource for example based machine translation.

Many believe that information is now doubling every two years. Machine summarization, intelligent indexing, and information mining are tools that will be needed for individuals to keep up in their discipline work, in their businesses, and in their personal interests. This large digitization project will enable extensive research in these areas.

## Philosophy of Content Selection

The Million Book Project envisages to develop a collection of one million digital books by adopting a staged approach as described below. The Million Book project will adhere to the U.S. copyright law.

U.S. collections will primarily include the following types of materials:

### *1. Coordination of Selection*

Creating one digital copy and mirroring it in different locations will suffice, and will support the multiple uses at any time. Preliminary discussions with OCLC as a host for a registry of scanned items are underway. Certain key projects, such as the Making of America project, are already represented in the OCLC database as digital books. Other large digitization projects may require some data entry of their content in order to avoid duplication.

### *2. Non-copyrighted materials*

Materials published before 1920 are in the public domain and may be scanned for this project. Several large academic libraries are considering shipping materials from their repositories of little used books to India or China. These books will be scanned there and then returned to where they came from. To reduce the costs of selection, the project will probably develop a strategy of selecting key topics and then removing large runs of books and journals from a selected repository. Having a reasonable turn-around time will be essential to the success of the project. A strategy has been devised to understand the logistics of shipping the materials and the impact of their absence from the home library.

The 1909 copyright law granted copyright for 28 years. Rights holders could then renew the copyright for another 28 years; many publishers and authors did not exercise that renewal option. Thus, some books published after 1922 (56 years prior to the 1978 effective date of the 1976 act) may be out of copyright. In order to provide for the efficient checking of status of these books, the copyright renewal records for books for these years have been scanned and made available online at www.ulib.org. Similar records for other formats, such as serials and audiovisual material, will also be made available as a part of this resource.

Government documents are also in the public domain and may be included in this project. Many participating libraries are repositories for full runs of government documents and could supply them to the project, as could the Library of Congress. The inclusion of these documents will allow for more recent material to enter the project legally and to become available to a broader audience and in a more accessible manner. Many government documents are currently available in digital form. The creation of these back files would enhance those resources.

The Chinese delegation is most eager to have technical reports and science and technology dissertations as a part of this project. Scholars and universities producing these scientific material have copyright interests in them. Gaining university permission might be fairly straightforward. A good-faith attempt would also have to be made to obtain the permission of the scholars. That could be a part of an externally funded copyright clearance project, but no pilot-study has been made to allow for an estimate of contact rate and subsequent success. If some arrangement could be made with University Microfilms to scan dissertations of selected universities from microfilm, which would be cheaper and easier to transport, such an initiative might satisfy a strong desire among all participants to increase science content.

### 3. Copyrighted materials

The 1998 Copyright law grants copyright to authors for their lifetimes plus 70 years or for 95 years. Patent law, by contrast, gives 20 years. A.W. Mellon's JSTOR project developed the concept of a moving wall that allowed the inclusion of materials over five years old. Journal publishers generally agreed that the economic value of that material was greatly reduced and granted permission for its inclusion in this most successful project. A similar broad publisher agreement about the point at which economic value of a print book declines is greatly needed. Books often go out of print in two or three years but remain in copyright and thus be unavailable for over 90 years.

Dr. Raj Reddy and Dr. Peter Shane, Director of the Institute for the Study of Information, Technology and Society recently had a conversation with a major book publishers to explore the possibility of taking a broad publisher approach to receiving copyright permissions. Certain publishers, including the National Academy Press, have had the experience that when they digitized their books, sales increased because attention was focused on the material and the users were not yet ready to read the books online. Authors' guilds will also be contacted to see if they would be interested in granting permissions.

Three conditions seem to be necessary to attract publishers to the scanning of their out of print but in copyright titles:

* Publisher should receive a tax deduction for contributing the title to this project. The tax deduction might reflect

revenues previously generated by the title.

* When a print on demand feature becomes a part of this project, publishers should collect royalties on books printed.
* If a book were to return to general popularity, as the effect of the movie Titanic had on the sales of out of print titles, the publisher should be able to withdraw the permission for a fee. The publisher might be expected to reimburse the project for the costs of digitizing the title and maintaining it online.

Dr. Michael Shamos, a Director of Carnegie Mellon's Universal Library project and an intellectual property attorney, recommends the following approach to copyright clearance: The million book project will make a good faith effort to clear copyright on appropriate materials by sending the publisher of record a letter asking for permission. Replies will be recorded in the administrative metadata. If the publisher has returned the rights to the author, the author will be contacted. Subsequent copyright holders will be contacted as needed.

### *4. Best books approach*

The project will seek publisher permission to scan books from Books for College Libraries (BCL), one source for core academic books in English. A previous study done at Carnegie Mellon University Libraries indicates that 22% of publishers granted permission for scanning and mounting on the web. The materials in the study were a random sample of Carnegie Mellon Libraries' books and included a broad range of dates, publishers, and in and out of print status.. Numerous difficulties from out of business publishers, lack of publisher records, return of copyright to authors, and other circumstances were identified. Subsequently, Carol Hughes, the collections development officer for Questia, corroborated Carnegie Mellon's experience.

OCLC owns a database of books from the latest edition of Books for College Libraries. BCL contains about 50,000 titles. A 22% success rate in clearing copyright would result in 10,000 of the best books for college students being included in the project. Clearing copyright is labor intensive and expensive. Bradd Burningham's recent article estimated those costs ("Copyright Permissions" in Journal of Interlibrary Loan, Document Delivery, and Information Supply, 11:2 (2000), 95-111). The BCL database, however, will allow for sorting by publisher so that permission requests can contain the names of several books. A quick sample indicates that as many as 25,000 publishers may be represented there. Despite the expense, this commitment to quality should be attempted. Carnegie Mellon University Libraries will seek private foundation funding to undertake this project.

Publishers increasingly see that digital presentation of their works can attract buyers. They are interested in exploring ways in which their out of print titles may be returned to profitability. Continued work with publishers through the course of this project may attract many of them to it. That would be most beneficial in enriching the content to be made available.

## Current Status

Now we will describe activities used to establish protocols, to select standards to be used, and to address issues of indexing and retrieval. Workflow and training programs to support the larger project are being developed. Both the content and the mechanisms for using it will be made available in open source code.

One of the key activities has been to work with libraries within United States who will participate in providing content for scanning for the Universal Library. Members of the U.S. Digital Library Federation met on November 15 and 16, 2001 to work out the logistics of selecting and transporting materials from U.S. collections. Participants included the executive director of DLF, representatives of the NSF, OCLC, the Center for Research Libraries, collection development officers, and other librarians from the Library of Congress, the University of Washington, the University of California Berkeley, Stanford University, University of Illinois, University of Chicago, Penn State University, and the University of Pittsburgh.

The collection development librarians discussed:

* Collection focus to achieve a consensus on how to select the million books to be digitized.
* Involvement of outside scholars in selection issues to consider how non-librarian scholars might participate in selection.
* Copyright considerations to consider seeking permission for a set of in copyright "best books", such as those in Books for College Libraries.
* Standards for the work to review the current Digital Library Federation standards with a view to rapid adoption.
* Registry issues to move forward with OCLC in establishing a registry for books selected.
* Methods of transport to consider alternative means of transport and return.
* Timing to weigh the advantages of air containers and sea containers.
* Level of participation to determine minimum levels for contributors to the project.
* Incentives for participation to establish means of

recognition for contributions through screen display and copies of the archives.

The outcome of this meeting was a plan for the selection and transmission of almost a million books to China and India over a multi-year period and a plan for assessing the success of the project annually.

The National Science Foundation's 2000 ITR grant cycle provided $500,000 for equipment to begin a Million Book pilot project. That grant will allow the purchase of 18 Minolta scanners to be located in India and China. These scanners have already been deployed to begin the scanning process. Additional scanners from other donors have permitted increase in the number of scanners deployed in India and China.

## Participation of China

In August of 2001, the Chinese University Presidents, a Ministry of Education officials, and Chinese Academy of Sciences leaders visited the U.S. to reach agreements and to form a steering committee. Dr. Michael Lesk and Dr. Stephen Griffin from NSF attended this meeting and also hosted the Chinese delegation at the National Science Foundation. Professor Pan Yunhe, President of Zhejiang University; Dr. Gao Wen, Deputy President of the Graduate School, Chinese Academy of Science; Professor Chi Huisheng, Vice President of Beijing University; Professor Hu Dongcheng, Vice President of Tsinghua University; Professor Xu Zhong, Vice President of Fudan University; Professor, Zhang Yibin, Assistant to the President, Nanjing University; Mr. Guo Xinli, Vice General Director, Ministry of Education of China; Mr. Chen Jianping, Vice Director, State Planning Commission of China; and Dr. Ching-Chih Chen of Simmons College attended.

## Indian Contribution

A delegation from India visited US in May of 2002. This

includes officials from from the Central and State Governments in India, Presidents of Universities and leading academicians. The Indian team included Prof MGK Menon, Chairman, Council of IIIT-A and IIT-B, Mr Yashwant Bhave, Jt Secretary, Ministry of Communication and Information Technology, Dr. IV Subbarao, Secretary Education, Government of Andhra Pradesh, Dr P. Krishniah, Executive Officer of TTD, and Mr Ajay Sawhney, Special Secretary for IT, Government of Andhra Pradesh, Dr Om Vikas, Senior Director, and Dr Chaturvedi, Director, of the Ministry of Communication and Information Technlogy, Government of India, Mr Surendra Bagde, Joint CEO MIDC, Mumbai. Dr. N. Balakrishnan, Chairman of the Division of Information Sciences, Indian Institute of Science, Prof Ashok Kolaskar, Vice Chancellor, Pune University, Dr MD Tiwary, Director, IIITA, Dr. Thangraj, Principal, AKCE, Mr Shreedhar, Secretary, AKCE, Dr Vaidhyasubramanian, Dean, SASTRA, representing the academia.

The meeting at CMU reviewed the current status of the work in India and created plans for the Million Book project in India, including technological challenges, legal and copy right issues, selection of books, meta data standards, search engines and server management. It was concluded that one of the Central Government agencies will take ownership of the Million Book Initiative in India, and will form a consortium that will give large impetus to the Indian efforts in a coordinated way.

## Logistic Challenges

Accessing, scanning and webhosting of a million books is a major logistical challenge. A million books can be expected to be about 300 to 500 million pages. Throughput of each Minolta PS7000 scanner is about 6,000 to 10,000 pages per day based on three-shift operation. Using a 100 scanners, and about a

1000 person workforce, we can expect to complete the task of scanning a million books in 500 working days, or roughly two years of three shift operation. Given the uncertainities of quality of workers, equipment failures and power failures, we anticipate the scanning to be completed in less than four year time frame. This website will provide a graphic visualization of the progress after full speed of operation.

**Movement of books from U.S. to India and China**

India and China have large academic libraries and will contain much of the material to be included as part of the Million Book project. Over 700 of these libraries are OCLC members whose holdings can be easily ascertained. Because the scanning centers can be established anywhere, It is planned to establish them close to the libraries so that the books can be transported with minimal difficulty. It may be feasible to locate some of the scanning centers within the academic libraries, space permitting.

The task of shipping materials from the U.S. to China and India has been examined. The current plan is to primarily use air containers rather than shipping containers so as to reduce the damage to books and time of absence of the books from their owning libraries.

The books can be packed at originating libraries in small vendor boxes. It may be desirable to shrink wrap the books to ensure their intact arrival. The basic cost of shipping per book is expected to be about one to two dollars per book. Some libraries may select some materials that do not need to be returned because they are in the process of being discarded, but the default will be that materials will return to their originating libraries.

The Center for Research Libraries is willing to supply some of its own books to the project. It might also serve as a collection place towards the end of the project when the quantity of material to be shipped falls below the whole container level.

### Future Sustainability

Sustainability is a long-term issue for this project; further research will be done on developing economic models to support this major contribution to education. Partial answers to this significant challenge are discussed below. Three establishments have potential for offering a sustainable model for this project—the Library of Congress and similar national libraries, OCLC, and other commercial concerns.

The million-book project will be a public good and as such must have a suitable repository that will continue to make it available to the public at no charge. That responsibility belongs most clearly to the national library in each country. Having a network of national libraries mirroring the resource around the world would be an appropriate and desired outcome.

### Library of Congress

In the United States, the Library of Congress whould be the natural choice to act as the repository of all knowledge, because the national interest is so clearly served. However, the Library of Congress is not the national library of the United States, although many people assume that it is. In the LOC's own words in its mission statement: "THE FIRST PRIORITY of the Library of Congress is to make knowledge and creativity available to the United States Congress." It is only a lesser goal to make knowledge available to the public, and that is why the million-book project had to be undertaken outside of the scope of LOC. LOC is also the guardian of the copyright office and is apparently unwilling and/or unable to digitize anything to which there might be a copyright claim.

In 2001, Congress appropriated 100 million dollars for Digital Preservation, contingent on LOC's raising of $75 million in matching resources. The law allows the acceptance of gifts in kind as a part of the matching funding. The possibility of pledging the million-book project to LOC as matching funding for the Digital Preservation initiative is being explored. Even if the value of the project were only assessed on its inputs (equipment and labor), the Million Book project represents a significant investment.

## OCLC

Another alternative might be for OCLC to maintain a free version of the resource. OCLC is a non-profit organization whose member libraries are committed to enhancing access to information. OCLC might cover its costs by charging member libraries a small fee when the million-book project is accessed through the 48 million-title database. For the millions of OCLC users, that convenience would be worth a small payment in an already existing fee relationship. OCLC's recent strategic planning initiatives identified the addition of more full text to the database, exploring archiving responsibilities, and becoming more international as important thrusts. OCLC would also be able to cover partial costs through some of the strategies listed below for publishers.

## Commercial alternatives

The marketplace for electronic books is chaotic at this moment. Questia, designed to be an online source with at least 50,000 of the best books with sophisticated software to support searching and the creation of footnotes, marketed itself directly to students at a $20-30 monthly fee. Although the project was well capitalized and attracted a great deal of media attention, its operations have been significantly scaled back over the past year. Librarians have long observed that charging for resources in the academic environment reduces use. Students' desire for the convenience of online information sends them to the web and to the much-used electronic resources of their own libraries. That love of convenience apparently does not extend to purchasing Questia under current pricing models.

During the same period, the company netLibrary has announced that it will provide new full textbooks online. NetLibrary marketed itself to libraries through consortia. Use of materials, thus, was at no direct cost to students and faculty. While students appreciated the convenience of being able to use the resource online, they had many complaints about its functionality—in particular they resented the fact that books could only be printed one page at a time and that books were unavailable if another individual were using them. The economic models behind netLibrary charges also seemed to reflect an adherence to those of paper books rather than recognizing the economies of digital materials. The assets of netLibrary have since been sold to OCLC.

At this time, the marketplace responses suggest that turning the million book project into a private, revenue-generating source would not offer a sustainable model. JSTOR, Project Muse, and other digital journal projects that offer online materials with superior functionality and sustainability continue to flourish.

**Publishers**

Another commercial alternative might revolve around relationships with publishers. As publishers find that making the book available increases sales, they might be willing to support the project. The Universal Library website would support "buy" buttons, in return for a small share of the revenues from print-on-demand sales of out of print materials.

## Funding Sources

Funding for the Million Book Project is coming from multiple sources. National Science Foundation is providing funding for equipment, India and China are providing manpower resources for scanning, indexing and hosting, and various companies and foundations are providing partial support.

National Science Foundation is providing funding for Scanners, Computers, Servers, and Software. These resources from NSF are augmented by China and India who are providing the manpower, about 2,000 man years of effort each, over a five year period, as their contribution to this project. This represents a twenty-to-one relative contribution by China and India to this project. They will assist in the selection of documents, software development and in digitizing of the books. English language materials already resident in those countries would be scanned first, before books are shipped from the United States. Chinese and Indian language based books would also be scanned where such material is available free of copyright restrictions. U.S. libraries, primarily members of the Digital Library Federation, would ship materials as needed, to be scanned and returned.

## Donations

Activities such as selection and acquisition of books, packing and shipping costs, and quality assurance of the content are unfunded, and would greatly benefit from your support.

## The Knowledge Conservancy

The Knowledge Conservancy is being created as a complement to the Universal Library Project. It is expected to help in the following ways:

★ Accepting undirected and directed gifts to digitize and make freely accessible the works of man. This includes gifts that guarantee specified numbers of books or specified collections under the rule that access is free to the people.

- ★ Funding the digitization of works and the ongoing upgrading of the digital works to the public. This funding can be directed to ongoing or new digitization projects. In addition, the funding will support one central master registry site that other sites will mirror.
- ★ Promoting awareness of these digital works, and their importance, to the public at large.
- ★ Selection and digitization of works may be at the discretion of the Conservancy, the projects it funds, or its donors.
- ★ For example, a donor might contribute money specifically for digitizing works in a particular subject area. Selection of works might also be made from lists drawn up by scholars, requests over the Internet, and books donated to the Conservancy.
- ★ Coordinating the efforts of digitization efforts. The Knowledge conservancy maintains a database to keep track of all book editions, music editions, art, and motion pictures that have been digitized and whether they have free access. This includes the capabilities to
- ★ determine through its catalog whether access to a known document is already available,
- ★ claim to be digitizing a document within a certain time period,
- ★ reference a document with a hyperlink that does not 'go bad,'
- ★ reference the content of a document based on accepted practice in document tagging, and

★ allow machine interpretation of copyright restrictions and other restrictions on access and use.

## Supporting Knowledge Conservancy

The Knowledge Conservancy seeks donations and support from people and organizations wishing to help make the cultural treasures of the world available to all.

## Rationale for the creation of Knowledge Conservancy

The mission of the Knowledge Conservancy is the preservation of the world's cultural, historical, and scientific works, and their free access to the world over the Internet. Many projects are already underway to put works on-line for general reading, including projects like American Memory, Project Gutenberg, and the Universal Library. While these projects are making some headway at preserving the world's cultural heritage, they still face major obstacles:

★ Digitization efforts are widespread but relatively small and too often associated with restricted access. Collection owners are not motivated to provide free access often through ignorance about available techniques for recovering costs.

★ Funding for the digitization of information — and for its ongoing preservation, maintenance, and delivery, once digitized — is less than needed to make a large-scale digital library of millions of items available to the global public.

★ There is no global organizations seeking only to provide coordination of digitization efforts, sharing of limited resources, and global public awareness.

★ A large portion of the world's cultural heritage is copyrighted. Thus far, projects have largely avoided using copyrighted material, because of the difficulty of acquiring rights. Many works risk being lost in obscurity long before the copyright expires. The result is that important bodies of work may be unavailable in widely accessible for for a long time, and possibly forever.

The Knowledge Conservancy promotes the widespread duplication of digital collections at many sites, to increase accessibility and minimize the risk of single-point failure.

Conservancy policy is that a digital copyright may be retained by the collection owner but the conservancy will have a perpetual right to provide free viewing access to the material through its universal library. Furthermore, free viewing access will be automatically and perpetually granted to any site that agrees to the conditions of copyright and agrees to solely bear the cost of the mirroring. The copyright owner will always have a right to a link defined on any of his pages viewed, as will the Knowledge Conservancy.

The Knowledge Conservancy will actively support and endorse, but will not fund, money making activities around the material that is free to read. Examples include ordering copies of a book or manuscript, paying to print, paying for high fidelity access, ordering CD or DVD ROMs, ebook editions, selling supplementary materials, searching tools, indexing tools, multilingual tools, and portals that provide new media presentations of the material.

The Knowledge Conservancy will fund (a) digitizing a work and (b) providing metadata about a work including cataloging metadata, metadata about the structure of the content inside the work (e.g., chapters, stanzas, link maps for images), metadata that controls copyrights, and full text (symbolic) conversion. It will not fund, but will strongly endorse and otherwise support, interpretative efforts.

The conservancy is not a standards making organization,

but will provide online cross-disciplinary support and assistance in order to improve quality in digitization, free-to-read presentations, and long-term preservation and migration of digital works. The conservancy may charge fees for this support or provide referrals to organizations that charge fees for such support.

### Copyright Disclaimer

All the books available at the Universal Library are either out of copyright or permission to scan has been granted. If this is incorrect the offending content will be removed on receiving information from the aggrieved party.

## 3. CALIFORNIA DIGITAL LIBRARY

The California Digital Library is the University of California's 11th University library. It was established in 1997 by University of California President Emeritus Richard Atkinson to build the University's digital library, assist campus libraries with sharing their resources and holdings more effectively, and provide leadership in applying technology to the development of library collections and services. Organizationally housed under the UC Office of the President, the CDL operates in close collaboration with all UC campuses and their libraries.

### Mission

The mission of the Library is to harness technology and innovation, and leveraging the intellectual and cultural resources of the UC, the CDL supports the assembly and creative use of the world's scholarship and knowledge for the UC libraries and the communities they serve. To achieve its mission, the CDL utilizes strategic partnerships and technical innovation to:

* **Focus on digital library collections** by investing in the means of developing, acquiring access to, and

persistently managing digital collections.

- ★ **Invest in applications** that help campus libraries and others build meaningful, cost effective, and customized services for the use of the University's scholarly, cultural, and learning resources.
- ★ **Provide collaborative leadership** in the development of new forms of scholarly communication.
- ★ **Leverage its investments** to influence the marketplace for scholarly information in the interest of the University, its libraries, and the communities they serve.

### Organization

Harnessing technology and innovation, and leveraging the intellectual and cultural resources of the University of California, the California Digital Library supports the assembly and creative use of the world's scholarship and knowledge for the UC libraries and the communities they serve. Established in 1997 as a UC library, the CDL has become one of the largest digital libraries in the world.

The California Digital Library is housed under the University of California Office of the President, and is directed by Daniel Greenstein, the University Librarian for Systemwide Library Planning and the CDL. UC library groups, CDL advisory groups, CDL staff, and third-party partners all contribute to the workings of the CDL. Because the CDL is one of the UC libraries, it participates in systemwide library groups. CDL advisory and working groups provide guidance for specific CDL programs and initiatives.

The CDL staff support the CDL's mission and programs. Many staff members also serve on advisory committees and working groups focusing on the development of digital libraries.

CDL staff departments include:

- ★ Administration
- ★ Built Content
- ★ Business Development
- ★ Communication
- ★ Digital Library Services
- ★ Digital Library Technologies
- ★ Digital Preservation Programs
- ★ Office of Scholarly Communication

**Collections & Services**

With more than 32 million items in their collective holdings, the UC libraries make up the largest university research library in the world. The Library provides access to scholarly materials, databases of journal article abstracts and citations, electronic journals, publishing tools, and reference databases for the University of California community.

The CDL also builds collections and provides public access to cultural heritage materials though a variety of innovative programs such as Counting California, which hosts digital government information, and the eScholarship program, which assists in the creation and dissemination of UC-produced scholarship.

In addition, the CDL pursues technological innovations that enhance services for accessing, sharing, manipulating, and integrating scholarly content in all forms.

CDL collections and services include:

- ★ **CaliforniaDigitalLibrary.org :** Provides a single point of access for the publicly available digital collections produced or managed by the UC.
- ★ **CDL Image Demonstrator :** Allows users to search and view a collection of art and architecture images

drawn from museum and art collections.

- **Counting California :** Offers "one-stop shopping" for government data and statistics about California.
- **Digital Preservation Program :** The CDL hosts the UC libraries' digital preservation program to ensure long-term availability and access to digital content.
- **Directory of CDL-Licensed Content :** Lists the CDL's extensive collections of digital resources, including article databases, electronic journals, and reference texts.
- **eScholarship Editions :** Provides access to digital texts and monographs, including more than 1,400 UC Press titles. A significant number of the electronic books are available for free to the public.
- **eScholarship Publications :** Showcases publications from the eScholarship program, including interactive publications from the Electronic Cultural Atlas Initiative, legacy online journals such as the Dermatology Online Journal, and monographs from the UC International and Area Studies Digital Collection.
- **eScholarship Repository :** This free, open-access repository infrastructure supports the full range of scholarly output, from pre-publication materials to journals and peer-reviewed series, by offering UC departments direct control of publishing.
- **Melvyl® Catalog :** A searchable catalog of library materials from the 10 UC campuses, the California State Library, the California Academy of Sciences, the California Historical Society, the Center for Research Libraries, the Giannini Foundation of Agricultural Economics Library, the Graduate Theological Union, the Hastings College of the Law Library, and the Lawrence Berkeley National Laboratory Library.

★ **Online Archive of California (OAC) :** Federates collections of digital materials (such as manuscripts, photographs, and art) held in the libraries, museums, and archives across California through a searchable database.

★ **Request :** Enables UC faculty, students, and staff to enter requests from the Melvyl Catalog and journal article databases for materials. Items not available at a user's home campus are delivered via interlibrary loan, while items available at a user's home campus are delivered through the document delivery service.

★ **SearchLight :** Allows simultaneous searches across multiple journal databases, book catalogs, and other information sources available through the CDL and the UC campuses.

★ **UC-eLinks :** Provides a way to easily move from an article or book citation in an article database to the full online content of the item, or, for print materials, to automatically look for a UC library location of the item.

**Programs**

The California Digital Library supports the assembly and creative use of the world's scholarship and knowledge for the University of California libraries and the communities they serve. To accomplish these goals, the CDL partners with the UC libraries, publishers, and other institutions in broad-based programs and initiatives. Programs host specific digital collections and services.

The CDL's programs include:

★ **Collections :** Acquiring scholarly content, hosting digitized materials from UC collections and non-UC library and museum partners, and enabling the publication of original scholarly materials.

* **Services :** Enhancing services for discovering, sharing, manipulating, and integrating scholarly content.
* **eScholarship :** Fostering innovation and faculty experimentation in digital scholarly communication.
* **Digital Preservation :** Focusing on the persistent management of digital information.
* **Education, Communication, and Assessment :** Furthering the understanding of digital library products and the digital library domain; discovering needs, testing usability, and evaluating the use and usefulness of digital collections and services.
* **CDL Technologies :** Supporting the UC campus libraries and others in the application of technology for the development of scholarly digital collections and services.

**Collections**

The University of California's scholars and students conduct their research and learning while drawing from a significant portion of the world's knowledge held in the UC's library collections. Those collections grow and become more convenient to use through the California Digital Library's program to acquire and host scholarly materials in digital form.

The CDL leads a large collaborative effort to license electronic scholarly materials on behalf of the UC, in co-investment with the campus libraries. In addition, CDL hosts digital content created by the UC libraries and California partners, and makes these materials available for public use.

**The CDL**

* **Provides the UC community with more digital material** than is available at any other university, including more than 8,000 electronic journals, tens of

thousands of electronic books, and more than 250 article and reference databases.

- ★ **Saves millions of dollars** compared to what would be spent by the campuses acting independently.
- ★ **Allows campus libraries to focus** on local research and curriculum by economizing on costs for commonly needed materials and acquisition processes.
- ★ **Provides a deep and broad collection of online cultural heritage materials** from UC and California libraries, museums, and historical societies via the Online Archive of California (OAC).
- ★ **Enables the experimental publication** of scholarly output in open-access repositories.
- ★ **Encourages interactive use** of government and social science statistics and data via Counting California.
- ★ **Forges partnerships** with university presses and societies to digitally publish scholarly works.

New activities and explorations are focusing on:

- ★ **Publishing scholarly monographs** in XML.
- ★ **Hosting digital image collections** managed by UC Visual Resource curators.
- ★ **Providing access** to local history collections.
- ★ **Cultivating the interchange** of California's botanical information resources.

## Services

Services allow scholars and students to search for and use items in the University of California collections and elsewhere. Services are the necessary complement to collections and to the activities of acquiring, managing, and preserving scholarly materials.

The California Digital Library pursues technological

innovations that provide solutions to the UC libraries for the discovery, integration, manipulation, and sharing of scholarly content in all forms. The CDL provides some direct online services and makes tools available to the UC libraries and others for the customization of local services.

The digital services program relies on systemwide collaboration to identify, build, and implement services and tools that benefit the UC libraries and other partners.

Existing services, tools, and activities concentrate on:

★ **Discovering print and digital materials** in the UC libraries and beyond, including the 32 million items in the UC libraries via the Melvyl® Catalog, and the large collections of cultural heritage materials from more than 70 California libraries and institutions in the Online Archive of California (OAC).

★ **Streamlining access to online and print materials** by linking from article citations to the full online content or to the locations for printed materials via UC-eLinks.

★ **Manipulating content** by providing tools to export citations to citation management software, or to create and export presentations using digital images.

★ **Creating and sharing scholarship** by providing faculty with experimental publishing tools and infrastructure.

★ **Influencing commercial products** by developing high-performance technical and functional requirements, and by working with UC subject specialist librarians, known as Resource Liaisons, who monitor and influence licensed products.

★ **Supporting UC librarians** by communicating with the Users Council, sponsoring workshops, and providing a Help Desk and guides for troubleshooting.

New activities and explorations are focusing on:

- **Digital image services,** with tools designed for classroom instruction.
- **Federated searching or portal tools** for the discovery and integration of disparate collections.
- **Instructional technologies** that integrate digital materials into learning and course management systems.
- **Delivery of digital books** to classrooms, labs, libraries, and individual readers.

## EScholarship

Scholarly communication is the foundation of all academic activities. The traditional model of scholarly communication is based on journal publications, and in the current age, it has become expensive, restrictive, and increasingly limited in its ability to make information accessible. To address these concerns, the eScholarship program was initiated by the California Digital Library at the University of California.

The eScholarship program facilitates innovation and supports experimentation in the production and dissemination of scholarship. Through the use of innovative technology, the program seeks to develop a financially sustainable model and improve all areas of scholarly communication, including its creation, peer review, management, dissemination, and preservation.

New modes of scholarly publication include:

- **Repositories for research and scholarly output,** including pre-publication materials and peer-reviewed content.
- **Web-based publications** of digitally reformatted content.
- **Electronic editions of academic monographs** of

interest to both scholarly and general-interest readers.

In partnership with librarians, scholars, publishers, information technologists, and professionals in other memory organizations, the eScholarship program has developed several key collections and services:

- ★ **eScholarship Editions :** Provides access to a growing collection of digital texts and monographs, including more than 1,400 UC Press titles. A significant number of the electronic books are available for free to the public.
- ★ **eScholarship Publications :** Publications from the eScholarship program, including monographs from the UC International and Area Studies Digital Collection, journals and peer-reviewed series in the eScholarship Repository, experimental interactive publications like ECAI, and legacy content like the DOJ.
- ★ **eScholarship Repository :** This free, open-access repository infrastructure supports the full range of scholarly output, from pre-publication materials to journals and peer-reviewed series, by offering UC departments direct control of publishing.

## Digital Preservation

The University of California libraries are committed to maintaining world-class collections of scholarly information. To this end, essential information resources must remain available and accessible into the future — a growing challenge in the days of digital resources that are increasingly ephemeral and at risk.

In partnership with the UC libraries, the California Digital Library established the digital preservation program to ensure long-term access to the digital information that supports and results from research, teaching, and learning at UC. Included are ejournals, web-based content, digitally reformatted materials from UC libraries and museums, and online teaching and learning materials.

A priority of the digital preservation program is creating a preservation infrastructure composed of tools, guidelines, and best practices. This infrastructure will support independent preservation efforts throughout the University, helping meet UC's needs for the reliable archiving, management, and retrieval of digital information.

Other digital preservation activities include:

★ **The UC Libraries Digital Preservation Repository:** The digital preservation repository will offers a set of services for the controlled, orderly deposit of digital objects and the delivery of those objects between authorized users and long-term storage. Grant funding for the digital preservation repository has been received from the Institute of Museum and Library Services.

★ **Preserving and persistently managing ejournals.** The UC libraries have invested heavily in licensed content, but do not directly control the content. Because of this, the digital preservation program is investigating methods to preserve and manage these materials.

★ **Preserving online government and political materials:** Funded by grants from the Library of Congress's National Digital Information Infrastructure and Preservation Program (NDIIPP) and The Andrew W. Mellon Foundation, these projects focus on identifying, collecting, and preserving web-based government and political information. In the process, they provide an understanding of strategies for web archiving in general.

★ **Press release :** CDL receives $2.4 million Library of Congress grant to preserve online government and political materials.

★ **Final report for The Andrew W. Mellon Foundation:** Evaluating solutions for the capture, curation, and preservation of web-based government information.

Developed in collaboration with national and international efforts, the digital preservation infrastructure adheres to established standards and open-source practices.

Preservation partners include the UC campus libraries and digital library and preservation researchers around the world.

**Education, Communication & Assessment**

The California Digital Library has a variety of education, communication, and assessment activities that introduce the organization to others and help further the understanding of digital libraries. Through this program, the CDL collaborates with staff at each campus to foster successful use of digital collections and services and informs University of California and its partners about the wide range of digital library services and developments.

In addition, the CDL considers it critical to understand the information needs of the UC community and characteristics of the use of its digital collections and services. These assessment activities are fundamental to the CDL's own education and the informed pursuit of improving service.

The education, communication, and assessment program allows the CDL to:

★ **Foster independent and successful use of CDL collections, services, and tools :** Activities include establishing usability tools for the selection and design of collections and services, and working with the Evaluation Liaisons, the Users Council, and other service staff on the campuses to develop outreach and instructional materials. User guides and help are included with all major collections and services.

- **Develop an understanding of the needs of CDL patrons and their use of CDL resources :** Projects include soliciting information from patrons, performing needs assessments for service design and enhancements, and coordinating the production of quantitative and qualitative use data.
- **Articulate CDL directions, goals, and activities for a variety of audiences :** Methods and venues include this web site and a variety of publications, press releases, and communiqués.

## CDL Technologies

The CDL Technologies group is responsible for the technical design, implementation, and operations of the California Digital Library in support of the plans and policies formulated by the University Librarian.

CDL technologies provide enabling infrastructure for campus libraries and other information organizations by:

- **Investing in technologies and applications** that help campus libraries and others build cost effective, customized services that support the use of the University's scholarly, cultural, and learning resources.
- **Continuously experimenting with innovative technologies** in the provision of scholarly information and in the development of new forms of scholarly communication.
- **Defining architecture guidelines and standards** in cooperation with the University community.
- **Implementing new systems** within this framework.

## Future Directions

Looking ahead, the CDL technologies group is working to develop the full range of infrastructures requisite to the ingest, preservation, and presentation of information to scholarly communities.

The CDL recognizes that new directions must be explored to leverage ingenuity in systems design for the delivery of content to users, and that these system's capabilities must be accessible, uniform, and well-characterized. The future lies in the services the CDL provides, not merely in the content the CDL preserves.

## Partners & Research

Collaboration is a core value for the California Digital Library. The CDL's continuing success in delivering and sustaining digital collections and services for the University of California's teaching and research depends on its collaboration with the UC campuses as well as state, national, and international partners.

The CDL provides leadership to the digital library community through founding memberships in key organizations that are working to define and analyze library challenges and technological innovations. CDL staff members are active within many key standards development groups and initiatives.

In addition, the CDL has a very successful record of acquiring grants to explore strategic innovations in digital libraries. Granters have included the Andrew W. Mellon Foundation, the Library Services and Technology Act administered by the California State Library, the Institute of Museum and Library Services, and the Library of Congress.

## Partners

The Library partners with the University of California's campus libraries and systemwide library planning to build and maintain a shared digital collection and a digital services infrastructure. In addition, the CDL partners with many other organizations based at UC, including museums, the UC Press, and the San Diego Supercomputer Center in order to expand the scope of its research and programs.

Outside of the UC, the CDL is deeply networked with national and international research, cultural, and education establishments. Through active memberships in several organizations, the CDL contributes to the development of digital libraries. Staff members participate in the definition of technical standards that support digital library activities, collections, and services.

## Memberships and Standards Work

The CDL is a member of:

- ★ Coalition for Networked Information
- ★ Consortium for the Computer Interchange of Museum Information
- ★ Council on Library and Information Resources (CLIR)
- ★ COUNTER
- ★ Digital Library Federation (DLF)
- ★ EDUCAUSE
- ★ International Coalition of Library Consortia (ICOLC)
- ★ National Information Standards Organization (NISO)
- ★ RLG
- ★ Scholarly Publishing Academic Resources Coalition (SPARC)

CDL staff contribute to standards development efforts, including:

- **Metadata Encoding and Transmission Standard (METS) :** CDL staff (Brian Tingle) serving on the editorial board.
- **Open Archives Initiative (OAI) :** CDL staff serving on the steering committee.
- **OpenURL :** CDL staff serving on the National Information Standards Organization (NISO) Development Committee.
- **Preservation Metadata: Implementation Strategies (PREMIS) :** CDL staff serving on this working group sponsored by the Online Computer Library Center (OCLC) and the Research Libraries Group (RLG).
- **Shibboleth :** CDL and UC staff serving on the Internet 2 development and implementation groups.
- **Z39.50 :** CDL staff serving on the Implementers Group Advisory Board.

### Research

With its partners, the California Digital Library is actively engaged in applied research that contributes to the development of digital library content and services and the progress of scholarly communication.

At the CDL, applied research takes several forms. Results have directly shaped digital library collections and services at the University of California and throughout California, and have had national and international impacts.

**Grant-funded initiatives :** Impacts of externally funded projects include refined digitization and encoding standards for cultural materials, best practices for creating and sustaining digital collections, deeper understanding of digital preservation methods and collaboration, expanded alternatives for scholarly publishing, and insights on user behavior toward print and digital materials. Grants totaling more than $1 million per year have been awarded from the Andrew W. Mellon Foundation, the Library Services and Technology Act administered by the California State Library, the Institute of Museum and Library Services, and the Library of Congress, among others.

**Co-development :** The CDL is in a unique position to help surface the interests and skills of stakeholder organizations, and support applied research and co-developments among them. For example, support from the CDL has helped California museums and libraries to develop their digital collections, the University's herbaria to collaborate in the creation of online collections and services, and the Electronic Cultural Atlas Initiative to build new tools.

**Standards development :** The CDL lends its staff to the principle community efforts to understand digital library technology and infrastructure requirements, and to define, test, and establish related standards. Staff have participated in standards work for content encoding, digitization, systems interoperability, and security and authentication. See a list of CDL memberships and standards work at the partners page.

Selective list of grant-funded activities:

★ **Preservation of web-based government information:** Investigating of the technical alternatives for harvesting, organizing, and preserving web-based government information. $150,000 grant from the Andrew W. Mellon Foundation.

★ **Management of mixed print and digital collections:** Systemwide Library Planning is exploring how scholars and libraries can best integrate and preserve collections of scholarly journals that are published in both print and digital forms. $670,000 grant from the Andrew W. Mellon Foundation.

- ★ **Preservation of UC library materials :** Creating a pilot digital preservation repository for multi-institutional use, based on the Open Archive Information System (OAIS) model for digital preservation. $374,736 grant from the Institute of Museum and Library Services.
- ★ **Contributions to the National Digital Library collection :** Supporting cooperation between the Online Archive of California (OAC) and the Library of Congress's National Digital Library Program. $600,000 grant from the Library of Congress.
- ★ **Best practices for digitizing cultural heritage materials and finding aids :** Supporting the creation of and permanent access to standardized metadata and digital images through the OAC. $488,148 awarded in three grants from the California State Library's Library Services Technology Act (LSTA).
- ★ **Alternative forms of scholarly communication :** Supporting experimentation in the dissemination of research findings. $167,836 grant from the Scholarly Publishing Academic Resources Coalition (SPARC).
- ★ **Extension of library standards to museums :** Evaluating the capabilities of Encoded Archival Descriptions, a digital finding aid technology, to integrate museum collection descriptions into the OAC collections. $828,533 awarded in two National Leadership grants from the Institute of Museum and Library Services.
- ★ **Establishment of the Japanese American Relocation Digital Archive (JARDA) :** Mining California's rich collections of Japanese American relocation materials to create JARDA. $358,724 grant from the Library Services and Technology Act,

administered by the California State Library.

* **National Science Foundation's Digital Library Initiative–Phase 2 :** The CDL is working with UC Berkeley, UC Santa Barbara, Stanford, and the San Diego Supercomputer Center on the "InterLib" suite of California projects in the NSF-funded Digital Library Initiative.

## 4. HARVARD UNIVERSITY DIGITAL LIBRARY

The Harvard University Library (HUL) is a department of the Central Administration that serves as the coordinating body for the more than 90 libraries that comprise the Harvard library system. HUL develops and implements library services and programs that are best provided centrally. These include the Office for Information Systems (which manages HOLLIS), the Harvard Depository (for off-site storage), the Weissman Preservation Center, the University Archives (including the Records Management Program), the Library Digital Initiative, and the Open Collections Program.

Harvard University launched the Library Digital Initiative (LDI) in July 1998 as a five-year program to develop the University's capacity to manage digital information by:

* creating the technical infrastructure to support the acquisition, organization, delivery, and archiving of digital library materials;
* providing a team of specialists to advise librarians and others in the University community on key issues in the digital environment;
* providing librarians and staff with experience in a wide range of technologies and digital materials; and,
* enriching the Harvard University Library collections with a significant set of digital resources

## The Harvard Depository Mission

The Harvard Depository is a climate-controlled media storage and retrieval facility, owned and operated by Harvard University, under the directorship of the Harvard University Library administration.

These guidelines and specifications were developed for the special conditions existing at the Harvard Depository and do not constitute recommendations to other entities. This document should not be utilized at other facilities without appropriate internal review.

The mission of the Harvard Depository is to promote effective use of space on the Harvard campus and the retention of financially and historically valuable resources by providing a secure, reliable, and cost-effective archival environment for the storage and retrieval of media.

### Goals

There are five overarching goals that support the Harvard Depository's mission:

- protect and preserve the collections entrusted to our care;
- meet or exceed client and archival storage industry standards for services;
- expend funds prudently to the maximum benefit of clients and the University;
- conduct ongoing qualitative and quantitative measurement and continual analysis and reporting of performance; and
- sustain a work environment that promotes teamwork, cooperation, and communication as values supporting our mission.

## Proposal for the Library

### *Introduction*

Digital information is transforming the conduct of teaching and research. There are debates about the speed of change and the nature of the change, but there is no doubt that the creation, transmission, accessing, and archiving of information will increasingly be digital. The Harvard Library is already moving into the world of digital information. Whether to move effectively and efficiently is an open question.

Harvard must and will develop a digital library capacity. There are a number of reasons why such a development is required:

### *Necessity*

Libraries, of necessity, reflect the world of scholarship and information. They acquire, disseminate, and preserve information in whatever form it is created by scholars and publishers; they provide teachers and researchers with materials in the forms those users desire. More and more of that material is being produced in digital form; more and more of users want access to such materials. Harvard has no choice but to develop the capacity to collect digital resources as it always has paper-based materials.

### *Functionality*

Digital information can be used in ways that paper cannot: it need not be tied to a particular location; it can be transmitted more easily to users; it can be consulted by many users at once; it encompasses many media from text to quantitative data to visual and audio materials, allowing these to be combined; it can be searched, copied, and manipulated in ways unknown to print. A full explication of ways in which digital information is changing and enhancing scholarship and learning would require a much longer paper, but the evidence is overwhelming. Numerous classes at Harvard-undergraduate, graduate, and professional-use digital information in the teaching process. In many cases, this is a more efficient way for teachers to provide information and students to obtain it through electronic reserves, on-line texts, and on-line visual collections. In many cases digital information represents more: the availability of digital information is transforming the teaching and learning process by allowing students to explore widely across information sources, to combine materials in new ways, and to be more active and creative participants in the learning process.

***Excellence***

Effective movement into digital information is needed to maintain Harvard's special position of excellence. The Harvard University Library is the greatest academic library in the world. If any metric sets Harvard apart from other universities it is the Library. Furthermore, it is not only that the library per se is a major resource for teaching and research; the library is directly related to the quality of the other major university resource: its faculty. The library is a major factor is attracting and keeping faculty. If the library declines in quality so does the University.

Every year, the Association of Research Libraries ranks its member libraries on a standard indicator of library scale. Every year, the data array looks the same: there is a smooth progression upward across the 100-plus academic libraries with a major discontinuity-Harvard-alone at the top level. The ranking is largely based on the size of collections and the scale of operations. No one can catch Harvard in that ranking. However, if one were to add criteria for performance in the digital world, it would likely rank one third of the way down-below a number of the major universities with which it competes. As time goes on, the faculty and students will more and more want performance in the digital library world commensurate with what they have come to expect from the paper-based collections. If Harvard is to maintain its quality-not merely for competitive purposes but because it value the highest levels of teaching and research-it will have to increase the efforts and change the way of doing things.

The proposal outlines the changes in library operation and structure caused by the digital revolution, and recommends a strategy for responding to these changes. It describes a project to develop the institutional capacity to acquire, deliver, and archive digital information and it argues for a more coordinated approach to these tasks than is the Harvard norm. Harvard has no choice but to move decisively into the world of digital information. The research and teaching obligations and the changing nature of the information needed to support those obligations require action and investment.

## A Coordinated Approach

Given that our many libraries must collect, deliver, and archive digital information, it needs a centralized University-wide project and not rely on distributed local activity, the norm for library operations at Harvard? A central, coordinated project is needed for at least three reasons:

### Digital information is different

When a book is acquired, it resides in a single library. When a digital resource is put on the network, it can be equally available to all. Further, traditional materials are sold in small units with a relatively low unit price, and purchasing decisions are virtually always local. Digital materials are being marketed in larger and much more costly units, and both decisions to purchase and the related cost-sharing negotiations frequently involve many separate Harvard units.

### Shared services are more efficient

The development of digital libraries involves a wide range of highly specialized technical skills, and duplicating those skills in each library would be both difficult and wasteful. Likewise digital libraries require a set of common infrastructure services, that need not be replicated in each individual library. Some hardware components exhibit significant economies of scale, including storage systems, one of the chief cost components of digital library systems. Software to support commonly used services can be licensed once for the entire University.

### Integration improves service

For the library user, having a unified and coherent way to find what is available, a single means of accessing secured resources, the fewest interfaces to digital materials, and the smallest set of required desktop applications represents significantly better service than if each library were to implement varied ways of doing similar things.

Harvard's libraries and library users have benefited for many years from the integrated, shared services of HOLLIS. The digital library will likewise benefit from coordinated development and common services. The absence of a coordinated infrastructure will inevitably generate duplicative and incompatible efforts in individual libraries, duplication that will (in the absence of a University-wide effort) happen soon in our current environment of exploding digital resources.

### Proposal Overview

The Harvard's digital library like other counterparts will be built over many decades as the world of digital information evolves. Rather it is proposed to launch Harvard's digital library effort, to give it the initial momentum, momentum that it is expected to be carried through regular library operations once digital libraries mature and digital formats become a norm. We are in a period of discontinuity, one where none of the old forms have been replaced, but new ones surround us, demanding attention. It is therefore proposed a one-time effort to provide special resources to help cope with these extraordinary times.

The proposed project will:

★ create the first-generation technical infrastructure to support storage of and access to digital library materials;
★ make available a staff of specialists to advise librarians (and other University personnel working in related areas) about a number of key issues related to digital materials, including digital reformatting, metadata, licensing, and archiving;
★ give librarians and technologists experience with a wide range of technologies and digital materials on which to base future decisions and development;
★ provide library users with at least one significant set of digital resources to support current teaching and research activities.

At the end of the five year period it is expected that Harvard will have the capacity to collect, organize, serve, and archive digital materials with the sophistication and ease with which it now manages traditional media, and that use of the digital collections will be part of the daily activity of students and scholars across the University. The acquisition, organization, and management of digital information should be on a firm footing as new information sources appear. The libraries will have a solid base for adaptation to the inevitable market and technical changes that will continue to take place in the digital world.

## Digital Libraries Elsewhere

Harvard is, of course, not alone in facing the need for an extraordinary initiative related to digital libraries. Most of the peer institutions have concerted programs underway, in some cases programs of considerable magnitude. Among the most notable are those at:

- The ***Library of Congress***, which has begun developing the National Digital Library, with a target 5-year budget of $60 million (including a $3 million annual appropriation from Congress and significant private contributions). The program has already generated a considerable collection of primary source materials related to the development of the United States, a collection receiving heavy use from around the world.
- The ***University of California*** system, which has recently created The California Digital Library program to acquire and archive digital materials for all 9 University campuses. The project budget for the initial year is $3 million, which does not include much of the infrastructure costs supported elsewhere in the University's budget.
- The ***University of Michigan***, which in 1993 initiated its Digital Library Program with the intention of creating a "comprehensive (i.e., campuswide in perspective), coherent (i.e., logical in its organization and scope), and coordinated (i.e., supported by systems and standards to promote effective access)" digital library collection. The digital material now available at Michigan are impressive in their scope and variety. Michigan's digital infrastructure has enabled it to win a continuing series of grants for content and program development.

★ The ***University of Virginia***, which has created technical centers specializing in a wide range of digital information, including: Digital Image Center, Digital Media and Music Center, Electronic Text Center, Geographic Information Center, Social Sciences Data Center, and the Special Collections Digital Center. Together these represent a wide array of resources (a fact that faculty coming to Harvard from Virginia have pointed out to Harvard librarians).

★ The ***UK Higher Education Funding Council***, which has mounted a 3-year, 15 million-pound, Electronic Libraries Programme to fund university-based digital library projects in a number of areas, including experimentation with electronic journals, digital preservation, and training.

The proposed program would not put Harvard at the "cutting edge" of digital library developments. Rather it is proposed to profit from the pioneering efforts of others who have invested in research and exploration of the many difficult issues in digital libraries. The program is intended to build on current knowledge to create a practical, large-scale infrastructure that will be of daily use in building our electronic collections as the world of publishing moves into the digital age.

## Project Activities

### *Developing Infrastructure*

Infrastructure is the collection of common systems and services that make it possible to store, organize, and access digital materials. Among the key elements to be addressed in the project are:

**1. Catalogs and indexes :** The hallmark of a library is organization, a structure that helps users identify and locate what is available. The HOLLIS catalog will be a key component of our infrastructure, but it is not adequate for many types of materials likely to be in the digital collections, including:

- ★ photographs, prints, and other visual materials
- ★ contents of archival collections
- ★ journal articles.

Building these separate catalogs and linking them in a coherent structure is critical to making the digital collections useful. It is a technical and intellectual task of considerable magnitude, and one made all the more pressing by the scale and breadth of Harvard's collections.

**2. Controlling access :** Much of the digital collection will likely be owned by others, and Harvard will only have a license permitting use. Other materials may be the property of Harvard, but we will want to control access for legal, contractual, or economic reasons. Securing access to digital materials can be thought of as a two-dimensional matrix composed of:

- ★ the user (how do we know for certain who this user is? what category is this user in?)
- ★ the digital item (which user classes can access this item? what use rights do they have to use this item: view a description? view a low-grade version? view a high-definition version? print a copy?).

**3. Storage :** Large digital collections involve many issues:

- ★ cost effective large-scale storage of hardware and software, including the capability to store digital items on a variety of devices with varying cost and performance characteristics
- ★ systematic back-up
- ★ disaster recovery plans and facilities
- ★ media migration to protect against data loss

★ coherence between stored objects and the data about those objects ("metadata") that makes them useable.

Scale changes storage requirements. Storing hundreds of thousands of digital objects and information about them requires tools, discipline, and systematic operations. A digital repository resembles in many ways the Harvard Depository-its nature is determined more by the scale of operation than by the specific nature of the materials stored. To work well, both require careful professional management.

**4. Interface.** The user interface for printed materials is inherent in the carrier (a book, a journal, a newspaper-each embodies its own interface). Digital materials are frequently separate from the interface, and the same object can be delivered through many different interfaces. One of the difficulties in the current environment is that there is a dramatic proliferation of interfaces, a proliferation that is causing user confusion and frustration. While one cannot hope to do away with the need to use many different system interfaces, a shared set of frequently used interfaces for such common actions as the following will noticeably simplify the use of the digital library:

★ searching bibliographic databases

★ viewing images of digitized journal articles or other page-based materials

★ navigating through descriptions of archival collections.

## Acquiring Digital Resources

The content of Harvard's digital collection will come from many sources, and will be distributed across many systems, within Harvard and without. Sources will include authors, commercial and non-profit publishers, government agencies, value-added aggregators, other universities and libraries, and scholarly societies. It anticipates that the landscape of players and products will evolve in complex and unexpected ways over the next decade. In this project they will both assist with the general acquisition and creation of content by Harvard libraries and begin creating a significant collection of content in specific areas.

The first two project activities relate to materials created outside of Harvard:

**1. Assistance with digital acquisitions :** The libraries are buying an increasing number of databases, digital reference works, and electronic journals. The acquisition process is increasingly complex, involving such questions as:

★ are there (or will there soon be) alternate sources for the same or equivalent materials?

★ will the delivery system fit Harvard's security and access systems?

★ is this the right interface for this material?

★ are there appropriate provisions for long-term, archival access?

★ is there adequate provision for "fair use"?

★ what parts of Harvard should share in the cost of providing this resource?

★ can this resource be effectively used over the Internet, or is a local copy needed?

★ are there adequate service guarantees in the contract?

★ does the contract protect Harvard against liability claims?

★ is the authorized user base defined appropriately for Harvard?

These issues are new to most librarians and addressing them requires specialized knowledge and understanding of both the technical and the legal environment.

**2. Integration of outside resources :** Much of the content of Harvard's digital collection will be held on systems outside the University. Because there are few standards or conventions for how such systems should operate, these systems tend to be designed in an astonishing variety of ways. Thus a significant effort is needed to integrate them into Harvard's local environment, in such areas as:

- ★ securing access
- ★ integrating with local interfaces
- ★ linking content and indexes
- ★ relating electronic content with Harvard's holdings of paper equivalents or of related materials
- ★ integrating searches across multiple related databases.

One of the key advantages of digital resources is that they can be functionally brought together for the user regardless of their physical location or technical format. Such integration however requires effort, both technical and intellectual, and the resulting smooth operation and navigation is one of the key contributions of libraries to the digital arena.

In addition to acquiring digital materials from elsewhere, there is an ever-increasing amount of interest at Harvard (not just within the libraries, but also in other areas including the museums, research projects, and classroom support) converting materials from traditional to digital format. Motivation for digital conversion includes the preservation of content when the original format is endangered, providing enhanced functionality, and improving access. This program will provide assistance in addressing many of the issues raised by these conversion projects.

Four additional project activities relate to materials converted locally:

**3. Conversion formats and methodologies :** Even something as seemingly straightforward as digital imaging, which is essentially the simple recording of a picture digitally, involves many issues. There are numerous recording formats, varying in the amount of detail captured, likely functional longevity (conventions and standards in this area evolve rapidly), the software that is required to capture, display, or print the image, the size of the resulting digital object, and the ability to render color. For the conversion of text, there are issues of markup (tagging added to text to identify and label its parts), for which varying standards and conventions are available, standards that affect usability, archivability, and the software needed for manipulation and display. For any digital format there are generally many conversion technologies available, again involving tradeoffs among functionality, cost, effort required, likely longevity, and compatibility with various technical environments. All of these issues involve technical knowledge and experience. The availability of appropriate technical assistance as the project is designed will significantly affect the utility of the product, the cost of the conversion, and the longevity of the result.

**4. Metadata :** To be useable by people or software, digital materials need to be described systematically:

★ For the user, this description is usually a catalog entry, providing index terms as well as a description of the item and location information. There are many differing practices in use today, both local ones and those adopted by various communities (current examples include standards adopted by research libraries, arts and cultural heritage museums, visual arts libraries, botanical or biological systematics collections, archives, and manuscripts libraries).

★ For the curator responsible for a digital object, there are many pieces of administrative information needed: information about the date and technique used for object conversion (of significance for media refreshing or format conversion), whether a copy is considered archival (which will affect how it is stored and formatted), and what access restrictions apply. Standards or conventions for which administrative information should be recorded, and how it should be encoded, are not yet common.

★ For software, the technical format of a digital object must be recorded (affecting what software is needed to render or use the object), how a given object relates to other digital objects (affecting how the interface provides navigation through a related set of materials such as images of the pages of a journal article), and the mark-up standard followed (describing the meaning of the tagging to be found in a text). There are an enormous number of examples and conventions for such "structural" metadata in use today, some standardized (e. g., the various "document type definitions" for text marked up in Standard Generalized Markup Language), many local or proprietary (such as the page-relationship data used in commercial electronic document management systems).

Again, this is an area where technical expertise and experience are required for intelligent decisions to be made in designing projects.

**5. Conversion process design :** Most conversion projects involve the expenditure of significant resources. A well designed workflow, the choice of the right technologies and service providers, and appropriate quality control standards and procedures are critical to controlling costs and conversion time, and improving the resulting product. This is an area where technical expertise and experience will make a significant difference in project design, affecting cost, usability, and longevity.

**6. Ownership marking :** When Harvard owns the rights to a digital object, there may be concerns about controlling legitimate reuse of that object. The University may want to allow general scholarly access to its resources, but to control (and perhaps profit from) their reuse in commercial publications. "Electronic watermarking" and similar technologies can provide ways of tracking the origin of an object and provide assistance in controlling the use and flow of owned resources. Such techniques are becoming available in the marketplace, but choosing the right strategy will require careful investigation and analysis.

## Project Structure

A 5-year project is proposed to be based in the University Library. The project would be managed under the direction of a governance committee of representatives from faculties and libraries. The committee would be responsible for setting priorities for project activities, for monitoring progress and costs, and for allocating the incentive fund (discussed below). In particular, it recommends that in addition to the normal month-to-month monitoring of the project, the governance committee conduct a formal review in the third year, to ensure that the project continues to be useful and its directions appropriate. The rapid evolution of the digital environment requires vigilance. Much will change over the course of the project.

The University Library would create a project team of systems developers and technical consultants, who would be responsible for the creation of the technical infrastructure and for providing assistance and consulting advice to library staff and others at Harvard developing or delivering digital resources. The University Library would also procure adequate hardware and software for operating the infrastructure and housing digital materials when needed.

Digital library developments must be driven by collection content and by relevance to the University's academic mission, not by technology. The work on infrastructure and integration discussed above cannot be done in the abstract, divorced from actual digital library materials.

Therefore a critical part of this project is the development of a digital collection that provides both ongoing utility to Harvard users, and experience on which to base sound design and development decisions. At Harvard, building library collections is a decentralized responsibility, with decisions about what to collect made at a level close to the researchers and students. A program to develop content therefore cannot be executed centrally. Instead, it is proposed the creation of a funding pool to be used to encourage the rapid development of a critical mass of digital materials, in order to:

- ★ provide real-world experience with the use of digital library resources
- ★ provide a set of materials on which to base infrastructure development
- ★ test and demonstrate the utility of Harvard's digital library developments.

This incentive fund would be used to help support digital item creation or acquisition by the individual libraries, based on the following criteria:

- ★ the materials would have to contribute meaningfully to building a critical mass of resources in a limited number of topical areas (we suggest using social science materials related to contemporary social issues or policy development, or materials related to one of the interfaculty initiatives, as these would be useful in all of the Harvard Faculties);
- ★ projects would need to utilize or, even better, contribute

to the development of the common infrastructure;

* materials should represent a variety of types of digital resources, so as to build experience at Harvard with a wide range of digital materials and to provide information on the relative utility of various resource types.

Most projects receiving support from the incentive fund are expected to involve significant matching effort or resources from the individual library (or libraries) involved.

**Costs**

There are three categories of costs to be considered for the digital library developments proposed here.

* First, there are the direct project costs for staff, hardware, software, HOLLIS II, and space and overhead. These are estimated to cost $7 million. In addition it proposed to have an Incentive fund of $5 million, for a total project cost of $12 million.
* Second, for digital libraries to succeed, the University will need to provide a number of other types of infrastructure applicable not only to digital libraries but also to other network and computing applications at Harvard. Examples of such infrastructure include network capacity, user authentication facilities, distributed printing facilities, support for local networks and workstations, and electronic classroom facilities and support. These are not directly attributable to the digital library but are a necessary condition for it to succeed.
* Third, the discontinuity of the digital revolution is causing severe strain on library collection budgets. The explosion of electronic resources on the market represents an increase in the pool of materials appropriate for the libraries to collect. Further, today little of the new material displaces traditional resources. For the next several years

at least, the libraries will therefore be faced with demands both to continue collecting as they have in the past and to acquire the new electronic formats. Since the proposed incentive fund is intended to be limited in both time and subject scope, libraries will be faced with the need to find significant new revenue to continue collecting as they have in the past, or they must reduce the scope of their collecting.

## Conclusion

The world of information-and the lives of those whose work depends on it-is being transformed. Key decisions affecting the ways in which online resources can be used, the standards, and the new solutions, are being shaped by the active participants. Work relating to digital libraries has been underway for over a decade. To date, Harvard has moved cautiously in digital libraries. The dramatic increase in the rate of development of electronic information in the past two years makes it inappropriate that they continue in this cautious manner. The explosion in the publishing and use of digital information requires to act now.

The development of a digital library for Harvard is not a threat to the remarkable history of its existing libraries. It is instead a powerful complement to those collections. If Harvard intends to be among the leading players in defining new directions for its outstanding academic programs, in shaping information policies for the digital world, and in creating the educational environment for the new millennium, it will need the best possible access to a full array of information resources, both print and digital. The development of a digital library, with the concomitant commitments to building a sound technological infrastructure and developing a community of highly skilled library and computing professionals, is a necessary step for the University.

For the libraries at Harvard, the years ahead will pose significant challenges to provide the best possible balance between print-based collections and digital resources. At present, the lack of a defined infrastructure for a digital library and the fragmented nature of digital content make it very difficult for the libraries to respond to the needs of the teaching and research programs of the University. The program so outline will allow the Harvard libraries to be effective providers of information to the users in the most cost-efficient way possible. Commitment to the coordinated development of a digital library program for Harvard will provide each of the libraries the opportunity to focus its attention on acquiring access to needed content, rather than crafting idiosyncratic solutions to maintain digital library developments. The libraries at Harvard are poised to carry out a vital role in assuring integrated access to both traditional and digital information resources. To do so effectively, there needs to be an institutional commitment to and a corollary investment in development of an operational infrastructure for a digital library.

## 5. DIGITAL LIBRARY OF GEORGIA

The Digital Library of Georgia is a GALILEO initiative based at the University of Georgia Libraries that works together with Georgia's libraries, archives, museums, and other institutions of cultural heritage to provide access to the cultural and historical resources of the state of Georgia. This primary mission is accomplished through the ongoing development, maintenance, and preservation of digital collections and online digital library resources.

The Digital Library of Georgia also provides digital library, photographic, and micrographic services, and supports the instruction, research, and service missions of GALILEO and the University System of Georgia through collaboration with university faculty, students, and staff, and through participation on local and national levels in the development of digital library standards, practice, and technology. The Digital Library facilitates cooperative ventures with other organizations and provides leadership for cooperative digital initiatives throughout the state.

The Library works together with Georgia's libraries, archives, museums, and other institutions of cultural heritage to provide access to the cultural and historical resources of the state of Georgia. This primary mission is accomplished through the ongoing development, maintenance, and preservation of digital collections and online digital library resources. These may include materials such as original manuscripts, typescripts, books, photographs, maps, sheet music, posters and broadsides, newspapers, primary source materials on microfilm, audio, video, and other formats.

The DLG participates on local and national levels in the development of digital library standards, practice, and technology, facilitates cooperative ventures with other organizations, and provides leadership for cooperative digital initiatives throughout the state.

The Digital Library of Georgia is also a department of the University of Georgia Libraries that provides digital library, photographic, and micrographic services, and supports the instruction, research, and service missions of GALILEO and the University System of Georgia through collaboration with university faculty, students, and staff.

The Library has four functional units:

**Digital Library of Georgia Production Center**

The Digital Library of Georgia Production Center supports the mission and goals of the Digital Library of Georgia by developing, maintaining, and preserving collections of digital content in collaboration with University of Georgia Libraries' and GALILEO staff.

## Digital Library of Georgia Teaching and Learning Center

The Digital Library of Georgia Teaching and Learning Center supports the mission of the Digital Library of Georgia by providing support for instruction and learning for University students, faculty, and staff. The Center provides a physical space and technology for instruction and works closely with University and Library faculty in the development of instructional materials and programs. These activities directly support the Digital Library of Georgia's mission to provide access to cultural and historical resources of the state of Georgia.

## Photographic Services

Photographic Services supports the mission of the Digital Library of Georgia and the University Libraries by working closely with the Digital Library of Georgia Production Center to provide digital imaging services for Digital Library of Georgia projects. Photographic Services also provides quality photographic and digital imaging services to patrons of the University of Georgia Libraries special collections libraries and University students, faculty, and staff.

## Micrographic Services/Georgia Newspaper Project

Micrographic Services supports the mission of the Digital Library of Georgia and the University Libraries by preserving collections of materials related to the history and culture of Georgia for ongoing access and providing micrographic reproduction services to Library patrons and University students, faculty, and staff. Micrographic Services has primary responsibility for the Georgia Newspaper Project, part of the United States Newspaper Program.

## Guiding Principles

**Usability and accessibility :** Build highly usable and accessible collections to make resources available to as wide a range of researchers, scholars, students, and the general public as possible.

**Standards and best practices :** Make use of standards, best practices, and open systems whenever possible to ensure longevity of and ongoing access to digital, photographic, and micrographic resources. Contribute to development of these standards and best practices by participation and collaboration with other digital library projects.

**Added value :** Provide not only digital facsimiles of historical and cultural materials, but strive to include rich background, contextual information, description, and metadata to promote deeper analysis and greater understanding of the collections and materials. Likewise, develop and implement digital library tools and services to promote enhanced interpretation, context, and understanding.

**Copyright :** Respect the rights of copyright owners by observing current laws and regulations regarding copyright and fair use. Monitor and observe developing legislation and support active involvement.

**Digital preservation :** Maintain and promote awareness and understanding of preservation of digital collections and take steps throughout the life cycle of digital materials to ensure ongoing access and usability.

**Appropriate use of technology :** Implementation of new technology will follow the mission and goals of the Digital Library, rather than technology for its own sake. The Digital Library will maintain awareness of digital library and technological developments.

## Goals of the Library

Build a sustainable and scalable digital library infrastructure.

Build comprehensive digital collections that reflect the full wealth of Georgia's history and culture and ensure fair representation of traditionally under-represented groups.

Preserve library collections, including sensitive cultural and historical resources through appropriate means such as photographic and micrographic reproduction.

Facilitate and cooperate in cooperative ventures with other organizations to build digital collections, resources, and services.

Contribute to the development of standards and best practices by participation at multiple levels including local, national, and international.

Provide high quality photographic and digital imaging services to University of Georgia library patrons and University students, faculty, and staff.

Promote instruction, teaching, and learning by providing instructional space and technology and working with university and library faculty to develop instructional resources and programs.

## Collection Development

### *Digitized Collections*

The Digital Library of Georgia, working together with Georgia's libraries, archives, museums, and other institutions of cultural heritage, provides access to the cultural and historical resources of the state of Georgia through ongoing development, maintenance, and preservation of online digital collections and resources. Original formats included may be text-based, including manuscripts, letters, diaries, and published works such as books and pamphlets, photographs, maps, art, artifacts, audio and video, graphic materials including architectural plans and drawings, and microfilm.

The Audience of the Digital Library of Georgia consists of five segments: Casual User, Student/K-12/Lifelong Learner, Information Seeker/Hobbyist, Scholar/Researcher, Government/Business Community. (More information)

Collections, materials, or items may be nominated for digitization by any interested party using the Digital Library of Georgia Digitization Nomination Form.

Collections nominated for digitization and/or inclusion in the Digital Library of Georgia will be judged based on the following criteria.

Proposed materials or collections must conform to the mission of the Digital Library of Georgia and be related to the culture and history of the state of Georgia. Materials that are restricted by the donor or other owner will not be digitized unless permission can be obtained.

Materials that are clearly in the public domain will be given priority for digitization. Where public domain status is questionable, a decision will be made on a case by case basis. When materials are under copyright restrictions, they will not be digitized unless permission is likely to be easily obtainable.

Materials or collections that are completely or partially described, captioned, labeled, processed, or cataloged will be given priority for digitization. Other instances will be handled on a case by case basis depending on factors such as the type and depth of description required, need for research, etc.

Materials that are hard to access due to preservation concerns or are only available to a limited audience due to security restrictions will be given priority for digitization.

Materials that are heavily used by researchers, other patrons, or staff will be given greater priority for digitization.

Materials that represent the cultural, political, social, geographic, and/or economic diversity of the state of Georgia will be given priority.

Materials that have high research, artifactual, or evidential value and/or are of particular interest to a key audience will have high priority for digitization.

Materials for which access will be substantially improved by digitization and which have a high potential for added value in the digital environment will be given priority. Examples of added value that the materials may lend themselves to include:

Creation and/or addition of supplemental resources to allow users to better understand, navigate, and use the collection

Linkages between materials

Virtual collections of materials based around a creator, topic, subject, or similar theme

New metadata, description, and finding aids in electronic form

The ability to search through the creation of electronic text

New ways to use or analyze the originals

## Duplication of Efforts

Materials that are publicly available in digital form elsewhere at a level of quality that meets the needs of the audience of the Digital Library of Georgia will not be digitized. Note that the DLG Portal Service may link to items related to the mission of the Digital Library of Georgia.

## Cooperative Potential

If the materials have the potential to be related to others held by different repositories or organizations, including materials already digitized or being considered for digitization, the priority for digitization is higher if it is likely that a cooperative or multi-collection digitization initiative may result.

**Availability of Local or Additional Resources**

Following on cooperative potential, if a repository or other organization can provide support in the form of staff time, equipment, or funding - especially at a local basis - to digitize materials to the standards required by the Digital Library of Georgia those collections may be given greater priority to take advantage of these opportunities.

**Technology**

Materials for which appropriate technology, processes, and best practices already exist for digitization will generally have priority. Projects that explore or require implementation of new technologies will be considered depending on the availability of resources and funding.

**DLG Portal Service**

The DLG Portal Service is a forthcoming project of the Digital Library of Georgia and is not currently active.

The DLG Portal Service links historical and cultural collections digitized by the DLG and held locally in GALILEO with digital collections, materials, sites, items or similar resources held by cultural and/or other non-profit organizations throughout the state and elsewhere by means of a selective portal service. The core of the portal service is a metadata catalog containing descriptive information about each resource.

The DLG Portal Service will record metadata about and link to sites meeting the following criteria:

★ Provides digitized resources or finding aids for collections in Georgia's cultural institutions or resources representing Georgia's history and culture
★ Makes the resource available at no cost
★ Has a plan for ongoing sustainability and maintenance

* Respects copyright by ensuring that materials are in the public domain or cleared for public distribution
* Priority will be given to sites containing cultural materials digitized in accordance with standard best practices for digital imaging recommended by the Digital Library of Georgia

## Ownership

The Digital Library of Georgia does not claim ownership of digital objects linked to from the DLG Portal Service. Ownership remains with the originating site. Note that collections digitized and mounted by the Digital Library of Georgia and GALILEO are linked to from the DLG Portal Service in the same way as other participating sites. Metadata created by the Digital Library of Georgia and included in the DLG Portal Service remains the property of the Digital Library of Georgia, but may be freely copied and shared as long as credit is given.

## Accuracy

Responsibility for accuracy of data, facts, and information presented rests with the institution providing the digital resource. The Digital Library of Georgia does not warrant any information on the sites linked to by the portal. The Digital Library of Georgia recommends that all sites have a means of collection information regarding the content accuracy and a polity for site review and revision.

## Accessibility

The DLG Portal Service strives to comply with accessibility standards developed as part of the Web Access Initiative of the World Wide Web Consortium available at http://www.w3.org/WAI/. However, the Digital Library of Georgia does not guarantee that sites linked to by the DLG Portal will comply with these accessibility standards.

## Removal Policy

A site may be removed from the DLG Portal at the discretion of the Digital Library of Georgia for one or more of the following:

- ★ Site is not consistently available and reliable
- ★ Inaccurate data, facts, or information
- ★ Proven violation of copyright
- ★ Site or content is no longer available for free to the public

## Copyright and Citation Information

The digital reproductions included in the Digital Library of Georgia have been made available for use in research, teaching (including distribution to classes), and private study. For these purposes one may reproduce (print, make photocopies, or download) materials from this web site without prior permission, on the condition of providing proper attribution of the source in all copies.

Because the materials in the Digital Library of Georgia come from a number of repositories within the state of Georgia, it uses the following form for citation:

[title of item when available], [name of collection], [name of repository], presented in the Digital Library of Georgia

**Examples:**

Men Picking Cotton, Robert E. Williams Photographs, 1872-1898, Hargrett Rare Book and Manuscript Library, presented in the Digital Library of Georgia

Cornelius C. Platter Civil War Diary, 1864 - 1865, Hargrett Rare Book and Manuscript Library, presented in the Digital Library of Georgia

The materials and pages included in the Digital Library of Georgia may be linked to freely from other Web pages and Internet resources.

## Frequently Asked Questions

### *Digitization of historical materials?*

- ★ More people can access and use unique, highly valuable, and often fragile materials
- ★ Users can view the materials from any computer connected to the Internet, any time of day
- ★ Searchable text allows users to conduct research in ways not possible before
- ★ Users gain an understanding of the context of the materials in history through associated supplementary resources such as timelines and historical overviews
- ★ Libraries can build "virtual collections" made up of related materials that are physically separated between repositories
- ★ Digitized Materials can be used in new and exciting ways for research and instruction when combined with the communications facilities of the Internet

**Digitization?** Selection of materials and collections to be included in the Digital Library of Georgia is guided by the Digital Library's Collection Development Policy.

### Georgia HomePLACE

The Georgia Department of Archives and History (Office of Secretary of State), the Office of Public Library Services (Board of Regents, University System of Georgia), and the Digital Library of Georgia and GALILEO (University System of Georgia) are collaborating on the long-range project called Georgia HomePLACE (Providing Libraries and Archives Electronically) to digitize valuable Georgia family and local history records and make them available as part of the Digital Library of Georgia and GALILEO. During the first phase of the project, the following resources will be made available:

*Vanishing Georgia* Historic Photograph Collection; Georgia County Marriage Records; Georgia Confederate Veterans Pension Application Files; Georgia Historical Map Collections; and other unique Georgia archival resources. The materials for Georgia HomePLACE will be coordinated locally by Georgia Public Library Systems under the Office of Public Library Services. The Digital Library of Georgia, while including the Georgia HomePLACE project, will also include collections and resources from Georgia's colleges and universities (especially the University System of Georgia), and other historical societies, museums, and cultural heritage repositories.

**Funding**

As a GALILEO initiative based at the University of Georgia Libraries, most of the funding for the Digital Library of Georgia comes from GALILEO, the University of Georgia, and other state sources. Grants from institutions such as the Andrew W. Mellon Foundation, the Institute for Library and Museum Services (IMLS), the Georgia Historical Records Advisory Board (GHRAB), the Taylor Foundation, and other sources also support current and past Digital Library Projects.

By nominating materials to be included in the Digital Library of Georgia, libraries, archives, museums, and other historical repositories throughout the state can help in the effort to obtain ongoing funding for the Digital Library.

**New projects and collections**

The Projects & Collections list provides information on newly available projects, ongoing resources, and forthcoming online collections being created by current DLG projects.

**Historical materials**

The Digital Library of Georgia is currently building a list of historical materials and collections related to the history and culture of Georgia from libraries, archives, museums, and other institutions of cultural heritage around the state. Selected collections may be digitized and made available online in the Digital Library of Georgia and GALILEO.

The DLG is planning the introduction of a Portal to Georgia History in the future to pull together high quality web sites relevant to Georgia's history and culture. More information on how sites will be selected may be found in the Digital Library's Collection Development Policy.

## Use of Library materials

The digital reproductions included in the Digital Library of Georgia have been made available for use in research, teaching (including distribution to classes), and private study. For these purposes you may reproduce (print, make photocopies, or download) materials from this web site without prior permission, on the condition that you provide proper attribution of the source in all copies. See the Copyright and Citation Information page for more information.

Those interested in publishing or other commercial uses of materials should contact the repository responsible for the custody of the original materials. Web pages for DLG collections include a link to the holding repository where the contact information may be found. Note that some DLG collections contain related materials from multiple repositories.

## Reproductions of materials

Because the items included in the digital library of Georgia come from a variety of repositories throughout the state, reproductions such as photographs, negatives, or photocopies of materials should be obtained directly from the holding repository. Availability of these services depends on the individual repository holding the original materials. Web pages for DLG collections include a link to the holding repository where the contact information may be found. Note that some DLG collections contain related materials from multiple repositories.

**Linking a site**

Anyone may link to the Digital Library of Georgia online collections without permission from the Digital Library of Georgia.

## 6. INDIANA UNIVERSITY DIGITAL LIBRARY

The Indiana University Digital Library Program (DLP) is dedicated to the production and maintenance of a wide range of high-quality networked resources for scholars and students at Indiana University and elsewhere. The Digital Library Program is a collaborative effort of the Indiana University Libraries, the Office of the Vice President for Information Technology, and the university research faculty with leadership from the School of Library and Information Science. This collaboration will capitalize on the institutional capabilities of this university, focusing university resources on digital library projects that support the teaching and research of IU faculty, support the learning and research of IU students, and foster research about the digital library.

The overarching benefit for the students, faculty, and staff of Indiana University will be access to an ever-widening range of digital library resources and services, including full-text online databases, faculty research, classroom materials, multimedia digital resources, electronic journals, and digital libraries from all over the world.

**Goals**

- ★ To increase the number and range of digital resources available for faculty and students;

- To offer digital library services and supporting technologies that are sustainable, scaleable, compatible with the university's technology infrastructure, and interoperable with national and international digital library initiatives;
- To promote and support the scholarly use of digital content and networked information resources by students and faculty at IU;
- To discover and promote currently available digital technologies that can revitalize teaching and enhance learning;
- To address key research questions from user-centered, collections-centered, and system-centered perspectives, their inter-relatedness and the importance of their balance;
- To conduct a program of research to advance the state of knowledge and practice in digital libraries, and the social, organizational, technological, and human factors involving the uses and users of digital libraries;
- To establish a national and international reputation for developing a premier digital library at Indiana University;
- To collaborate with colleagues at other colleges, universities, and research libraries, nationally and internationally in the development of an inter-institutional and international federation of distributed digital libraries.

**Participants**

The Digital Library Program encompasses all campuses of Indiana University. The program is directed through the steering committee comprised of three partners, the Libraries, University Information Technology Services (UITS), and the School of Library and Information Science (SLIS). The current

Administrative Team includes librarians, staff and information technologists from the Bloomington and Indianapolis Libraries and UITS.

## Program Areas

The IU Digital Library Program (IUDLP) will continue focus on a limited number of high priority program areas that include already successful digital library initiatives, development of new digital library services, research and development into digital library technologies, and various collaborations and partnerships.

The criteria for selecting digital library activities for support include:

- ★ Existing digital services that have demonstrated their usefulness to students or faculty.
- ★ Current projects to which it has committed resources.
- ★ New projects that offer widespread benefits to students or faculty.
- ★ New projects that contribute to teaching and learning, and offer research opportunities to faculty.
- ★ New projects that contribute to teaching and learning, and offer technology development opportunities for librarians or technologists.

The activities meet one or more of these criteria. To expand list the Digital Library Program Team solicits other project ideas and offers interested individuals help in planning and obtaining funding for other projects that fall within the scope of digital library initiatives.

## Ongoing Digital Library Services

**School of Music Digital Audio Library :** The Variations Project will expand its collection of digitized audio to meet instructional and research needs. In addition, the project will begin to provide access to image-based content, including CD booklets, liner notes, and musical scores. Changes to the current audio client and server will be made to migrate audio delivery to current protocols for multimedia delivery and resource reservation over IP. Access to Variations will be expanded from delivery in the Music Library, to other locations within the campus and university as network and intellectual property issues permit, including student computing labs, other libraries, faculty offices, and student housing. Experiments in providing inter-institutional access to music collections will be pursued in cooperation with other universities. URL: http://www.dlib.indiana.edu/variations/.

**Electronic text Resources for the Humanities :** LETRS will expand its SGML encoded electronic collections available over the WWW. In addition to providing access to commercially published collections, LETRS will expand its electronic texts by participating in and supporting new projects, using as a model the ongoing Victorian Women Writers Project. LETRS will also investigate collaborating with the Preservation Department, which is creating and storing digital page images for preservation, in the conversion of page images to full-text searchable collections. LETRS will also explore collaboration opportunities with Indiana University faculty scholars and the IU Press. Further, IUL and UITS will review and redefine the mission of LETRS with respect to its provision of public services and its role in developing and managing a specialized digital (CD-ROM) collection of works in the humanities, including English, Classics, Religious Studies, Philosophy, History, Languages, Linguistics and more. URL: http://www.indiana.edu/~letrs/.

**DIDO (Digital Images Online) :** The Digital Library Program supports a collection of low-resolution (72 dpi) digital images selected from the Slide Library collection of over 300,000 images. The image database, created in 1996, represents all historical periods and all media. As of August 2001, the database contains over 17,000 images, which are used to support upwards of 10 class-oriented web pages in the Art History Department each semester. Beginning fall semester 2001 it is expanding access to anyone an Indiana University campus for other educational purposes, via keyword searching and browsing. It is appointing an advisory group that will meet through the coming academic year to advise on enhancements to DIDO and ways to provide improved service to users outside the Department of Art History, on all campuses. Currently, image selection for DIDO is determined by the teaching needs of the School of Fine Arts.

### Digital Media and Image Center

The Digital Media and Image Center (DMIC) was established by the Digital Library Program in January 1998 to digitize images, sound, and videorecordings. Imaging for several major grant-funded projects has taken place in the DMIC, including photographs, correspondence, sheet music, lyric sheets, and personal effects from the Hoagy Carmichael Collection housed in the IU Archives of Traditional Music and the University Archives, negatives from the Frank M. Hohenberger Photograph Collection housed in the Lilly Library, and prints from the U.S. Steel Photograph Collection housed in the Calumet Regional Archives at IU-Northwest.

Smaller imaging projects have also been planned and completed in the DMIC, including approximately 600 negatives and prints of the Wylie House, camp manuals documenting procedures of Camp Chickagami for Girls in Winter, Wisconsin, and IU's holdings of the Indiana University Librarians' Association Newsletter in its various forms since 1969.

Staff at the DMIC is also attempting to establish baseline procedures for common types of imaging projects, including resolution requirements, output formats, and quality control procedures. It also provide consulting services for IU departments considering imaging projects.

## Current Digital Library Program Projects

### *Bloomington*

**Victorian Women Writers Project :** The Victorian Women Writers Project started in 1995, and is devoted to creating electronic editions of works by 19th century British women writers. Women published anthologies, novels, political pamphlets, and volumes of poetry and verse drama, yet it is only now that many of these writers and their works are receiving critical attention. There are currently almost 200 texts available, out of the many thousands to be done, and work is progressing with the help of English Department undergraduate interns. The collection receives an average of 40,000 uses per month. URL: http://www.indiana.edu/~letrs/vwwp/index.html.

**Wright American Fiction Project :** Nine universities in the Committee on Institutional Cooperation (CIC) are participating on a project to digitize 3,000 works of American fiction published between 1851-1875. This collection is based on Lyle Wright's bibliography American Fiction 1851-1875: a Contribution Toward a Bibliography (San Marino, CA: The Huntington Library, 1965). The titles in this bibliography, including works by Mark Twain, William Dean Howells, Herman Melville, Harriet Beecher Stowe and Louisa May Alcott, will be digitized and made freely available, providing a view of American literature, culture and history of this momentous period. The nine participating libraries are: Indiana University, Michigan State University, The Ohio State

University, University of Illinois at Chicago; University of Illinois at Urbana-Champaign; University of Iowa; University of Michigan; University of Minnesota; and University of Wisconsin. URL: http://www.letrs.indiana.edu/web/w/wright2/.

The Indiana University Digital Library Program has received a three-year, United States Department of Education Title VI Technology Program grant to digitize and offer on the World Wide Web a twenty-year portion of the Letopis' Zhurnal'nykh Statei (1956-1975), a serial publication that indexes Soviet periodicals from 1926 to the present. It covers more than 1,700 journals, series, and continuing publications of academies, universities, and research institutes in the fields of humanities, natural sciences, and the social sciences, and it also covers the popular periodical literature. Once digitized and made available on the World Wide Web, it will provide access to the periodical literature for an essential time in modern Russian history, beginning with the period of the Khrushchev "Thaw" following the 20th CPSU Congress and continuing through the first half of the so-called Brezhnev "Period of Stagnation."

## U.S. Steel Photograph Collection

The University received funding from the Indiana State Library/LSTA to digitize the 2,250 photographs in the U.S. Steel Photograph Collection in the Calumet Regional Archive at IU Northwest in Gary. In addition to the photographs the site will feature supplemental texts to provide context for the images and learning activities for students in grades 4-12, developed by Indiana teachers.

## Cushman Collection

The University also received a two-year grant from the Institute for Museum and Library Services (IMLS) to digitize and publish on the Web 18,000 slides from the Cushman Collection in the University Archives in Bloomington. This collection includes Kodachrome slides from 1938-1969, which includes a time when few photographers shot color. Mr. Cushman was a highly-skilled amateur photographer who not only photographed people and places around the world, he meticulously documented his work in notebooks. The project continues from October 2000-September 2002.

### Digital Music Library

The University received funding from the National Science Foundation and the National Endowment for the Humanities was received through the Digital Library Initiatives 2 program to create a digital music library. Building upon VARIATIONS, the project aims to establish a digital music library testbed system containing music in a variety of formats, involving research and development in the areas of system architecture, metadata standards, component-based application architecture, and network services. This system will be used as a foundation for digital library research in the areas of instruction, usability, human-computer interaction, and intellectual property rights. The project will run four years, from October 1, 2000-September 30, 2004.

### Inscriptions from the Land of Israel

Michael Satlow from the Department of Religious Studies proposes developing a research and demonstration prototype of a web site that presents the material culture of the Land of Israel from the Second Temple period to the Arab conquest (c. 450 BCE – 614 CE). The heart of the site will be the corpus of inscriptions. This prototype will focus on Jerusalem. Both LETRS and the Digital Library Team in Indianapolis are providing support for this project. LETRS is providing e-text and web development; the Indianapolis team is providing map digitization and GIS consultation.

## Frank M. Hohenberger Photograph Collection

The University planned and implemented an image digitization project in partnership with the Lilly Library. The first 500 photographs in the Frank M. Hohenberger Photograph Collection have been digitized. A web site for the project offers the complete finding aid, the images, and contextual information about Hohenberger and Brown County. The contextual information includes a biographical essay about Hohenberger written by former Lilly librarian Cecil K. Bryd for an Indiana University Press book of Hohenberger photos and a contemporary article written about Hohenberger and published in the American Magazine in 1933. It is adding subject descriptors to the finding aid in order to increase the consistency of subject searching and continuing to digitize images. URL: http://www.dlib.indiana.edu/collections/lilly/hohenberger/index.html.

## Electronic Atlas of Central Indiana

The Atlas is a Web-based repository of maps and GIS (Geographic Information Systems) data covering Central Indiana. The primary goal of the Atlas is to acquire, archive and make available data for the Indianapolis Metropolitan Statistical Area and the nine county region of Boone, Hamilton, Hancock, Hendricks, Johnson, Madison, Marion, Morgan and Shelby counties. The Atlas project is funded by grants from the Indianapolis Foundation. These data include the social and economic data created by the SAVI Project as well as maps and datasets produced by other providers. To date, these providers consist of the U.S. Census Bureau, the U.S. Geological Survey, the IUPUI Center for Earth and Environmental Science, The Polis Center, the United Way of Central Indiana and the Natural Resource Conservation Service. Maps are currently available as images (PDF files which allow some limited interaction with the data) and as downloadable files (for experts who want to manipulate the data on their own computers).

The Atlas encompasses several digital library initiatives including Geographic Information Systems development, the Historical Aerial Archive, the Indiana Geographic Information Catalog, and Historical Maps.

**Geographic Information Systems**

An object oriented spatial database is under development. The system will facilitate the development of an online mapping system. The retrieval and delivery system being developed for the Atlas will also provide a dynamic data download and decompression application.

**Historical Aerial Archive**

Digitized historical aerial photographs of six of the nine counties of Central Indiana have been incorporated into the Atlas. An image server allows users to pan or zoom on the image. Future enhancements will include address-matching capabilities.

**Historical Maps**

Funded in part by the Ayres Foundation, the Historical Maps section of the Atlas will include a selection of maps from Indianapolis and the Central Indiana region. The team has consulted with the Indiana State Library, the Indiana State Museum, and the IU Geography and Map Library on the project.

**Indiana Geographic Information Catalog**

The development of the catalog is funded in part by a grant from the Federal Geographic Data Committee of the US Geological Survey. Metadata records from local and state agencies are being added to the catalog. These metadata records contain information about geo-spatial data created within the State and that data's location. The catalog will eventually be connected to the National Geospatial Data Clearinghouse, http://130.11.52.184/, operated by the Federal Geographic Data Committee.

IUPUI University Libraries Community Project: in Collaboration with Central Indiana Schools, Museums, and Public Libraries

Funded by a National Leadership Grant from the Institute of Museum and Library Services (IMLS), IUPUI University Library offers access to digital image databases to public libraries and K-12 educational institutions. The Indianapolis Museum of Art has joined IUPUI University Library as the main supporting partner on the Community Project whose purpose is to enrich the lives of members of the community through visual arts. Other museum supporters of the Community Project are The Eiteljorg Museum of American Indians and Western Art, The Indiana State Museum, The Children's Museum, and The Indiana Historical Society.

## Philanthropic Studies Index

The Philanthropic Studies Index (PSI) is an online reference tool to literature on voluntarism, nonprofit organizations, fundraising, and charitable giving. PSI, for the present, provides access to periodical articles, both current and retrospective. In the future, coverage will increase to include relevant books, dissertations, working papers, and other information sources relevant to the ever-growing field of philanthropy. PSI covers 1940 to 1999. PSI was migrated into an Oracle database structure in 2000. A web interface for citation editing and data loading have been incorporated into the management system. Future enhancements will include development of advanced searching functionality, development of new data entry screens, and gathering and delivery of detailed search statistics.

## New Digital Library Initiatives

**Integrating Access to Electronic Resources :** The Digital Library Program will work with others in the IU Libraries, at IUB and IUPUI and elsewhere in the university, toward the goal of integrating existing electronic resources into a more comprehensive and accessible source. These currently include full text reference sources (Encyclopedia Britannica, OED), bibliographic indexes (Expanded Academic Index), and full text journals (MUSE, JSTOR and some journals within EAI). Each of these resources looks and works differently; it needs to plan to get these resources to work together better.

**Indiana University proposes three areas of research:** (i) digital libraries as complex (technological, social, organizational and human) systems; (ii) streaming audio and video data as digital library services; and (iii) the relation of testbed digital libraries to networked learning environments and collaborative work spaces. The proposed electronic reserve system above offers but one set of digital library opportunities. Research focusing on the electronic reserve project could advance the state of knowledge and practice in digital libraries through the contributions of IU's research faculty in areas of human-computer interaction and systems design, instructional systems technology, social and organizational informatics, and others. Other areas with research potential include innovative user services, digital collections management, digital library system design, and streaming media.

**Streaming Digital Media :** The Digital Library Program will undertake a program of research and development in the network delivery of audio and video content, for example: IP-video and IP-audio, Quality of Service, and network infrastructure; user interaction and usability; metadata for discovery and retrieval of video and audio; scaleability; authentication and intellectual property; security; other technology issues. This work will build on IU's experience in delivering networked audio and video library services (through the Variations Project and the IMDS-Interactive Media Distribe to explore with the Indiana University a project to digitize their entire database of documentary films and license it to academic institutions. This project would have potential on a number of levels, serving both the academic community and the distributors of documentary films. It would give Indiana University a unique opportunity to explore the necessary technology to provide this service. It would also lend itself to an interesting program of research. It would have a testbed for a number of business models related to distributing a "full-text database" of moving images and would hope to gain valuable information about how students and faculty use networked motion pictures.

**Network Access to Unique Collections :** The Digital Library Program will undertake projects to provide network access to digitized resources — specialized texts, rare books and manuscripts, ephemeral or pre-publication literature, and other texts and artifacts from the collections of the IU Libraries.

**Digital Library Seminar Series :** The Digital Library Program will offer a seminar series, highlighting issues related to digital libraries. Some of the seminars will be offered over the lunch hour once a month. Others will be larger and use national speakers, perhaps twice a year. We will also explore the possibility of sponsoring a national teleconference, similar to Networked Information and the Scholar (October 1994). This teleconference would bring together digital library experts from a number of fields. The purposes of the seminar series are (1) to increase knowledge about digital libraries throughout Indiana University; and (2) to increase the visibility of Indiana University as an international participant in digital library developments.

## Infrastructure for Digital Libraries

**Inter-institutional Collaboration :** The Digital Library Program will collaborate with colleagues at other colleges, universities, and research libraries in the development of an inter-institutional and international federation of distributed digital libraries. Special emphasis will be given to long-standing collaborative partners, such as institutional members of the CIC, and through partnerships within the Digital Library Federation of which IU is a member. These collaborations will take the form of digitization projects, such as the Wright American Fiction Project, software development with the University of Virginia on FEDORA, and Perry Willett's work on TEI guidelines.

**Digital Library Architecture and Infrastructure :** The Digital Library Program will develop and help implement a common architecture for digital libraries at IU. The DLP will advise or directly support individual centers devoted to creating and managing digital collections or delivering networked information services, and will seek to integrate these into a common design architecture that is scaleable, sustainable, and interoperable. University Information Technology Services (UITS) will develop and deliver technology infrastructure services in support of the DLP: campus and wide-area networking, data center operations and management, application design and development, or others. UITS and SLIS can provide support for user requirements analysis, user-centered design, and usability testing. The Advanced Information Technology Laboratory (AITL) in UITS will provide technology assessment, evaluation and testbed development in support of the DLP.

**Consultation and Advisory Services :** The Digital Library Program cannot directly guide or manage every project in the wide array of digital library services that will be developed and implemented at Indiana University. For projects not under its direct guidance, the role of DLP is to provide advice and consultation as requested regarding the direction taken by such digital collections and services and to help assure their integration with other digital library services and with the IU digital library architecture. The Digital Library Program staff will work with Library Information Technology and other units to delineate specific areas of responsibility. They will also develop a plan for communicating their services throughout the university.

## 7. SMETE DIGITAL LIBRARY

The Science Mathematics, Technology and Engineering (SMTE) Digital Library is a dynamic online library and portal of services by the SMETE Open Federation for teachers and students to access a wealth of teaching and learning materials as well as join this expanding community of science, math, engineering and technology explorers of all ages. SMETE opens up the worlds of science, mathematics, engineering and technology education to teachers and students anytime, anyplace.

The goal of the project is to provide access to high-quality teaching resources and learning activities that reflect the museum's foundation of playful exhibit-based inquiry in science, art, and human perception. The collection is suitable for educators in both classroom and out-of-school settings; for peer institutions such as museums, science centers, and universities; and for individuals. Funding was received from the National Science Foundation to launch the Learning Resources Collection.

The SMETE Open Federation was formed to promote the teaching and learning of science, mathematics, engineering and technology at all levels. The Federation was built with funding by the National Science Foundation, National STEM Education Digital Library program and partnerships with nationally recognized professional educational organizations, academic institutions and private e-learning companies. The SMETE Open Federation community fosters the ongoing collaborative development among partner organizations, provides tools and services to support collection and service providers, and ensures stability, sustainability and scalability of the Federation's programs and projects.

SMETE.ORG. SMETE.ORG is the gateway to a comprehensive collection of science, math, engineering and technology (SMET) education content and services available to learners, educators, and academic policy-makers. By serving as the integrative organization that distributes pedagogical material through the establishment of a federation of digital libraries and providing direct access and delivery of instructional resources, SMETE.ORG meets the growing and changing needs of the participatory communities of learners and educators. A collection of collections and a community of communities – SMETE.ORG.

**Vision Statement**

The SMETE Open Federation takes a global leadership role in technology in the service of learning. As a membership organization, it promotes, advances, strengthens and improves the teaching, learning and comprehension of science, mathematics, engineering and technology (SME&T) education in K-12 and higher education. The primary mission of the

SMETE Open Federation is to establish universal access to academic excellence in SME&T education. Serving and representing the community of administrators, learners, and educators, the SMETE Open Federation is the premier digital collection of resources and services for the nation and the world in SME&T e-learning. Among the nation's leading digital libraries, the SMETE Open Federation is recognized for advanced technology, leading-edge research, premier educational collections and active community involvement. The SMETE Open Federation and its participating libraries and services responds to its community's needs in order to advance SME&T education worldwide.

To these ends, the SMETE Open Federation is characterized by:

★ A whole that is greater than the sum of its parts, in which each member has a clearly focused and valued mission and all contribute to a network of premier educational resources.

★ A diverse community of educators and staff who use new technologies, evaluation techniques and curricular innovations to enhance student learning.

★ A technological infrastructure based on leading-edge research that provides open access to expertise, tools, technology and services.

★ Active partnerships that foster ongoing collaborative development with business and industry, cultural and social organizations, and research and educational institutions to ensure stability, scalability, and sustainability.

★ Learning communities that engage in universal freedom of access to knowledge.

★ Communities of individuals having a common disciplinary interest.

* Leadership in establishing higher achievement in SME&T education.

To ensure that this vision becomes a reality, the SMETE Open Federation strives to attain the following goals:

* To be a leader in innovative digital library technology and education.
* To provide users with a full spectrum of interoperability at the content, procedural and transaction levels.
* To establish, maintain, and grow a digital library that responds to the educational needs of end users.
* To support the creation and evolution of the National SMETE Digital Library.
* To establish a diversified funding model that sustains the SMETE Open Federation.
* To develop a community of learning communities who validate, use, contribute to, and support the SMETE Open Federation.

## Organization and Governance

The SMETE Open Federation is a federation of organizations and research projects that span science, mathematics, engineering and technology (SME&T) education. These organizations include various SME&T disciplinary digital libraries, K-12 science libraries, services that support digital libraries, professional development organizations for SME&T teachers and faculty, as well as SME&T publishers and professional and disciplinary societies. The SMETE Open Federation as a voluntary membership organization depends upon the reciprocal agreements among and between Federation members. A Board of Directors representing the membership of the Federation provides direction and oversight to the organization; it facilitates collaboration among the members, establishes future directions for the Federation and guides the work of the SMETE Open Federation operations unit

Currently, the SMETE Open Federation is an unincorporated entity. Initially, the Board of Directors assumed an advisory role until a plan for sustaining the organization has been developed and implemented. During this period one representative from each SMETE Open Federation Partner will sit on an interim Board of Directors. The role of the Board of Directors is to set policy, derive and monitor the Federation's purpose and goals, and conduct strategic planning for the short and long term. It is also responsible for working with the SMETE Open Federation operations unit to ensure fiduciary solvency and sustainability of the organization.

**Alliance Members and Affiliates**

**Access Excellence @ The National Health Museum** (www.accessexcellence.org)

Access Excellence is a national educational program that provides high school biology and life science teachers access to their colleagues, scientists and critical sources of new scientific information via the Internet.

**American Association for the Advancement of Science** (www.aaas.org)

AAAS is America's premier professional society dedicated to the advancement of scientific and technological excellence across all disciplines, and to the public's understanding of science and technology.

**Association for Women in Science** (www.awis.org)

The Association for Women in Science is dedicated to achieving equity and full participation for women in science, mathematics, engineering and technology.

**Biology Education Online** (www.accessexcellence.org/LC/BEOn)

Biology Education Online, a joint project of Access Excellence @ the National Health Museum and the National Association of Biology Teachers, is an online, peer reviewed journal of science teaching resources.

**BioQUEST Curriculum Consortium** (www.bioquest.org)

BioQUEST is a national consortium of over 100 college biology educators and computer software developers who have developed and are continuing to produce quality biology curricular materials, simulations and tools.

**Biosci Ed Net** (www.biosciednet.org/)

The Biosci Ed Net (BEN) Collaborative, spearheaded by the American Association for the Advancement of Science and composed of 11 professional societies and coalitions for biology education, is developing a revolutionary approach for transforming biology teaching and learning in undergraduate and graduate institutions, as well as in professional schools.

**Computing and Information Technology Interactive Digital Education Library** (www.citidel.org/)

The Computing and Information Technology Interactive Digital Education Library (CITIDEL), is a collaborative project among universities and professional societies, to establish, operate and maintain a digital library for the computing education community in all its diversity and at all levels.

**Coalition for Networked Information** (www.cni.org)

The Coalition for Networked Information is jointly sponsored by the Association of Research Libraries and Educause. Comprised of over 200 member organizations, CNI focuses on issues associated with developing networked information content; transforming organizations, professions and individuals; and building technology, standards and infrastructure.

**Computer Science Teaching Center** (www.cstc.org)

The Computer Science Teaching Center (CSTC) is an Internet-based repository of peer-reviewed teaching resources for computer science educators. Endorsed by the Association of Computing Machinery, the CSTC is designed to facilitate access to quality teaching materials developed worldwide.

**Digital Library for Earth Systems Education** (www.dlese.org)

The Digital Library for Earth Systems Education is conceived as an information system dedicated to the collections, enhancement, and distribution of materials that facilitate learning about the Earth system at all educational levels. It is being built as a community effort; collections, services and tools will be developed and maintained by numerous partners that reflect the broadest possible participation from the Earth system educational community.

**Education Development Center** (www.edc.org)

With over 325 projects worldwide, the Education Development Center (EDC) is one of the world's leading non-profit education and health organizations. EDC brings researchers and practitioners together to create tools and conditions for learning, reaching people of all ages, backgrounds and abilities.

**Eduprise** (www.eduprise.com)

Eduprise provides a complete range of services that helps colleges and universities build Internet-enabled instruction quickly and effectively, and provided project management services to IMS.

**Eisenhower National Clearinghouse for Mathematics and Science Education** (www.enc.org)

ENC provides K-12 teachers with a central source of information and curriculum materials on mathematics and science.

**iLumina** (www.iLumina-dlib.org)

iLumina, a collaborative project between Eduprise and university partners, is a digital collection of small scale undergraduate teaching materials developed by faculty for science, mathematics, technology and engineering education.

**Instructional Architect** (ia.usu.edu)

The Instructional Architect, developed by Utah State University, is a suite of online services for automatically recommending learning resources and providing instructional support to allow users to combine existing learning resources into their own lesson plans.

**Interactive University** (iu.berkeley.edu/iu/)

The Interactive University Project enables UC Berkeley to make its unmatched resources of people and knowledge available on the Internet. It serves learners and educators, targeting K-12 teachers, students, their families, and local communities throughout the Bay Area and California.

**Internet Scout** (scout.cs.wisc.edu)

The Internet Scout Project provides timely information to the education community about valuable Internet resources. The Scout Report, their flagship product, has been continuously published every Friday since 1994.

**Learning Matrix** (thelearningmatrix.enc.org)

The Learning Matrix, administered by the Eisenhower National Clearinghouse, will use the web to support an innovative experience of professional inquiry into the teaching and learning of mathematics and science. It will include peer-reviewed electronic resources for teaching future mathematics and science teachers and information about best practices in undergraduate teaching and assessments, course syllabi and interactive learning materials.

**Learning*Online* Network with CAPA** (www.lon-capa.org)

Learning*Online* Network with CAPA (LON-CAPA) initiative aims to create and sustain a cross-institutional distributed platform for content creation, sharing and delivery. LON-CAPA will allow groups of organizations (schools, departments, universities, commercial business) to link their online instructional resources in a common marketplace, thus creating an online economy for instructional resources.

**Mathematical Association of America** (www.maa.org)

The Mathematical Association of America is the largest professional organization in the world that focuses on undergraduate mathematics education.

**Mathematical Sciences Digital Library** (www.mathdl.org)

The Mathematical Sciences Digital Library (MathDL) is an online resource managed by the Mathematical Association of America and hosted by the Math Forum. MathDL provides online resources for both teachers and students of collegiate mathematics including the Journal of Online Mathematics and its Applications (JOMA), a catalog of mathematics and commercial products and digital classroom resources.

**Math Forum** (www.mathforum.org)

The Math Forum is an online knowledge building community for the teaching and learning of mathematics, with almost one million visitors per month. The Math Forum Web site provides teachers, mathematicians, students, parents and others with a range of services-such as mentoring projects, public forums, an online mathematics library, ask-an-expert services and online educational materials.

**Merit Network** (www.merit.edu)

Merit Network is a nonprofit corporation that promotes computer networking in Michigan and beyond. Merit's Center to Support Technology in Education develops educational and support programs aimed at assisting and promoting the infusion of learning technologies into educational institutions, with a focus on K-12 schools.

**Michigan Teacher Network** (mtn.merit.edu)

Michigan Teacher Network (MTN), a project of Merit Network, provides easy access to K-12 education related Web resources that have been carefully evaluated for quality, relevance and effectiveness. MTN describes thousands of high quality resources that can be effectively used with students in the classroom, for professional development or for educational planning and problem solving.

**MERLOT-Multimedia Educational Resource for Learning and Online Teaching** (www.merlot.org)

The Multimedia Educational Resource for Learning and Online Teaching (MERLOT) is an international cooperative for high quality online resources to improve learning and teaching within higher education. The cooperative connects systems, consortiums, institutions of higher education, professional organizations of academic disciplines and individual members to form a community of people who strive to enrich the teaching and learning experience.

**National Center for Supercomputer Applications** (www.ncsa.org)

The National Center for Supercomputing Applications earned and maintains an international reputation in high-performance computing and networking and in developing innovative software applications.

**National Engineering Education Delivery System** (www.needs.org)

NEEDS is an digital library of courseware and other instructional software for engineering education. At NEEDS, teachers, students, and lifelong learners can search, access, and download educational learning resources over the Web as well as comment on them or join in on-line discussions regarding engineering education.

**Online Computer Library Center** (www.oclc.org)

The Online Computer Library Center (OCLC) is a nonprofit membership organization serving over 40,000 libraries in 76 countries and territories around the world. A world leader in digital library services, OCLC helps libraries serve people by providing economical access to knowledge through innovation and collaboration.

**Project Kaleidoscope** (www.pkal.org)

Project Kaleidoscope is a nationally respected, informal alliance working to build strong learning environments for undergraduate students in mathematics, engineering and the various fields of science.

**SRI International, Center for Technology in Learning** (www.cilt.org **and** www.escot.org)

SRI International Center for Technology in Learning conducts research on all aspects of learning technologies. Their current efforts include various multi-institutional projects such as the Tapped-In online teacher professional development community (with nearly 8,000 members) and the Center for Innovative Learning Technologies (CILT) partnership of researchers, practitioners, policymakers, and industry.

**TeacherLIB** (www.teacherlib.org)

The TeacherLIB project, a joint project of Merit Network and Eastern Michigan University, strives to ensure that as the National SMETE Digital Library develops, a focus on K-12 teachers is maintained.

**University of California Teaching, Learning and technology Center** (www.teacherlib.org)

The University of California Teaching, Learning and

technology Center (TLtC) is working with SMETE.ORG to develop a webzine and online forum to provide visibility to campus and faculty efforts in the development and use of teaching and learning technologies across the University of California system.

**University and Corporate Members**

California State University at Sacramento (www.csus.edu)

Cisco Systems (www.cisco.com)

Eastern Michigan University (www.emich.edu)

John Wiley & Sons (www.wiley.com)

Sun Microsystems (www.sun.com)

University of California, Berkeley (www.berkeley.edu)

University of California Office of the President, Academic Initiatives (www.ucop.edu/acadinit/)

University of Florida (www.ufl.edu)

University of Maryland, Baltimore County (www.umbc.edu)

Utah State University (www.usu.edu)

Virginia Polytechnic Institute and State University (www.vt.edu)

**Technology**

The SMETE Open Federation technology services allow participating SMETE collections and services to form a cohesive digital library community that embraces and represents the fundamental diversity of our members. The technical foundation of the SMETE Open Federation is a set of sophisticated protocols and specifications to permit any SMETE collection or service to leverage the combined collections of the our members. Our approach offers a range of options for collections to use for participating in the SMETE Open Federation. Collections and services will be able to negotiate their participation to meet their needs from a set of options bounded by the following two endpoints of a continuum.

## Tools for Interoperability

Through collaboration with the SMETE Open Federation, member collections and services will have free access to shared technology. One of the principal pieces of technology is software tools for interoperability at three levels: content, e.g., shared metadata; protocol, e.g., federated search and metadata harvesting; and transaction, e.g., digital rights management.

## Content Interoperability

**Cataloging :** One of the principal technical hurdles to overcome in digital library interoperability is a cooperative cataloging approach for resources within the digital library collections so that people and computers will be able to find relevant objects by searching, as opposed to browsing the entire digital library one collection or object at a time until they find the right one.

To support collections and authors in creating metadata for their digital learning resources, we have compiled a list of metadata authoring (cataloging) tools that permit the creation of metadata through various means appropriate to the type of learning resources available to the author. The end-objective is to create a comprehensive metadata creation and management service for SMETE collection developers and end-users.

## Protocol Interoperability

**Federated Search :** To expand the network of resource collections, we provide a federated search application programming interface (API) to enable search over multiple, remotely hosted SMETE collections simultaneously. Our approach allows for search over all participating SMETE collections from the SMETE Open Federation premier gateway at www.smete.org, as well as enables search from any participating peer to any participating peer. Thus member collections benefit from having a value-added gateway from their local collections into the full range of participating SMETE collections.

The SMETE Open Federation has implemented a generalized federated search mechanism for educational digital libraries. The technical details are described in the SMETE Search API. (This work is based upon original testing conducted between the SMETE.ORG Portal, ENC and the Utah State University Instructional Architect project, using the originally proposed specification. This prototype demonstrates the type of search fields the libraries should support and the format of the search results. The original specification is loosely based on the Simple Digital Library Interoperability Protocol (SDLIP-Core).)

**Hosting Services**

The SMETE Open Federation will also catalog metadata and host collections as needed. This service is necessary in order to help incipient collections that do not yet have the technical infrastructure to host their own collection initially, but would like to share their resources and make them available to the SMETE Open Federation. Furthermore, some collections that meet the broad criteria for inclusion in the SMETE Digital Library, may wish to have their metadata replicated so that new, value-added services may be built around them.

**Transactional Interoperability**

Transactional interoperability permits member collections and services to integrate their back-end systems such as digital rights management systems, with other members' systems. This is one area of new development for the SMETE Open Federation.

## Education and Outreach

To build a SMETE Digital Library that is both useful and used, it is essential to engage a broad community of SMETE educators, learners and other stakeholders in order to develop the technical and social infrastructures of the SMETE Open Federation. It is important to recognize the SMETE Digital Library is more than just a technical infrastructure; it is also a community.

The SMETE Open Federation, through is Education and Outreach program area, support the expansion and development of collections and services within and beyond the SMETE Digital Library community. We reach out to educators and learners at all levels to engage them in the use, re-use, review and development of the resources made available through the SMETE Digital Library. It supports improved teaching and learning as a primary outcome of our efforts.

The primary vehicles for Education and Outreach are workshops and focus groups at conferences and individual consulting with organizations. Using these vehicles, it can assist both the development and dissemination of content and services for the SMETE Digital Library. It will help identify the needs, priorities, and evaluations of incipient collections to identify how to make them educationally relevant for the SMETE Digital Library as well as evaluate existing collections to identify gaps, that is, materials that are needed but missing from the current collection. It can consult with service providers interested in providing their service for the SMETE Digital Library. Finally, it will educates teachers and administrators on how to use digital learning materials available from the SMETE Digital Library.

## Evaluation

In order to evaluate the SMETE Open Federation effectively,

we must create strong collaborations focused around common goals and outcomes. The evaluation program area establishes a structure that will ensure the SMETE Open Federation (and ultimately the National SMETE Digital Library) collects the information necessary to track and monitor its own activities and provides individual members with data they need to evaluate their own activities, but not interfere with individual evaluation efforts.

To accomplish this, we bring together evaluation experts to establish the SMETE Open Federation as a center for evaluation education resources. This center:

★ Coordinates planning for an initial set of educational workshops for SMETE Open Federation members defining the critical dimensions of SMETE digital library evaluation.

★ Identifies formative evaluation needs of SMETE Open Federation partners.

★ Encourages collaboration and consultation among evaluation experts and novices.

★ Fosters and disseminates digital library evaluation 'best practices.

SMETE Digital Library is one of the very few digital libraries that cater to the academic and research needs of the scientific and technological communities. It has grown rapidly and is all set to be grow fastly in the time to come.

## 8. DIGITAL SOUTH ASIA LIBRARY

The Digital South Asia Library provides digital materials for reference and research on South Asia to scholars, public officials, business leaders, and other users. This project builds upon a two-year pilot project funded by the Association of Research Libraries' Global Resources Program with support from the Andrew W. Mellon Foundation. Participants in the Digital

South Asia Library include leading U.S. universities, the Center for Research Libraries, the South Asia Microform Project, the Committee on South Asian Libraries and Documentation, the Association for Asian Studies, the Library of Congress, the Asia Society, the British Library, the University of Oxford, the University of Cambridge, MOZHI in India, the Sundarayya Vignana Kendram in India, Madan Puraskar Pustakalaya in Nepal, and other institutions in South Asia.

The Digital South Asia Library project (DSAL) together with the Digital Dictionaries of South Asia (DDSA) have instituted a plan for archiving and preserving their resources. This plan considers much of the recent literature concerning these. The problems of digital archiving are widely described elsewhere and will be summarily referred to here.

In order to avoid the difficulties of proliferation and obsolescence with regard to compression software, DSAL avoids compressing and decompressing data as much as possible. Some of the files are large, but the continuing reductions in the price of digital media make this approach practical. Images from the Web site are currently either gifs or jpegs. However, DSAL archives tiff files for these images because tiffs contain the most information of any image format. DSAL does not touch up tiffs, gifs or jpegs.

The server for DSAL and DDSA uses two tape systems as well as another server to backup the entire Web site. Back-ups occur daily. In order to further secure the data against the possibility of damage to the facility where the back-ups occur, a copy of the data is stored away from the site each week. In addition to the data on the Web site, archived material such as the tiff files used to prepare gifs and jpegs are also backed-up on CDs. The data storage plan also includes the following procedures to ensure the integrity of the storage media.

- ★ Periodic checks of completeness and functionality of the media.
- ★ Periodic refreshing and/or copying the resources in order to guard.against the degradation of media.
- ★ Migration to new media or new formats.
- ★ Saving files in their primary format.
- ★ Preserving the technology used in the creation/storage of the files.

Naming conventions are established and documented so that resources can be consistently identified and found. DSAL naming conventions include:

- ★ Only lowercase for file names.
- ★ Use of Primary Key field names in the file names whenever possible.
- ★ Linking of parts of a file name with an underscore ( _ ).
- ★ The inclusion of dates in file names (date of the original resource).
- ★ Files are grouped together on storage media using the structure of the DSAL Web site (resources can be labeled as reference, maps, indexes, images, bibliographies, statistics, or books and journals).
- ★ Jewel cases are labeled with complete file names (in runs) and include the dates of the CD creation or the DLT creation.
- ★ Tapes and CDs themselves are also labeled with abbreviated file information.

**Works Referenced**


- ★ Research Library Group: *Preserving Digital Information: Final Report and Recommendations.* http://www.rlg.org/ArchTF/.
- ★ National Library of Australia: *The Role of Preservation*

*and the Library of the Future.* A paper presented by Colin Webb, Director Preservation Services, at CONSAL 2000, the 11th Congress of Southeast Asian Librarians Conference, Singapore, 26th - 28th April 2000. http://www.nla.gov.au/nla/staffpaper/cwebb9.html.

- Neil Beagrie and Daniel Greenstein (King's College London). *A Strategic Policy Framework for Creating and Preserving Digital Collections.* http://ahds.ac.uk/manage/framework.htm.
- David Haynes, David Streatfield, Tanya Jowett and Monica Blake *Responsibility for Digital Archiving and Long Term Access to Digital Data.* http://www.ukoln.ac.uk/services/papers/bl/jisc-npo67/digital-preservation.html.

**Partners**

The Digital South Asia Library is a global collaborative effort to make important and rare resources available to the international community. Partners include:

- In the United States
- Center for Research Libraries (home)
- University of Chicago (lead institution)
  - The ARTFL Project
- American Institute of Indian Studies
- American Institute of Pakistan Studies
- Asia Society
- Association for Asian Studies
- Center for South Asia Libraries
- Columbia University
- Council of American Overseas Research Centers
- Library of Congress
- Triangle South Asia Consortium
- University of Minnesota

- ★ University of Washington
- ★ Urdu Research Library Consortium
- ★ In Europe
- ★ British Library (lead institution)
- ★ University of Oxford
- ★ Wellcome Library
- ★ In South Asia
- ★ Roja Muthiah Research Library (lead institution)
- ★ Centre for Studies in Social Sciences, Calcutta
- ★ Library of Congress Field Office-New Delhi
- ★ Madan Puraskar Pustakalaya
- ★ Maraimalai Adigal Library
- ★ MOZHI
- ★ Mushfiq Khwaja Library and Research Centre
- ★ Sundarayya Vignana Kendram
- ★ Tamil Nadu State Archives
- ★ Urdu Documentation Centre
- ★ Urdu Research Centre
- ★ In Australia
- ★ Curtin University of Technology
- ★ International Organizations
- ★ Electronic Cultural Atlas Initiative (ECAI)
- ★ South Asia Regional Team
- ★ South Asia Through Official Eyes (SATOE)

## Digitizing the Collection

Due to the variety of materials involved in the project, various scanners are used. The microfilm materials are scanned using a Wicks and Wilson 4100 Roll Film Scanstation. Film is scanned at 400 dpi in grayscale. The resulting tiffs are compressed with the recognized standard, the LZW algorithm. Unbound books are put through a Canon DR-3020 Document Scanner. Tiff images are created at 300 dpi. Serials and manuscripts are scanned using a Minolta PS 7000 overhead scanner. Photographs are scanned using a Hewlett Packard ScanJet 4C3C flatbed scanner. 35 mm. film is scanned using a Nikon Super Coolscan 4000. This scanner is also used to scan mounted slides. Tiffs are created for all images. Three types of tiffs are created. First, in some instances, uncompressed tiffs are created. In addition two categories of compressed tiffs are created, LZW lossless tiffs and G4 fax compression tiffs. The latter are used with Optical Character Recognition (OCR) software for the creation of full text items. All original, untouched tiffs are archived in at least two types of media-either DLT tapes or CDs as well as copies on the server.

Adobe Photoshop is used to create the jpegs and/or gifs for Web delivery. Images in grayscale are saved as gifs with 8 colors. Using grayscale alleviates some of the bleed through (the situation when type from the back of a page is visible when looking at the front of a page) often associated with older materials.

Oversized maps are photographed at one of the labs at the University of Chicago Hospitals. 4 x 6 positives are created from this process and these are then scanned with a full flood scanner. In addition, maps may be digitized on a Contex full scale color scanner located in the Advanced Lab of Social Science Research Computing at the University of Chicago.

**Unicode**

In order for any language to be displayed on a computer, the symbols (alphabet and numbers) that comprise that language must be transformed into numbers, the digits that make up the digital language of computers. Before computers were widely and intensively networked, there was less impetus for uniformity in the development of digital representations for the various languages of the world. A plethora of diverse digital character sets were developed for specific languages. These character sets could not practically represent the symbols of other languages and were not compatible with a variety of operating systems or software applications. With the advent of the Internet and the World Wide Web, the desirability of a uniform system for encoding the symbols of all the languages of the world became evident. To this end, a uniform system of encoding the symbols of languages into a single digital character set, a Unicode, was developed. Because Unicode establishes unique values for language symbols, Unicode can be used across a variety of computer operating systems and software applications. For a full description of Unicode please see their Web site http://www.unicode.org. Given the diversity of languages in South Asia and the global audience envisioned for DSAL, the use of Unicode for material presented on the Web site is an imperative.

**ISCII**

DSAL and DDSA use the Indian Standard Code for Information Interchange, ISCII, for the encoding of Indic texts into data files. ISCII was developed and adopted by the Government of India and is widely used in South Asia for languages written in the various scripts derived from the Brahmi script. Indic languages written in Perso-Arabic script can not be encoded with ISCII. The ISCII files are then translated into Unicode for display on the Web. The translation from ISCII to Unicode is made simpler by the participation of the Government of India in the Unicode consortium. According to the Unicode consortium, "for any given Indic script, the consonant and vowel letter codes of Unicode are based on ISCII." http://www.unicode.org/unicode/faq/indic.html#1.

## Dublin Core

The technical term metadata refers to data describing information sources such as those on a Web site like DSAL. This data allows search engines to find and classify resources. The creation of widely accepted standards for the structure and content of metadata has been an important recent development in information technology. The DSAL and DDSA projects have decided to implement the Dublin Core as the metadata system for these projects in accordance with guidelines outlined by the Library of Congress, http://lcweb.loc.gov/marc/dccross.html. Among the various metadata standards, Dublin Core is being widely adopted in the academic world. DSAL also incorporates generic metadata to ensure that crawler-based search engines can access the metadata. All DSAL and DDSA first and second level pages will have metadata.

## PURL

One important issue in the evolution of digital resources on the World Wide Web has been the ability to track a resource in spite of changes in location. For a variety of reasons, the address or Uniform Resource Locator (URL) of a resource may change. In order to facilitate the tracking of resources, DSAL and DDSA have decided to use OCLC's PURL service. PURL stands for Persistent Uniform Resource Locator. Instead of pointing directly to the location of an Internet resource, a PURL points to an intermediate resolution service. The PURL can remain consistent even if the URL varies so that users can link to a resource without updating their

As part of the effort to conform to the World Wide Web Consortium (W3C) standards and recommendations, DSAL and DDSA are attempting to prepare for the use of XML (eXtensible Markup Language). Most documents on the Web are written in a form of HTML (HyperText Markup

Language), but shortcomings in HTML with regard to data exchange and manipulation have led to a call by the W3C for the eventual use of XML (eXtensible Markup Language). In the short term, the W3C have recommended the adoption of XHTML (eXtensible Hypertext Markup Language) as a step toward that end. XHTML is designed to be compatible with XML standards as they are more widely adopted. DSAL and DDSA strive to keep abreast of recommended practices in order to ensure that the site remains easy to use.

**Web Accessibility Initiative**

In 1998, Congress amended the Rehabilitation Act to require Federal agencies to make their electronic and information technology accessible to the disabled. Recent legal interpretations of the act have extended the scope of the law to all state-controlled colleges and universities. The criteria for compliance with regard to Web-based technology and information are based on access guidelines developed by the Web Accessibility Initiative of the World Wide Web Consortium (W3C). These standards consider the needs of users with a variety of disabilities. People with visual disabilities will find it easier to use reading browsers because of the labeled graphics, described video, marked up tables, and guidelines for the use of color and movement. People with hearing disabilities will benefit from the captions included with audio files. Those with physical disabilities that limit their capacity to use a mouse can more easily navigate Web sites by means of keyboard and/or single-switch support for menu commands. Because users with cognitive or neurological disabilities often need a more consistent structure of information, WAI includes recommendations about data structure and display such as consistent navigation, concise language, and the elimination of flickering tags.

The World Wide Web Consortium has identified three levels of compliance with WAI. Level One compliance will remove the major barriers for users with specific disabilities. Levels Two and Three will incrementally improve the transfer of information. DSAL and DDSA Web pages will strive for Level Two compliance

There are coincidental benefits of the WAI for Web users without disabilities. For example, he various modalities of the WAI offer text only options for the users of Web phones or palm pilots with either small or even text only display screens. Clear and concise Web pages are beneficial to all users.

## Specifics

After reading and reviewing a number of articles on the WAI, DSAL and DDSA have put together a brief list of the main points of WAI that affect our site.

HTML should help to convey meaning through its layout and presentation.

★ The layout should be consistent throughout an entire site.

★ Documents should be organized so that they can be read without style sheets. For example, when an HTML document is rendered without associated style sheets, it must still be possible to read the document.

## Color

★ All information conveyed with color should also be possible to interpret without color, either from context or markup.

★ Color blind individuals might not distinguish red from green from yellow. If you use color in Web design, use clearly contrasting colors such as blue and black and white and yellow.

* Eschew instructions based on color, such as 'push the red button'.

**Fonts**

* Choose tags that emphasize translatable structure. Speech synthesizers are unable to interpret some forms of visual representation (such as 'italic'). Instead, use tags such as STRONG, EM, and H1 to add structure to documents.
* Avoid deprecated, that is to say outdated, font tags, for example (font color="blue")
* Separate navigation items with a space, a " | ", and a space in order to avoid overtaxing screen readers.

**Hypertext.**

* Use phrases that are comprehensible out of context.
* Link text should be concise.
* Added accesskeys may help users without mice and work well with the audio browsers needed by some disabled users.

**Tables**

* Explain table contents by use of the summary attribute in the table tag.
* Make line by line reading comprehensible.
* Use the summary tag for graphs and charts as well.

Declare the language of the document, for example (HTML lang="eng").

* This helps the computer or assistive device present information in a manner appropriate to that language and also helps software that translates text from one language into another.
* Use three letter ISO 639-2 language codes rather than two letter codes. The ISO list is available at http://lcweb.loc.gov/standards/iso639-2/englangn.html.

Avoid using frames as these cause problems for indexing and searching via search engines because of the way in which some spiders work.

Every image, sound, applet, and script should be accompanied by alternative textual descriptions.

- ★ For example, for an image used to describe membership in a document, the gif file referring to membership information should be accompanied with a textual desciption in following manner, img src=" littlemembership.gif" alt="Membership Information" border="0"
- ★ Other options for text accompaniments, such as D-links or longdesc. are not currently recommended.

Provide alternative content for scripts, applets, and plug-ins in case active features are inaccessible or unsupported. Avoid tags that cause screen flicker. Flickering can initiate seizures or other unintended consequences for some users.

## Works Referenced

- ★ Web Accessibility Initiative (WAI) from W3C http://www.w3.org/WAI/.
- ★ Checklist for complete instructions http://www.w3.org/TR/WCAG10/full-checklist.html.
- ★ Federal Information Technology Accessibility Initiative http://www.section508.gov/ .
- ★ Designing for the Color-Challenged: A Challenge http://www.InternetTG.org/newsletter/mar99/accessibility_color_challenged.html.
- ★ Web Monkey http://hotwired.lycos.com/webmonkey/97/11/index4a.html, and http://hotwired.lycos.com/webmonkey/design/site_building/tutorials/tutorial5.html.

**Tools**

- ★ http://www.delorie.com/web/lynxview.html Shows you what a given page would look like in Lynx, a text only browser. This can be a good place to start checking for compliance with WAI.
- ★ http://www.delorie.com/web/purify.html Check the level of HTML compliance.
- ★ http://www.cast.org/bobby/ this tool will check one page at a time for the various levels of compliance (1 - 3).
- ★ http://watson.addy.com/ Dr. Watson is a free service that estimates download
- ★ times and checks link validity, site popularity,and spelling.

## 9. DIGITAL LIBRARY OF INDIA

Digital Library of India is a digital library of books, which is free-to-read, searchable, predominantly in Indian languages, available to everyone over the Internet. Very soon it is expected that this portal would provide a gateway to Indian Digital Libraries in science, arts, culture, music, movies, traditional medicine, palm leaves and many more. This project is a collaboration between different Indian institutes and Universities and Carnegie Mellon University under Universal Digital Library Project.

### Vision

For the first time in history, all the significant literary, artistic, and scientific works of mankind can be digitally preserved and made freely available, in every corner of the world, for education, study, and appreciation and that of all future generations.

Up until now, the transmission of our cultural heritage has depended on limited numbers of copies in fragile media.

The fires of Alexandria irrevocably severed our access to any of the works of the ancients. In a thousand years, only a few of the paper documents we have today will survive the ravages of deterioration, loss, and outright destruction. With no more than 10 million unique book and document editions before the year 1900, and perhaps 100 million since the beginning of recorded history, the task of preservation is much larger. With new digital technology, though, this task is within the reach of a single concerted effort for the public good, and this effort can be distributed to libraries, museums, and other groups in all countries.

Existing archives of paper have many shortcomings. Many other works still in existence today are rare, and only accessible to a small population of scholars and collectors at specific geographic locations. A single wanton act of destruction can destroy an entire line of heritage. Furthermore, contrary to the popular beliefs, the libraries, museums, and publishers do not routinely maintain broadly comprehensive archives of the considered works of man. No one can afford to do this, unless the archive is digital.

Digital technology can make the works of man permanently accessible to the billions of people all over the world. J.N.Tata and other great philanthropists, and visionary information scientist like Dr S. R. Ranganathan, in past centuries have recognized the great potential of public libraries to improve the quality of life and provide opportunity to the citizenry. A language independent digital library, widely available through free access on the Internet, will improve the global society in ways beyond measurement.

The technological advances today make it possible to think in terms of storing all the knowledge of the human race in digital form by the year 2008.

**Mission**

The mission is to create a portal for the Digital Library of India which will foster creativity and free access to all human knowledge. As a first step in realizing this mission, it is proposed to create the Digital Library with a free-to-read, searchable collection of one million books, predominantly in Indian languages, available to everyone over the Internet. This portal will also become an aggregator of all the knowledge and digital contents created by other digital library initiatives in India . Very soon we expect that this portal would provide a gateway to Indian Digital Libraries in science, arts, culture, music, movies, traditional medicine, palm leaves and many more. The result will be a unique resource accessible to anyone in the world 24x7, without regard to socioeconomic background or nationality.

Typical large high-school libraries house fewer than 30,000 volumes. Most libraries in the world have less than a million volumes. One million books, therefore, is more than the holdings of most high-schools, and is equivalent to the libraries at many universities and represents a useful fraction of all available books.

One of the goals of the Digital Library of India is to provide support for full text indexing and searching based on OCR (optical character recognition) technologies. The availability of online search allows users to locate relevant information quickly and reliably thus enhancing student's success in their research endeavors. This 24x7 resource would also provide an excellent test bed for language processing research in areas such as machine translation, optical character recognition, summarization, speech and hand writing recognition, intelligent indexing, and information retrieval in Indian languages.

It is expected that the Digital Library of India will be mirrored at several locations worldwide so as to protect the integrity and availability of the data. The DLI will also partner with other country specific Digital Libraries initiatives as part of the Universal Library Project ( www.ulib.org ) spearheaded by Prof. Raj Reddy and Carnegie Mellon University.

### Goals

The primary long-term objective is to capture all books in digital format. It is believed that such a task is impossible and could take hundreds of years, and never be completed. Thus, as a first step we are planning to demonstrate the feasibility by undertaking to digitize 1 million books (less than 1% of all books in all languages ever published) by 2005. We believe such a project has the potential to change how education is conducted in much of the world.

A secondary objective of this project will be to provide a test bed that will support other researchers who are working on improved scanning techniques, improved optical character recognition, and improved indexing. The corpus this project creates will be one to three orders of magnitude larger than any existing free resource.

### Benefits

The principal benefit of the Universal Library will be to supplement the formal education system by making knowledge available to anyone who can read and has access. Libraries have played a vital role in the advancement of human society. Societal advance depends on young people having access to books via libraries and other means. We expect that making this unique web resource available free to everyone around the world will enhance the learning process.

Libraries are unevenly distributed around the world and within each country. In the U.S., the NCES Survey noted that in 1996, 3,408 of 3,792 institutions of higher education had libraries holding 806.7 million volumes. The 112 largest university libraries in the United States and Canada each have at least 1.8 million books. They are members of the Association for Research Libraries. Massachusetts has about 25 million volumes; New York has about 31 million volumes, and California has about 40 million volumes in their ARL Libraries (Association for Research Libraries, 1999/2000). Other states, such as North and South Dakota, have no large libraries. A few large public libraries have several million volumes. However, most junior colleges, high schools, and public libraries have much smaller collections. Making this large knowledge repository can revolutionize research at all levels of education and give a much-needed boost at minimal cost to our national educational infrastructure. This impact will be further enhanced given the convenience of online access, and the benefit of full text searching at word and phrase levels.

A secondary benefit of online search is to make locating the relevant information inside of books far more reliable and much easier. Student success in finding exactly what they seek will increase and increased success will enhance student willingness to perform research using this large resource. NCES reports that 84 percent of libraries around the country are open between 60 and 80 hours a week. This digital library would be open all the 168 hours the week on a 24x7x365 basis. More than one individual will be able to use the same book at the same time. Thus, popular works will not be checked out and thus unavailable to others.

This million-book project will produce an extensive and rich testbed for use in further textual language processing research. It is hoped that at least 10,000 books among the million will be available in more than one language, providing a unique resource for example based machine translation.

Many believe that information is now doubling every two years. Machine summarization, intelligent indexing, and information mining are tools that will be needed for individuals to keep up in their discipline work, in their businesses, and in their personal interests. This large digitization project will enable extensive research in these areas.

## Philosophy of Content Selection

The Million Book Project envisages to develop a collection of one million digital books by adopting a staged approach as described below. The Million Book project will adhere to the copyright law.

### *1. Coordination of Selection*

Creating one digital copy and mirroring it in different locations will suffice, and will support the multiple uses at any time. Preliminary discussions with OCLC as a host for a registry of scanned items are underway. Certain key projects, such as the Making of America project, are already represented in the OCLC database as digital books. Other large digitization projects may require some data entry of their content in order to avoid duplication.

Books denoting ancient historical events of India, cultural and social books in different languages are digitized. These materials are obtained from authorized university public libraries in India. Palmleaves, journals and manuscripts are also digitized. Microfische, Microfilms also can be digitized and processed under this project.

### *2. Non-copyrighted materials*

Materials published before 1940 are in the public domain and may be scanned for this project. To reduce the costs of selection, the project will probably develop a strategy of selecting key topics and then removing large runs of books and journals from a selected repository. Having a reasonable turn-around time will be essential to the success of the project. A strategy has been devised to understand the logistics of shipping the materials and the impact of their absence from the home library.

If the published books are identified to be under copyright, the book will be removed within a duration of two months after the claim of the book on the website.

***3. Best books approach***

The project will seek publisher permission to scan books from Books for College Libraries (BCL), one source for core academic books in English. A previous study done at Carnegie Mellon University Libraries indicates that 22% of publishers granted permission for scanning and mounting on the web. The materials in the study were a random sample of Carnegie Mellon Llibraries books and included a broad range of dates, publishers, and in and out of print status.. Numerous difficulties from out of business publishers, lack of publisher records, return of copyright to authors, and other circumstances were identified. Subsequently, Carol Hughes, the collections development officer for Questia, corroborated Carnegie Mellon's experience.

Publishers increasingly see that digital presentation of their works can attract buyers. They are interested in exploring ways in which their out of print titles may be returned to profitability. Continued work with publishers through the course of this project may attract many of them to it. That would be most beneficial in enriching the content to be made available.

**Current Status**

In this section we will describe activities used to establish protocols, to select standards to be used, and to address issues of indexing and retrieval. Workflow and training programs to support the larger project are being developed. Both the content and the mechanisms for using it will be made available in open source code in due course of time.

The Process workflow is summarized in terms of three major process elements:

* Pre Scanning Process
* Scanning Process
* Post Scanning Process

**Pre Scanning Process**

* Books Procured are enlisted using the Regular Meta Data information
* Books are then submitted to the "Digital Library of India system" for duplication verification
* The system checks for the duplicates and generates the barcode for only non duplicate books
* The barcode assigned books are then issued to the contractors for the scanning operation

**Scanning Process**

* The books are scanned at a particular location or centre with an allotted Scanning machine and an operator
* The operator creates the structural meta information for the book he / she scans
* The operator/ meta data entry operator enters the admin meta information for the books scanned on a particular day
* The Scanned books undergo processing and OCR and also Quality control is done by the Contractors/ Supervisors
* The scanned and processed books are copied onto the hard disks and DVDs

* The DVDs are submitted to the source / location / scanning centre
* The Hard disks are brought to the central server location for web enablement

**Post Scanning Process**

* The contractors/supervisors upload the Meta information obtained in two formats: Admin and Structural to the central server.
* The system admin coordinates the meta information and the actual content obtained and allocates a server for the same
* The Quality assurance team works on the content before they are uploaded onto the server.
* If the Quality assurance certifies the quality of the content and meta information then the content is uploaded
* Else it appears offline unless the content is corrected based on the defects found

**Tools used**

The following are the specialty tools that are developed, customized and used for the Digital Library Project:

(a) Meta Data Software
(b) Pre-Scanning Meta Form
(c) Post-Scanning Meta Form
(d) OM transliteration Software
(e) Indian Fonts and iTrans manual and mapping table for Indian Languages
(f) Quality Assurance Software Package
(g) Duplication Checking Tool
(h) Image Quality Checking Tool
(i) Meta Data Quality Checking Tool

(j) Server Management Tool
(k) Server Software and its services
(l) Workflow management Software

**View Status of Books Online**

- ★ By Language wise
- ★ By Centre wise

**People**

***Credits***

- ★ The Principal Scientific Advisor to the Government of India.
- ★ Dr. Raj Reddy, Founder and Director of the Universal Digital Library (UDL), Carnegie Mellon University, USA
- ★ Dr. M G K Menon, Chairman, Council of Indian Institute of Technology-Bombay (Mumbai)
- ★ Dr. V S Arunachalam, Vice Chairman, Planning Commission, TamilNadu, India
- ★ Dr. N. Balakrishnan, Principal Investigator and Executive Director of the India-US Million Book Project, Indian Institute of Science Bangalore

***Academia***

- ★ Dr. Rajeev Sangal, Director, International Institute of Information Technology, Hyderabad
- ★ Dr. C. V. Jawahar, Project Investigator, Regional Mega Scanning Centre, IIIT, Hyderabad
- ★ Dr. M. D Tiwari, Director, Indian Institute of Information Technology, Allahabad
- ★ Dr. Ashok Kolaskar, Vice Chancellor, Pune University, Maharashtra
- ★ Mr. Sridharan, Secretary, Arulmigu Kalasalingam College of Engineering, Tamil Nadu

- M R. S. Vaidhyasubramanian, Dean, Shanmugha Arts, Science, Technology & Research Academy, Tanjavur, Tamil Nadu
- Dr. S Venkadesan, Indian Institute of Science, Bangalore
- Dr. Thangaraj, Principal, Arulmigu Kalasalingam College Of Engineering, Tamil Nadu

**Other Contributors**

- Dr. Y .S.Rajan, Vice Chancellor, Punjab Technological University, Punjab
- Dr. A.Vagiswari, Head Library, Indian Institute of Astrophysics, Bangalore
- Dr. P.V Konnur, Goa University, Goa
- Mr. V.R Gowri Shankar, Sringeri Mutt, Karnataka
- Dr. Udaya Kumar, Anna University, Chennai
- Mr. Vasant Mehta, Sri Kanchi Kamakoti Peetham, Tamil Nadu

**Government**

- Mr. Chandrasekhar, Joint Secretary, Ministry of Communication and Information Technology, Govt. of India
- Dr. Om Vikas, Senior Director, Ministry of Communication and Information Technology, Govt. of India
- Mr. Ajay Sawhney, Special Secretary for IT, Government of Andhra Pradesh
- Mr. A. P. V. N. Sharma, Government of Andhra Pradesh
- Dr. A. K. V. S. Reddy, Government of Andhra Pradesh
- Dr. A. N. Reddy, Government of Andhra Pradesh
- Dr. P. Krishnaiah, IAS Secretary for Education, Government of Andhra Pradesh

- Dr. S. Ravi Kumar, Director or Public Library, Government of Andhra Pradesh
- Mr. P. Y. Rajendra Kumar, Director of Public Library, Government of Karnataka
- Mr. B.S. Reddy, Director, SVDL, TTD

**Other Contributors**

- Dr. Ajeya Kallam, IAS
- Mr. Kamal Kant Jaswal, Secretary, Ministry of Communication and Information Technology
- Mr. Yashwant Bhave, Additional Secretary, Ministry of Communication and Information Technology
- Dr. G. V Subbarao, Director of Libraries, Government of Andhra Pradesh
- Dr. I. V. Subbarao, IAS
- Dr. P. K. Chaturvedi, Director, Ministry of Communication and Information Technology, Govt. of India
- Dr. R.K. Arora, Ministry of Communication and Information Technology, Govt. of India
- Dr. Gulshan Rai, Executive Director, ERNET
- Dr.V. N. Shukla, Director(Special Applications),CDAC
- Dr.R. K. Varma,Executive Director,CDAC-Noida
- Dr.A. B. Saha,Executive Director,CDAC-Kolkata

**Carnegie Mellon University**

- Dr. Michael Shamos, Director of UDL, Intellectual Property
- Dr. Jaime Carbonell, Director of UDL, Language Technologies
- Dr. Gloriana St. Clair, Director of UDL, University Librarian, Content Selection

### Other Contributors

- ★ Dr. Robert Thibadeau, Director of UDL, Privacy and Security
- ★ Gabrielle V. Michalek, Carnegie Mellon University
- ★ Madhavi Ganapathiraju, Carnegie Mellon University, USA
- ★ Eric Burns, Carnegie Mellon University, USA
- ★ Ed Walter, Carnegie Mellon University, USA
- ★ Krishna Konduru, Carnegie Mellon University, USA
- ★ Kishore Madhav, Carnegie Mellon University, USA
- ★ Walt Schearer, Carnegie Mellon University, USA

### US Advisors

- ★ Dr. Ching-chih Chen, Co-Principal Investigator, China-US Million Book Project
- ★ Dr. Peter Chen, Executive Director of the China-US Million Book Project
- ★ Dr. Daniel Greenstein, Executive Director of the Digital Library Federation
- ★ Dr. Brewster Kahle, President, Internet Archive
- ★ Dr. Victor Zue, Professor, LCS, MIT
- ★ Dr. Michael Lesk, Professor, Rutgers University
- ★ Dr. Stephen Griffin, National Science Foundation

### China

- ★ Dr. Pan Yunhe, President of Zhejiang University
- ★ Dr. Gao Wen, Deputy President of the Graduate School, Chinese Academy of Science
- ★ Mr. Guo Xinli, Vice General Director, Ministry of Education of China
- ★ Mr. Chen Jianping, Vice Director, State Planning Commission of China

- Dr. Chi Huisheng, Vice President of Beijing University
- Dr. Hu Dongcheng, Vice President of Tsinghua University
- Dr. Xu Zhong, Vice President of Fudan University
- Dr. Zhang Yibin, Assistant to the President, Nanjing University

## The Indian Team

- Kiran Kumar, Planning Director, UDL, Bangalore
- Vamshi Ambati, Project Manager, Regional Mega Scanning Centre, IIIT, Hyderabad
- Lakshmi Pratha Hari, Regional Mega Scanning Centre, IIIT, Hyderabad
- C.S.N Mohan, Thrinaina Informatics Limited, Regional Mega Scanning Centre, Hyderabad
- Ajay Reddy, PAR Informatics Limited, Regional Mega Scanning Centre, Hyderabad
- T N Sreenivas, TTD, Regional Mega Scanning Centre, Hyderabad
- K. Vamsi Krishna, Regional Mega Scanning Centre, IIIT Hyderabad
- Chandrasekhar, Veerababu Bandarupalli Supervisors, Regional Mega Scanning Centre, Hyderabad

## Other Contributors

- Nazeer Hussain, MSIT, IIIT Hyderabad
- Mahender Kandukuri, MSIT, IIIT Hyderabad
- Kishore Maramraj, MSIT, IIIT Hyderabad
- Vishwa s Sharma, Indian Institute of Science, Bangalore
- Kochurani Mathew, Indian Institute of Science, Bangalore
- Pradeepa, Mini Balakrishnan, Sheik Dawood, S.Venkatesh and Anandh (till 2004)

* Jiju Varghese, Indian Institute of Science, Bangalore

**Partners**

*Coordination and Research Centre in India*

* Indian Institute of Science, Bangalore
* International Institute of Information Technology, Hyderabad

**Academic Institutions**

* Anna University, Chennai, Tamil Nadu
* Arulmigu Kalasligam College of Engineering (AKCE), Srivilliputur, Madurai, Tamil Nadu
* Goa University, Goa
* Indian Institute of Astrophysics, Bangalore,Karnataka
* Indian Institute of Information Technology, Allahabad, Uttar Pradesh
* International Institute of Information Technology, Hyderabad, Andhra Pradesh
* Osmania University, Hyderabad
* Punjab Technical University, Punjab
* Shanmugha Art, Science, Technology & Research Academy, Tanjavur, Tamil Nadu
* University Of Hyderabad, Hyderabad
* University of Pune, Pune, Maharashtra

**Religious and Cultural Institutions**

* Kanchi University, Kanchi, Tamil Nadu
* Poornapragna Vidyapeetha, Bangalore
* Salarjung Museum, Hyderabad
* Sringeri Mutt, Sringeri, Karnataka
* Tirumala Tirupati Devasthanams, Tirupati, Andhra Pradesh
* Tibetan Monasteries and Literature on Jainism

**Government and Research Agencies**

- ★ Academy of Sanskrit Research, Melkote, Karnataka
- ★ CDAC- Noida
- ★ Maharashtra Industrial Development Corporation (MIDC), Mumbai, Maharashtra
- ★ Rashtrapathi Bhavan, New Delhi

**United States of America**

- ★ Carnegie Mellon University
- ★ Louisiana State University

**China**

- ★ Beijing University
- ★ Chinese Academy of Science
- ★ Fudan University
- ★ Ministry of Education of China
- ★ Nanjing University
- ★ State Planning Commission of Chin a
- ★ Tsinghua University
- ★ Zhejiang University

**Industrial Partners**

- ★ Thrinaina Informatics Ltd., Hyderabad, Andhra Pradesh
- ★ Par Informatics Ltd., Hyderabad, Andhra Pradesh
- ★ SV Infosys, Tirumala Tirupathi Devastanams, Tirupathi, Andhra Pradesh
- ★ Microsoft

## 10. VIDYANIDHI

Vidyanidhi ("Treasure of Knowledge" in Sanskrit) began as a pilot project to demonstrate the feasibility of Electronic Theses and Dissertations in the Indian context This project got underway in the year 2000 at the Department of Library and

Information Science, University of Mysore, Manasagangotri, Mysore, sponsored by the National Information System for Science and Technology, Department of Scientific and Industrial Research, Ministry of Science and Technology, Government of India.

Vidyanidhi, in many ways, is an attempt to implement the directives of content development outlined by the Action Plan of the National Task Force on Information Technology and Software Development, of the Government of India as far as the university theses are concerned. The policy initiatives identified in the Plan make it mandatory for all universities or deemed universities across the country to host every thesis/ dissertation on a designated website. This national policy has provided a policy framework for initiating a digital library of ETDs in India.

Currently Vidyanidhi is evolving into an Information Infrastructure and portal for strengthening and augmenting the doctoral research capacities of Indian Universities.

The Vidyanidhi also has the strategic support from the University Grants Commission.

Vidyanidhi Project's vision is to build and strengthen the research capacities and enhance the quality of doctoral research research in India and the mission is to prepare the future generation of scientists to be better equipped to harness the power of ICTs to work and play a more effective role in the creation, accessing and use of knowledge. The vision is to help usher in the E-paradigm of academic life and work culture, there by exploiting the immense possibilities of digital libraries. Digital library technologies offer enormous advantages over traditional print world. The digital library is not just a storehouse of knowledge and information but a dynamic landscape for the creation and use of knowledge.

**Premise**

- ★ Convenient and seamless access to information improves the quality of higher education and research
- ★ The academic milieu is transiting towards e-paradigm and students and research scholars are to be able to move towards e work culture
- ★ An enabling framework and mechanism for the above is to be in place
- ★ Digital libraries are the bulwarks of such an enabling framework
- ★ Universities have to develop and partner in developing digital libraries

**Goals**

- ★ To evolve into an information infrastructure and enabling framework for enhancing the quality of doctoral research output
- ★ To develop a mechanism for depositing and accessing Indian electronic theses/digital theses from anywhere, anytime.

**Ojectives**

- ★ To evolve appropriate policy frameworks and mechanisms that would advocate and promote ETDs in India
- ★ To sensitise, encourage and train doctoral students in India to create their doctoral research works electronically. The training programmes would help inculcate good practices in scholarly writing, e publishing, accessing and using scholarship.
- ★ Facilitate the creation of doctoral theses in electronic form by offering tools and resources for accessing knowledge resources and creating & depositing doctoral

research works. This would enable the doctoral students to adopt and follow good practices in scholarship.

* Develop tools and resources for E-learning, E-scholarly publishing and online repositories. The tools and resources include manuals, tutorials, style guides and others. This would focus on fostering the adoption of good practices.
* To increase the availability of university research to society and to preserve it electronically by procuring, collecting, archiving and disseminating doctoral research in India. This would not only enhance the visibility of Indian academic research as well as help archive the same.
* Host and maintain the Vidyanidhi Digital Libraries Portal- offering the above resources and facilities.

**Indian Doctoral Research**

India with its enormous system of higher education spanning two hundred and eighty one universities (including deemed universities) is a reservoir of extensive doctoral research in the country. Hard statistics regarding doctoral research output is not available as there is no system/mechanism to deposit, catalogue and archive the Indian theses. Estimates of doctoral research output can only be extrapolations of available statistics. Based on such extrapolations we estimate that annually 25,000 to 30, 000 doctoral theses are produced in India.

Today most doctoral students in India get their theses produced electronically, get the printout and submit the required number of copies to their respective universities. For lack of systematic efforts-individual as well as institutional, the far versatile electronic version is generally not maintained and archived while the dumbed down version - the print version is supposedly maintained at the respective university libraries. Those hard copy versions of theses remain locked in the libraries. They are consigned to be frozen assets. Vidyanidhi project is an effort in the direction of spreading the ETD movement in India and to facilitate the creation, access, and use of Indian doctoral research.

Doctoral research represents the beginning of a great scholarly and academic journey. It is a journey that is rigorous and also fraught with many a challenges- from selecting a topic to writing the thesis. It is also a long and arduous one- involving long hours of intellectual labour. The labour and the rigours of thesis writing challenge even the most able students It is rather unfortunate that the doctoral students are expected to complete the process without the support of adequate tutoring, mentoring, requisite guidelines, resources& tools. Students in Indian universities do not have convenient access to many of the resources and tools that would make this great journey a very enriching experience. Vidyanidhi is positioned as a portal that will help make this pedagogic journey very exciting and rich with its facilities, resources and tools.

## Vidyanidhi Strategies

The Vidyanidhi strategies revolve around- evolving a policy framework, organizational model, and implementation mechanism.

In other words our strategy is centred on the following four areas of activities -

- ★ Policy framework (Through meetings, participation, liaison and other methods)
- ★ Education and Training (Best research practices, Information Literacy and E-publishing)
- ★ Content building (Full text, Metadata, and doctoral information)
- ★ Resources and tools development (Online depositing software and interfaces, Online thesauri and others)

Our strategy is to follow a multi pronged and parallel approach for all of the above four areas of work. Further more, these areas of activities are also complementary to one another. For example effective policy implementation and education and training facilitate and strengthen content building. Better resources and tools also help education and training as well as content building.

It is currently focusing on the four areas of activities- Developing Policy framework and advocacy; Content Building; Awareness, Education and Training, and; Resources and tools development.

A Round Table of Vice Chancellors of universities is scheduled on June 14, to deliberate on the issues/concerns relating to strengthening doctoral research in India and the possible role that ETDs can play. More specifically, the objective is to come up with a policy initiative and a modus operandi for evolving into a national collaborative system for ETDs in India. University Grants Commission (the apex body for regulating, monitoring, facilitating, funding and coordinating Government agency for higher education in India) is involved in this effort. Dr. Arun Nigavekar, Chairman, UGC will be chairing the Round Table.

### *Round Table Objectives*

To sensitize the participants on the immense possibilities of e-theses and deliberate on the issues regarding the creation and depositing of research works at a designated Website. The main issues are-

- Address concerns- such as plagiarism, copy right and other misgivings and apprehensions
- Copy right and University research-help develop a clear cut copy right policy on university research - especially doctoral research

- ★ Building an E-commerce model in order to eventually make the programme a self-sustaining one as well as provide cost incentive to the students and participating institutions.
- ★ Possibility and feasibility of forming alliances with publishers for publishing of theses

Evolve an organizational mechanism for the implementation of the policy. The organisational mechanism that has been envisioned for Vidyanidhi is the 'distributed collaborative model'- where in Vidyanidhi would be the nodal agency for the repository, metadata database, policy framework, and development of tools and resources. Given the imbalances in the network infrastructure for ETDs in Indian Universities, Vidyanidhi is positioned as a repository for the participating universities, if need be.

- ★ Solicit the participation of the institutions in the Vidyanidhi project
- ★ Develop guidelines and frameworks for participation
- ★ Evolve and have an MOU with the participating institutions

## Strategies

- ★ Identify and select institutions/universities which are strong in their research capacities
- ★ The identification and selection process of institution is based on the following general criteria-
  - ★ Doctoral research out put in different disciplines of Social Sciences (Top 25 universities in each of the Social Science disciplines have been identified)
  - ★ Publications output ( Identifying the top 25 Indian academic institutions using the ISI Social Science Citation Index)

- ★ Willingness to participate in this collaborative endeavour

★ solicit participation of these 25 universities

The final selection of 15-25 institutions (we assume that all those identified may not be forthcoming in their willingness to participate) would be based on their willingness to participate and to a certain extent regional representation and other factors

## Content Building

The Vidyanidhi Digital Library is conceived as having two layers- Metadata database and full text of theses. We are currently focusing on building both these layers. Currently we have nearly 50,000 records in the metadata database and 300 full text theses. The Vidyanidhi metadata database is a truly multilingual database with records in English and Indian Languages as well. Vidyanidhi has implemented the Unicode standard for Indian Languages and scripts.

The Vidyanidhi architecture is represented in figure1.

## *Awareness, Education and Training*

As outlined above, there is an urgent need to bridge the digital divide created by digital illiteracy, by training the students and faculty in E-Publishing and E-Archiving.

Our plan is to offer three one week long training programmes either in Mysore/Bangalore/ or other cities in collaboration with other institutions.

The training programmes are envisaged at two levels/ phases of doctoral research process

★ The first phase -the first year of doctoral studies-more like an orientation programme. This would also help us to build a sensitized community of doctoral students.

At this stage the objective is to sensitize and excite the doctoral students to the immense possibilities and benefits of E-theses. The course content would focus on orienting the doctoral students towards creating documents in electronic formats. Thus the course would be introductory in nature.

★ The second phase would be typically in the third or fourth year of doctoral studies-at the thesis writing stage. At this stage the objective is to facilitate the doctoral students in creating their thesis in E-format by exploiting the versatility and richness of digital creation and formatting. The course content would focus on hands on and 'do it yourself' kind of tool kits

  ★ As a first step, training modules would be prepared and made available
  ★ Call for participation through different means
  ★ Identify the doctoral students for training programmes
  ★ Organise and conduct 5 day long intensive hands on training

The education and training programme would also be a kind of community building exercise, having the participants to be part of the ETD community. It plans to initiate a ETD List serv to act as a platform for exchange and communication of information, keeping track, and update each member of the group. The participants would be encouraged to subscribe to the ETD list serv and thus plan to keep in contact continuously.

Though it would be ideal to have the second level advanced training programme as a sequel to the first, that is-restrict it only for the participants who have undergone the orientation programme, it expects that it may not be a wholly feasible approach. All students who register for doctoral programme may not complete. The 'drop out' rate among doctoral students is fairly significant. It is also possible that some students may be already familiar with the basics and may not require the orientation programme. Therefore, we feel that it cannot restrictive and be made conditional. A pragmatic approach would be to strive towards the ideal but have a flexible policy. It plan to have the two kinds of training independent of each other, but attempt to make it a follow up as far as possible.

**Accessing and searching the Vidyanidhi Database**

Currently the Vidyanidhi website and the search interfaces are in English (Indic Language web pages are in the pipeline). However searching is facilitated in English as well as Indic Languages. There are two possible ways of searching the Vidyanidhi database. One can search the integrated database that has all the records irrespective of language/script or the respective vernacular database having records of theses in that language only. The difference between the two approaches is -one affords search in the English language and the other in the vernacular. The first approach also provides for viewing records in Roman script for all theses-search output- that satisfy the conditions of the query and also an option for viewing records in vernacular script for theses in vernacular. The second approach- enables one to search only the vernacular database and thus is limited to records in that language. However, this approach enables the search to be in the vernacular language and script.

Access to and the search interaction in the Vidyanidhi Database is facilitated in the following manner. When one gets to the Metadata Database one can choose to search by language, either -

- ★ All
- ★ Hindi
- ★ Kannada

While the 'All' option facilitates the searching of the integrated database, the other two- Hindi and Kannada limits the access and search to only the respective languages. It will illustrate the search process with the following example-

* Select all
* Select the field -
  * Author
  * Keyword
  * Title
  * University
  * Subject
  * Guide
  * Language
  * Year

Further narrowing of the search is also provided- where in one can combine any two fields. Once the database is queried using any of the above conditions, then the search results indicates the number of records output under - All, Hindi, Kannada. The searchers will have the option to click on their choice and view records in either Roman script only or Roman as well as respective

## Vidyanidhi Promotional Activities

Vidyanidhi is following a multi pronged approach toward the realization of it mission and objectives. It is advocating, liaising, promoting the concept of ETD within the Indian academic milieu. It is following in parallel the top down as well as bottom up approach. It has involved the apex body for higher education - UGC to promote the ETD through its regulatory arm, the heads of academic institutions to implement the policy frameworks and also targeting the Students to sensitize and enthuse them. The promotional flyers and brochures targeting all the three segments are being readied.

# 2 Indian Digital Libraries

## 1. ARCHIVES OF INDIAN LABOUR

The Archives of Indian Labour is a unique digital project initiated at the V.V. Giri National Labour Institute, in collaboration with the Association of Indian Labour Historians (AILH). The archive, which aspires to be the prime repository of labour related records in the country, was designed and instituted to address the urgent need for preservation of rapidly decaying documents and material on labour. The archive, apart from being a repository of sources and documents, builds collections and initiates research in the field of labour history. The collections are generated through projects commissioned at the programme and institutional documents donated by various organisations. Documents related to labour movement (generated by workers' organisations, state and business enterprises) are preserved at the archive, in addition to personal narratives and memories of leaders of Indian labour movement and workers.

A unique feature of this archive is the integration of historical and contemporary records. Organised around special collections, it provides historical depth to contemporary issues and situates historical changes from a contemporary perspective.

The archive also assumes importance due to its emphasis on informal sector labour. The technical specialty of the Archives of Indian Labour is its stress on digital storage and retrieval of material. This is the first fully digital archive in the country. The digital mode was opted considering its advantages in terms of financial & spatial economies, durability of storage, and improved access to material.

The Archive is an Integrated Multimedia Storage and Retrieval System, which enables to store records and material in different media formats- such as text, audio, video and digital- and provide access to these through an integrated delivery system. The organisation of material and its delivery are realised through a open source code software, Greenstone, developed by New Zealand Digital Library. The software is customised considering the requirements of the archive in a user-friendly manner. The system is designed to enable fast and meaningful delivery of documents through different access modes- such as offline networked PCs, CDs, and the World Wide Web.

The web site of the Archives of Indian Labour (www.indialabourarchives.org) was formally inaugurated by Shri Sharad Yadav, Hon'ble Union Labour Minister, on May 1, 2002, the International Labour Day. With this, a much wider public now have access to the information gathered at the archive.

The materials, which are now available on World Wide Web, amounts to 7 Giga Bytes, comprising of 8 major collections (nearly 50,000 printed pages; and 100 hours of taped interviews). These collections include records and reports of all the Commissions of Labour from 1931 till 1991 (including the complete collection on the First National Commission on Labour, 1969); records and publications of central trade unions such as AITUC, BMS, CITU and INTUC; records and reports on the unorganized sector labour movement in regional centres. A large number of interviews of workers and labour activists and documents of labour movement in the informal sector can also be accessed. Apart from this, a detailed inventory of material and sources on labour history and write ups on technical aspects of digital archiving are available in the web site.

The search facility instituted to the web site enables greater access directly to the documents right to the level of page, section, word or a tagged audio and video clip. It also allows non-linear search across collections. By default, the search facility is across all the collections and user has the option of setting preferences for particular collections(s). The navigation of the web site is made simple through a write up that provides instructions for using the help menu.

Brief descriptions are given on every collection explaining the source, contents and its structure. Each of the collections comprises of various sections that classify the documents thematically at the sub-collection level. The sub-collection is further divided into individual physical documents. Depending on its nature, the document could be navigated at different levels.

## 2. ADVAITA SHARADA PROJECT

A unique project in knowledge management, known as the '*Advaita Sarada project*', has been launched by *Sri Sri Jagadguru Sankaracharaya Mahasamsthanam*, Sri Sarada Pitham, Sringeri, Chikkamagaluru District, Karnataka. It is for digitization of ancient manuscripts other & south Indian Languages pertaining to the vedas, vedangus, upanishad and other sastric studies by Sri Sri Jagadguru Shankaracharya Mahasamsthanam Dakshinamanga Sri Sharada Peetham, Sringeri. Project has been completed and scanned data web enabled on www.new.dli.ernet.in

Sri Sarada Pitham, founded about 1200 years ago by Sri Adi Sankara, the great Indian philosopher, is a renowned centre of learning. His Holiness Sri Sri Bharati Tirtha Mahaswami, the present Sankaracharya and 36th *Pithadhipati*, a sage of great learning, has been imparting knowledge contained in ancient Indian literature to all seekers who come to him from many parts of the world. His Holiness, on becoming aware of the potential of information and communication technology, desired to make this knowledge available to all those who wish to learn, wherever they are, in any part of the world where information and telecommunication technologies can reach them.

The *Advaita Sarada Project,* conceived and blessed by him, seeks to create a knowledge base from more than 25,000 *Granthas* or books available in Sringeri and from audio and video recordings of classroom proceedings, *Vidvat Ghosht*is (scholarly debates) and the like that are regularly conducted in this village.

Many of the more than 25,000 *granthas* in the libraries of Sri Sringeri Math date back a few centuries. The *granthas* are available in the form of ancient *tala patras* (palm leaf manuscripts), *kadatas* (a form of manuscript made from a long piece of cloth, conditioned by smearing on it powdered tamarind seeds and charcoal, and then folded into pages), paper manuscripts, and printed books. The subjects/ topics they deal with include Vaidika Dharma, philosophy, logic linguistics, science, mathematics, medicine, stories from the *puranas* and *itihasas,* literature, arts and many other subjects, and are in many Indian languages such as Sanskrit, Kannada, Telugu, Tamil, Malayalam and Marathi. However, it is not uncommon to find transcripted books - that is, the language of the text of the book and the script in which it is written are different. An example is Bhaskaracharya's *Lilavati*, the Sanskrit *slokas* or verses (containing mathematical problems) of which are written in Telugu script.

The objective of the project is to create a universal, free-to-read, digital library on the Internet that can be accessed by students and scholars alike. In addition to the books which, we now know, provide explicit knowledge, the Advaita Sarada Project has set a goal of providing tacit knowledge by making it possible for the seekers to interact with scholars, experts and teachers. This interaction known as 'socialization' in modern knowledge management terms will help students gain a correct understanding of *granthas*.

In addition to the above, informed *Tippani* (annotation) will be written and created at the book level and at the section/chapter level. These annotations will guide the student about contents of the book, its relative importance in the gamut of literature available on the subject of study, profile of the author, pre-requisites for studying the book, and also suggest related and advanced books on the subject.

The *granthas* are scanned using a high performance scanner, and its pages stored as images in a powerful computer system, known as the knowledge server, using a modern Database Management System (DBMS). The DBMS has the capability to store images, audio and video recordings as well as texts (words and sentences that can be understood by computers and hence can be processed, that is, indexed, searched, located and retrieved). DBMS also has the capability to serve hundreds of users simultaneously with the information they want, without interfering with one another.

In order to design a knowledge base that can be represented and stored in modern DBMS, it is necessary to conceptualize the knowledge base, which in this case consists of *granthas*, audio and video recordings. A model is a mental picture of the concept; therefore, the knowledge base model is a mental picture of it.

While modeling a knowledge base, as consisting of various entities about which to know something. Examples of entities associated with the knowledge base under discussion are:

- ★ Books (*granthas*) in various physical forms (palm leaf manuscript, paper manuscript, *kadata*, printed books etc);
- ★ Authors, who are associated with the *grantha* as its creators, or as persons who have written commentaries on it, or as those who have edited and brought out a critical edition of it.

These entities about which one wants to know are known as *'Objects'* in computational terminology. Examples of a few more objects are: taxonomy, which represents a hierarchical categorization of various subjects (or disciplines of study); sub divisions of a *grantha* into sections/chapters (eg: *kandas, parvas, prakaranas or adhyayas*).

Details that needed about various objects are known as the '*Attributes*' of those 'objects'. It certainly does not want to know every detail about an 'object' - only those details that are relevant for the purpose. For example, in the case of books, one may need to know its name, author, language, subject etc. Similarly, about an author, his name, period and a brief profile of him is needed.

All 'objects' that share common properties and that exhibit similar behaviour are classified together into what are called *'Classes'*. Therefore, 'classes' consist of 'objects' that are similar and an 'object' becomes an example of a 'class'. Bhaskaracharya's book on Mathematics, *Lilavati,* is thus an example of a 'class' called 'Book' and Bhaskaracharya is an example of a 'class' called 'Author'. 'Objects' of a 'class' may be interrelated with other 'objects' in another 'class'. In the knowledge base,

1. Books are interrelated with Authors, as it is they who have created the Books.
2. Subdivisions of a Book are related to Books.
3. Books are related with other books on the same subject.

In conceptual modelling, to put it in a simple manner, it is concerned with identification of 'Classes', 'Objects', their 'Attributes' and their interrelationships. There are many other aspects as well, which however is not required for understanding of a model as far as this discussion is concerned. It is said that Indian Logic (*Tarka*) also sees the world around us in terms that are similar to what is used in modern knowledge management, though in a more elaborate manner.

Since the *granthas* are captured as images, for a detailed search of the contents in the Library, the page images should converted into 'Texts' that can be understood, or 'read', by the computer. 'Optical Character Recognition (OCR) converts the images of lines of a book into a series of words or texts. An OCR technology for Sanskrit and other Indian languages is still being perfected.

Unlike English, where each word is distinct, in Sanskrit - and many Indian languages - words can be combined (*sandhis* and *samasas*). Any OCR software, which reads the picture of words in a line, should also be able to determine whether the words have been combined and if so how? Only then can these words or phrases be indexed for facilitating links and retrieval. A person who can develop effective OCR software for Sanskrit should necessarily have some knowledge of its grammar to know how words can be combined so that they can be split individually, keeping the meaning in tact.

The scope of the *Advaita Sarada Project,* basically is to tell why it is important to learn Sanskrit and how this learning can be relevant to Science and Technology. Knowledge Management of ancient Indian knowledge provides both opportunities and challenges to those who are interested in learning from past so as to be a step ahead of their peers in the future. For, only persons or a group of persons who are well versed in both Sanskrit and Technology can build a suitable solution that will enable millions to mine profitably the knowledge in ancient texts.

## 3. CSCS MEDIA AND CULTURE ARCHIVE

The Centre for Study of Culture and Media Society was established in 1996 by a group of scholars interested in developing new approaches to studying culture in India. This interest has been energised by the sense that the social sciences and humanities disciplines as they exist are no longer adequate to the task of engaging seriously with the problems of time. Today both the political frameworks of the post-colonial nation-state (democracy, secularism, development) and the institutional structures they endorse are clearly in crisis.

Many of the crucial problems confronting today - relating to questions of gender, caste, comumunity, ethnicity - used to be traditionally relegated to the realm of 'culture' rather than being seen as political issues. And when the disciplines dealt with them it was often in orientalist frames, by way of explaining the cultural specificity of Indians, especially those who were "non-modern". The dominant social science framework in India, which was one of modernity - development, saw caste and community as embarrassing obstacles for the new nation to overcome. At the same time, the dominant framework in which 'culture' was viewed in the humanities was that of national culture and national identity.

The major thrust of CSCS has been to understand culture in its most inclusive sense - as encompassing the diverse attempts of people to produce meaning of various kinds. Such an endeavour will pose a serious challenge to the existing disciplines, and have a significant impact on cultural policy as well as alter the place occupied by 'culture' in political understanding. The phrase 'culture and society' is used to emphasize that culture must be seen not as a transcendent entity but as part of a network of social and political relations, indeed as integral to the formation of such relations.

**Media Archives**

This component of the CSCS Media Project assembles what could be the definitive media archive of post-Independence India.

By media we mean film, radio, television, and video; satellite and related communications technology; telecommunications; computer technology. Material on these subjects will include: press clippings, including reviews; pamphlets, reports and papers by government agencies, independent organisations, and individual work; visual images, including advertising, publicity leaflets, etc; market research reports; downloading from the Internet; a video archive.

This material will be compiled from already existing sources as well as assembled by independent research commissioned by CSCS. We intend to cover both conventional and non-conventional sources as well as generate new material informed by the broad research interests of CSCS.

Currently being scanned and indexed are :

Newspaper clippings on media from 10 mainstream newspapers.

**Media and Law :** Complete texts of legal acts from the Dramatic Performances Act - (1876) and the Indian Telegraph Act (1885) down to the Cable Television Networks Regulation Act (1995).

**Telugu material :** complete issues of select journals from the 1950s, clippings covering the post-Independence history of Telugu film and pamphlets, letterheads and other material from the Fans Associations of movie star Chiranjeevi.

Forthcoming material includes :

★ Material on Tamil cinema assembled during the Tamil Film Workshop (Chennai, 1997)

★ Dossier on the Shiv Sena-owned newspaper Samna.

★ Dossier on Gujarati newspapers including Mumbai Samachar, Samkaleen, Gujarat Samachar, Sandesh, Janmabhoomi, Pravasi and Chitralekha.

★ Marathi cinema.

The material is being assembled and stored both in image and text format (wherever possible: exceptions being mainly non-English material), and archived in CD-ROM discs, in which form they will be made available to researchers both in-house and selectively with collaborating institutions, as well as on the Internet.

The faculty of the Centre for the Study of Culture and Society has assembled a database that intends to cover the field of culture, politics and society in contemporary India. The database itself currently has over 20,000 records (2 Gigabytes), including text files and visuals, supported by over 12 Gigabytes of scanned images that form the record of the original sources of this documentation.

The database is presently available on http://www.cscsarchive.org as an IP address and Password-protected website.

## 4. DGITAL LIBRARY OF AYURVEDIC MEDICINE

Centers for Digital Archiving and creation of rare knowledge pertaining to Ayurvedic Medicine, integrating & show casing of the content created through Digital Library outlet for Uttaranchal State Govt. by C-DAC Noida have digitized manuscripts & Information related to Ayurvedic and forestry. The project has been completed and the scanned data web enabled on www.dli.cdacnoida.in

After having successfully completed the project to construct a digital library of the 36,000 medical formulations contained in traditional ayurvedic texts to prevent bio-piracy, the Council of Scientific and Industrial Research is all set to prepare a similar library of the traditional knowledge database of South Africa.

A compact disc (CD), which presents a glimpse of the ayurvedic digital library was released which will be useful for research. They were under way to get important patent offices across the world to use the library as part of their search tools while examining applications for patents. It would be of benefit to them also as they too would like to ensure that patent applications approved by them were not challenged later, as it would harm their reputation.

Besides, a committee of experts has been set up to formulate proper procedures with regard to access to the library to ensure that the knowledge contained in it is used for further development of medicines, without harming India's interests. The committee would interact with experts, academicians, NGOs and other stakeholders, including the pharmaceutical industry.

The digital library, which provides information about ayurvedic formulations in five languages — English, French, German, Spanish and Japanese — has been constructed as a follow up to the controversy over the U.S. patent office granting a patent for use of turmeric for wound healing and also in the wake of repeated litigations on products such as basmati and neem. The project was implemented by the CSIR's National Institute of Science Communication and Information Resources and was co-sponsored by the Health and Science and Technology Ministries.

## 5. DIGITAL LIBRARY OF INDIAN INSTITUTE OF MANAGEMENT, KOZHIKODE

This digital library developed by IIMK library holds documents on management, economics, sociology, etc and IIMK staff publications. The number of documents included are less as the library is in development stage. The Indian Institute of Management Kozhikode, IIMK is the fifth Indian Institute of Management. Established in 1996 by the Government of India in collaboration with the Government of Kerala, it provides education, training, consulting and research facilities in management.

Established in 1996 by the Government of India in collaboration with the Government of Kerala, it aims to provide education, training, consulting and research facilities in management. It is a Central Autonomous Body registered under the Societies Registration Act XXI of 1860, and is managed by a Board of Governors. The Director is the Chief Executive Officer of the Institute.

IIMK is located at Kozhikode, in south western India, a location made famous by the entry of Vasco Da Gama to India. The Institute operates from it's own, newly constructed campus, in the scenic ambience of approximately 100 acres in the Kunnamangalam locality of Kozhikode.

Indian Institute of Management Kozhikode seeks to achieve excellence and a leadership position in management education.

It aspires to :

* inculcate a spirit of life long learning
* strengthen capabilities of integrating concepts with applications and values
* contribute towards the development of communities of dependable, capable, caring and fair minded individuals.

IIMK is dedicated to offering world class programmes in management education. Its academic programmes encompass a range of long term full time diploma programmes such as the Post Graduate Programme in Management, and a number of short duration executive education programmes

The Institute seeks to achieve excellence and a leadership position in management education and to become a major learning resource centre in the Asia-Pacific region.

The Institute seeks to inculcate a spirit of lifelong learning. It aspires to strengthen the capabilities of integrating concepts with applications and values. It aims to contribute towards the development of communities of dependable, capable, caring and fair-minded people.

The Institute's activities presently include teaching, research and consulting. The Major programmes and activities of the Institute are:

* Post Graduate Programme in Management
* Management Development Programmes
* Research
* Consultancy Services
* Seminars and Workshops

Digital libraries are now being developed almost in all disciplines of study. India has no dearth of technical manpower and it is hoped that the digital libraries will soon appear and consolidate their information resources for education and research activities in the country.

## 6. DIGITAL LIBRARY OF INDIGENOUS KNOWLEDGE

South Asian countries decided to create a digital library of the region's traditional knowledge and develop laws to prevent such knowledge being misappropriated through commercial patents. The plan was announced at a workshop held in Delhi by the South Asian Association for Regional Cooperation (SAARC). Participants at the workshop have begun drawing up a technical framework for classifying the region's traditional knowledge and linking it to the international patent classification system. The aim is to create a composite digital library comprising individual Traditional Knowledge Digital Libraries (TKDL) from each country in South Asia.

The library contains information on 36,000 formulations used in *Ayurveda* — India's 5,000-year-old system of traditional medicine. The information - presented in English, French, German, Spanish and Japanese — was created in a format accessible by international patent offices to prevent the granting of inappropriate patents.

The database set international standards for registries of traditional knowledge, which were adopted by the intergovernmental committee of the World Intellectual Property Organization (WIPO) in 2003.

In 2001, India developed a system for classifying resources used in traditional knowledge that is similar to that used by the International Patent Classification (IPC). The IPC has agreed to include the Indian system in its own classification, which will be expanded to include about 200 sub-groups of drugs derived from Indian medicinal plants.

According to delegates at the Delhi meeting, this is likely to significantly aid patent offices searching the databases to ensure that proposed patents are truly novel and have not been reported before.Documenting traditional knowledge has become important as most of it is in the public domain and is easy to misappropriate, says Raghunath Mashelkar, director general of the Council of Scientific and Industrial Research (CSIR).

India's National Institute of Science Communication and Information Resources (NISCAIR) found that in 2000, almost 80 per cent of the 4,896 references to individual plant-based medicinal patents in the US Patents Office related to seven medicinal plants of Indian origin. In 2003, there were almost 15,000 patents on such medicines in the US, European and UK patent offices' registries. However, none of the 131 academic journals used by patent examiners when deciding whether to grant a patent is from developing countries such as Brazil, China or India.

South Asia possesses significant traditional knowledge that affects biotechnology, agriculture, pharmaceuticals and health care. More than 80 per cent of its 1.4 billion population have no access to modern health care services and medicine, and rely on traditional medicine, the Delhi meeting heard. The region shares a common heritage in traditional medicine — Bangladesh, India and Pakistan share the *Unani* system of medicine, whereas *Ayurveda* is used in India, the Maldives, Nepal and Sri Lanka. India's NISCAIR has prepared and circulated a practical guide for classification of traditional knowledge to other South Asian countries.

The Indian digital library of traditional knowledge has also attracted attention from other regions. Representatives from South Africa, the Commonwealth West African Education Delegation, the African Regional Industrial Property Organization and International Property Office in Singapore have discussed with India the possibility of creating similar databases.

The participants at the meeting, including staff of the SAARC Documentation Centre in Delhi, NISCAIR, and WIPO also discussed creating new laws to prevent misappropriation of traditional knowledge. Mikhail Makarov, deputy director at WIPO's technology retrieval systems service told SciDev.Net that WIPO is working towards a new legal instrument to protect traditional knowledge, using a combination of existing intellectual property laws and *sui generis* laws unique to individual circumstances of the countries developing them. Brazil, Costa Rica, India, Panama, Peru, the Philippines, Portugal, Thailand and the United States are among those that have adopted *sui generis* laws that protect some aspects of traditional knowledge. Regional organisations in the South Pacific and Africa are trying to define specific rights relating to traditional knowledge and strategies to protect them.

## 7. DIGITAL LIBRARY OF IIT KHARAGPUR

Initiated as a modern in-house Electronic Library in 1994, it is renamed as Digital Library. It has involved various digitization activities of the old documents for digital archiving. It has large number of electronic resources such as EiTech index, Compendex, IEEE / IEE journals in full text, INSPEC, Current Contents, Chemical Abstracts, Biotechnolcgy Abstracts, Agricultural Abstracts, Library and Information Science Abstracts, ASTM standards and ABI. A large number of video courses produced by the Centre for Education technology, 11T, Kharagpur are made available to the users for browsing by using a good number of VCRs.

Institutional Repository at IIT Kharagpur collects, preserves and disseminates in digital format the research output created by the IIT Kharagpur research community. It enables the Institute community to deposit (self archiving) their preprints, postprints and other scholarly publications using a web interface, and organizes these publications for easy retrieval. At present, the access of Institutional Repository is restricted within the IIT Kharagpur campus LAN only and submission of documents to this repository is also limited to the IIT Kharagpur research community. Institutional Repository is running on Dspace open archive software, a freely distributable archive system available from dspace.org complies with the Open Archives Initiatives (OAI) framework allowing publications to be easily indexed by web search engines and other indexing services.

INDEST Consortium (Indian National Digital Library in Engineering Sciences and Technology) was set up by The Ministry of Human Resource Development (MHRD). The Ministry provides funds required for subscription to electronic resources for 38 institutions including IISc, IITs, NITs, IIMs and a few other centrally funded Government institutions. The following IP-enable e-resources are available for online access for IIT Kharagpur users.

Full Text Databases (7000 journals): ABI / Inform Complete, ACM Digital Library, ASCE Journals, ASME Journals, Capitaline, EBSCO Databases, Elsevier s Science Direct, Emerald Full-text, IEEE / IEE Electronic Library Online (IEL), Indian Standards, Nature, ProQuest Science, Springer Verlag s Link

Bibliographic Databases COMPENDEX on EI Village, INSPEC on EI Village, J-Gate Custom Content for Consortia (JCCC), JET, MathSciNet, SciFinder Scholar, Web of Science.

## 8. GYANDOOT

Gyandoot (meaning "messenger of knowledge") is a new intranet-based digital library in the Dhar district of the state of Madhya Pradesh connecting rural public cybercafes. A corresponding website is an extension of Gyandoot intranet providing giving global access via a portal.

Gyandoot project was launched on November 29, 1999 and it was officially commissioned on January 1, 2000. Thus, from concept to commissioning, the entire Gyandoot DL project was executed in the short space of 51 days for a cost of $57,000 USD. The selection of services to be provided, the local youth to be trained for operating it, the design and testing of the software were all done through repeated meetings with the constituency: rural villagers.

Each day several hundred villagers travel to government offices from remote villages to obtain information, submit applications, meeting officials, obtain public records, and obtain information regarding prevailing prices in commodity market yards etc. This travel represents a significant hardship – usually involving loss of day's income, cost of transportation, uncertainty regarding availability of the relevant official/record/information on the day of the visit, repeated visits for expediting or picking up the desired information, and lastly harassment at the hands of corrupt public officials who hold a de jure monopoly over most government services.

As an example of the power of Gyandoot information consider that Dhar is a typical Indian district with most people dependent on farming. To sell their produce, farmers in Dhar traditionally rely on trader who are known to quote rates far below the market price and keep the difference. Farmers otherwise have to travel long distances to find a wholesale market that offers more competitive rates. With Gyandoot farmers can cut out the middleman and find the highest prices for their produce since Gyandoot gives them access to the latest market quotes, produce exchanges, and other information vital to farming. The reported impact has been that villagers

The Gyandoot Project is already in the process of being replicated. The Indian Government issued a state-wide tender on January 30, 2000 for setting up such kiosks across the state of Madhya Pradesh. The Governor announced in the State Government's annual address to the State Legislature on February 3, 2000 that information kiosks similar to the Gyandoot project will shortly be set up across the state.

The impact of Gyandoot is beyond the state, indeed the Indian Government is replicating the Gyandoot model nationwide with a national project called Drishtree (which means "vision"). Drishtree will provide market information to all Indian farmers as well as create a web-based citizen government interface to provide public administration, education, and healthcare services. With 700 million of India's one billion population living in villages, drishtree.com is poised to become the world's largest digital community.

## 9. INDIAN NATIONAL DIGITAL LIBRARY IN ENGINEERING SCIENCE AND TECHNOLOGY (INDEST)

The INDEST Consortium is an initiative by the Department of Secondary Education and Higher Education, Ministry of Human Resource Development (MHRD), Government of India. The Ministry of Human Resource Development (MHRD) has set-up a "Consortia-based Subscription to Electronic Resources for Technical Education System in India" on the recommendation made by the Expert Group appointed by the ministry. The consortium is named as the Indian National Digital Library in Science and Technology (INDEST) Consortium. "Shared subscription" or "Consortia-based subscription" to electronic resources through consortia of libraries is a feasible strategy to increase the access to electronic resources across Institutions at a lower cost. The consortia-based subscription can be successfully deployed to meet the pressures such as diminishing budget, increased user's demand and rising cost of journals.

The Ministry of Human Resource Development (MHRD) set-up the "Indian National Digital Library in Engineering Sciences and Technology (INDEST) Consortium" on the recommendation made by the Expert Group appointed by the ministry under the chairmanship of Prof. N. Balakrishnan. The Ministry provides funds required for subscription to electronic resources for (37) institutions including IISc, IITs, NITs, IIMs and a few other centrally-funded Government institutions through the consortium headquarters set-up at the IIT Delhi. Besides, (60)Government or Government-aided engineering colleges and technical departments in universities have joined the Consortium with financial support from the AICTE. Moreover, the INDEST-AICTE Consortium, as an open-ended proposition, welcomes other institutions to join it on their own for sharing benefits it offers in terms of highly discounted rates of subscription and better terms of agreement with the publishers. All electronic resources being subscribed are available from the publisher's Website. The Consortium has an active mailing list and a Web site hosted at the IIT Delhi.

The INDEST-AICTE Consortium is the most ambitious initiative taken so far in the country. The benefit of consortia-based subscription to electronic resources is not confined to 38 major technological institutions in the country but is also extended to all AICTE-accredited and UGC-affiliated institutions. (97)engineering colleges and institutions have already joined the consortium on their own. Recently (387)engineering colleges and institutions joined under self support- new scheme For further details, click at Join.

The Indian National Digital Library in Engineering Sciences and Technology (INDEST) is a very ambitious initiative, which will subscribe to electronic resources to achieve optimal use of these resources through the participating libraries. The consortium will have cooperative subscription, resource sharing/ILL, Training and technology support as well as other shared activities for better user services and help in sustenance and continuity of the digital libraries.

## 10. KALASAMPADA

The Indira Gandhi National Centre for the Arts, established in memory of Smt. Indira Gandhi, is visualised as a centre encompassing the study and experience of all the arts — each form with its own integrity, yet within a dimension of mutual interdependence, interrelated with nature, social structure and cosmology.

The arts are here understood to comprise the fields of creative and critical literature, written and oral; the visual arts, ranging from architecture, sculpture, painting and graphics to general material culture, photography and film; the performing arts of music, dance and theatre in their broadest connotation; and all else in fairs, festivals and lifestyle that has an artistic dimension. In its initial stages the Centre will focus attention on India; it will later expand its horizons to other civilizations and cultures. Through diverse programmes of research, publication, training, creative activities and performance, the IGNCA seeks to place the arts within the context of the natural and human environment. The fundamental approach of the centre is all its work will be both multi-disciplinary ana interdisciplinary.

Recognizing ,the need to encompass and preserve the distributed fragments of Indian art and culture, a pioneering attempt has been made by Indira Gandhi National Centre for the Arts (IGNCA) to serve as a major resource centre for the arts, especially written, oral and visual materials. One of the programmes of this centre, in collaboration with UNDP, is to utilize multimedia computer technology to create a wide variety of software packages; that communicate cultural information. Multimedia technology allows the user to interact and explore the subject in a non-linear mode by combining audio, text, graphics, animation and video on a computer.

Cultural Informatics Laboratory (CIL) , is a pioneering unit of the IGNCA, established in 1994 with UNPP assisted multimedia documentation project titled "Strengthening National Facility for Interactive Multimedia Documentation of Cultural Resources" has emerged as world-class documentation unit that demonstrates the manner in which the heritage can be recreated virtually, in the holistic and integrated perception of culture. It also acts as a focal point of digitisation of manuscripts, slides, books, audio and video to preserve the entire repository of its present and future holdings in digital mode and to disseminate the contents in various digital formats to the scholars, researchers and the people in general. The contents developed by CIL. which serves as the end-point in the assembly line of the IGNCA's activities are presented to the world through the thematic multimedia CD-R0M(s), inhouse developed Kalasampada (Digital Library-Resources of Indian Cultural Heritage) and website (www.ignca.gov.in). The UNDP project completed successfully in 2001.

A digital repository of content and information integrated with a user-friendly interface, has been developed to encompass and preserve the rare archival collections of the IGNCA. The Kalasampada facilitates the scholars (users) to access and view the materials over a couple of lakh of manuscripts, over one lakh slide, rare books, thousands of rare photographs, audio and video along with highly researched publications of the IGNCA, from a single computer interface (window).

The Project aims to use multimedia computer technology to develop a software package that integrates variety of cultural information and helps the users (students, scholars, artists and Research & scientific Community etc.) to interact and explore the subject available in image, audio, text graphics, animation and video on a computer in a nonlinear mode, by a click of mouse. The system aims at being a digital repository of content and information with a user-friendly interlace. The knowledge base such created will help the scholars to explore and visualize the information stored in multiple layers. This will provide a new dimension in the study of the Indian art and Culture, in an integrated way, while giving due importance to each medium. The IGNCA's archival collection includes manuscripts, slides, rare books, photographs, audio and video along with highly researched publications of books, journals and newsletters.

These rare manuscripts, collected from different institutions of India and abroad are mainly in the form of microfilms and microfiche. Approximately 12000 rolls of microfilms (out of about 20000) have been digitised. The digitisation of microfiche started recently. Similarly, slides (View Digital Images) are collected from the institutions like ACSAA, British Library, Victoria and Albert Museum etc. Slides over 100000 have been digitised. Rare Photographs digitised includes Rajah Deen Dayal collection, Sambhu Nath Sana collection etc. About thousand hours of Audio / Video Film & Video Documentation (online audio / video) is available in digital form out of total collection of over 10000 hours. A part of the IGNCA's publications (electronic books available) with the various volumes of News Letters (Vihangama) and Kalakalpa: Bi-annual Journal have been digitised.

The major activities of the project includes the digitization of materials, post digitization editing, high capacity storage & backup system, designing and development of effective retrieval system etc. Technology used for this development is based on Open standards using Unicode, a multilingual standards for fonts, accepted worldwide with open type fonts. Search is available both in English and Hindi (Devanagari). User have the option to select the material of his interest either from a specific type of collection like books, manuscripts, slides, audio, video etc or from the entire collections.

The facility is currently available only on intranet, for the very fact that these materials are priced possession, Intellectual Property Rights, and copyright issues, etc. Although, partial information can be accessed from the IGNCA's.

## 11. MUKTABODHA DIGITAL LIBRARY AND ARCHIVING PROJECT

The Muktabodha Digital Library and Archiving Project is an attempt to build a digital library in Indian languages specially the ancient texts on palm leaves, birch tree barks etc. It started in 1995 as a manuscript microfilming project focusing mainly on photographing at-risk and rare palm-leaf Vedic Shrauta Ritual manuscripts from both private collections and from libraries. Since that time the technology used and the focus have evolved into digitally capturing both Vedic Shrauta Ritual and medieval Shaivite manuscripts. Libraries photographed from include:

- ★ Mysore Oriental Research Institute
- ★ Puliyannur Tantric collections, Calicut Univ.

* Rashtriya Sanskrit Vidyapeetha, Tirupati
* Academy of Sanskrit Research, Melkote, Karnataka
* Oriental Research Institute, Trivandrum, KE
* Sri Chandrasekharendra Saraswati Visva Maha Vidyalaya, in Enathur, Kanchipuram
* Sri Venkateswara Univ. Oriental Research Institute, Tirupati
* Dakshinannaya Sharada Pitham, Sringeri, Karnatak
* Nedumpilli Mana I - Irinjalakkuda, Kerala

As phase II of Muktabodhas, its goals is to make available on the world-wide web important texts from our archives. The initial phase of this goal was realised in July 2003 when the core texts of Kashmir Shaivism were made available to the international scholarly community by publishing 75 volumes of the Kashmir Series of Texts and Studies in our on-line digital library. The success of this first phase of the on-line digital library was indicated in its first two years of existence by the downloading of over 5,800 texts by individuals and institutions in 54 countries. A particularly high use of the library is from India, Eastern Europe and countries of the former Soviet Union, indicating that Muktabodha's digital library is functioning as a source of indological texts for individual scholars and institutions that have neither the resources nor the access to obtain these texts by other means.

As a continuation of phase II the most important texts of the K.S.T.S. series not already available on the world-wide-web as searchable e-texts were data entered and made available as searchable e-texts in our digital library. An important part of this phase was also the publication of editions of important texts edited by Mark Dyczkowski, mainly but not exclusively in the Krama school.

Having secured the core texts of Kashmir Shaivism in

phase II of the digital library in 2003, the next focus is on securing and disseminating the Shaivite texts that formed the milieu from which Kashmir Shaivism drew to form the synthesis of Kashmir Shaivism. The two poles of this focus are the texts of Shaiva Siddhanta on the one side and the Trika-Kaula texts on the other side. Other traditions forming this milieu such as texts of the Virasaiva, Srividya and Matsyendranatha traditions have also been added.

Muktabodha has recently completed digitally photographing the collection of 1144 devanagari transcripts of mainly Saiva Siddhanta manuscript bundles prepared by the scholars of the French Institute in Pondicherry (IFP) under the direction of N.R. Bhatt in the 1950's and 1960's. These transcripts comprise over 2000 individual texts, most never published before, and form an important part of the Saiva manuscripts of the IFP which is the largest collection of Saiva Siddhanta texts in the world and has recently received recognition as a UNESCO MEMORY OF THE WORLD collection. Under an agreement between Muktabodha, the IFP and the Ecole Francaise d'Extreme-Orient these transcripts will be made available on both the Muktabodha and IFP websites. Muktabodha will also be continuing to add Tantric texts including texts of the Trika-Kaula edited by Dr. Mark Dyzckowski.

## 12. NALANDA DIGITAL LIBRARY

Nalanda is the result of the ongoing Digital Library initiative at National Institute of Technology, Calicut Library. Nalanda Project aims at a full-fledged Digital Library at NITC to cater to the increasing demand for information resources from the Campus User Community as well as from Remote Users from rest of the Country. Some resources are open to all, otherwise they are resistricted to NITC campus and their recognised users. At present, it is in evolving stage.

NITC Library was started during 1963, with skeleton staff, inside NITC Campus with books as its major holding. During that period NITC was offering only Undergraduate Programs with a total strength of 180 students per batch.During 70's the Institute started Post-Graduate Programs in various disciplines and this led to the improvement in library facilities too. The Library started a separate Text Book Bank Section for the students during this period. Even though the effective area of the library remained same at 1340 sq.m, the holdings of the library increased substantially.

During 1980's, the student strength at NITC increased considerably both at Undergraduate and Post graduate level. NITC Library widened its operations in order to meet the consequent increased requirement for the library facilities.A separate section for weaker sections of the society(Scheduled Caste and ScheduledTribes)was introduced with the help of the State Welfare Board for SC/ST.Library also started subscribing to a number ofIndian and Foreign Journals to keep abreast with the technological and scientific developments in the world. The collection of the library also grew about three times its level during 1970's. The intake of students increased in Undergraduate programs and 3 new UG programs in Computer Science & Engineering Production Engineering and Management and Architectural Engineering were started during the period. The Post-Graduate programs also doubled to 6 from the 1980 level of 3 programs. In addition to these, NITC started a Master of Computer Applications (MCA)Program during 1988. All these developments saw more users for library and library holdings increased substantially during the period. The library also increased its floor area to almost double that of 1960 level.

The operations of the library increased manifold during 1990-97. The holdings of the library increased to double the level of 80's and the area of library also increased with the addition of a new block. The demand on library also increased during this period due to the increase in student strength. The Institute had started a number of part-time programs and short-term training and executive development programs, increasing demand on the services of library. Even though the number of journals decreased during this period, the expenditure on this head had increased considerably as the library started subscribing to a number of important international journals. A separate reference reading room for the benefit of the users was started during this period. Similarly a full-fledged D.T.P centre with a graphics studio to meet the publishing needs of the Institute, and a separate Xerox centre were started during this period. A video section with more than 100 titles was started during this period in order to improve the learning resource collection. The services of the library to the weaker sections of the society also increased substantially. The holdings of books reserved separately for the use of students belonging to SC/ST communities had increased during this period.

## 13. NATIONAL RESOURCE CENTRE FOR WOMEN

The National Resource Centre for Women set up by the Government of India is conceptualized as a Virtual Resource Centre on Women's issues. The portal would function as a decentralized, participatory and partnership oriented entity aiming at giving access to digital catalogues of different libraries dealing with women's issues, reports of diverse nature, statistics, events, legislations pertaining to women etc using different media to reach a very broad based clientele at different levels.

Major efforts and investments are essential for the establishment of a Virtual Resource Centre as one of the major resource centres of prime importance. Sustenance of the efforts, in tune with the ever changing objectives and targets of the dynamic and virtual organization like NRCW, over the years, are highly desirable. Action Plans with quarterly targets are required to be devised and to be implemented to effectively reach the designated milestones. Training, orientation and motivation of the personnel are the essentials. In this endeavour if required the personnel may require to be trained professionally in all the fields of concern to make them effectively plan and execute the tasks. The personnel of the stake holders are also required to be involved in the ambit of personnel management to effectively meet the targets, as they are partners of the business. The efforts should be continued to equip the organization with all the facets of development by provision of the requisite resources as demanded in different critical situations. A suitable Economic Business Model is required to be evolved for effectively meeting the resource requirements.

It is very vital for the sustenance of the NRCW continued capacity building and provision of the requisite skill sets to enable the sustenance of the project on long term plan. All stake holders should form the primitive group and work in tandem with core NRCW teams to have the project reach the designated milestones. The focused areas could include all the areas covered above and also on the enhancement and diversifying the of the content management system. It is also very vital to draw the annual/quarterly work charts to accomplish the capacity building across all levels. In this regard the following activities are proposed:

Organinising regular training programmes in all fields of relevance for effective and efficient working of the environment. If it is felt necessary, the exposure may be provided in institutions of reputation, working in the areas of concern to have a quick learning curve.

The training areas should not only cover the actual subject of concern but also the areas IT – Digital Documentation, preservation, Web technology and Systems and software maintenance. Virtual Course material for training and orientation is required to be designed and developed by adopting international standards.

## 14. PERIYAR UNIVERSITY DIGITAL LIBRARY

The Periyar University has signed a MoU with the Information and Library Network centre, UGC and ERNET for getting the UGC-Infonet connectivity. In the first phase, Rs. 5 lakh has been allotted for subscription of online journals and databases. In the second phase, it is being planned to digitalise the university theses and dissertations. Periyar

Periyar University will soon join the select band of higher education centres with a digitised library. This knowledge bank will ensure its students and researchers latest information on a variety of subjects through the University Grants Commission's (UGC)-Infonet connectivity. As a part of the efforts to set up a 'digital library. It will also help the students to access more than 2,600 e-journals on various subjects.

The objective of getting the UGC-Infonet and establishing a digital library is to enhance the higher education and research programmes with the current and retrospective information with the support of latest technology. The connectivity will be established shortly. The digital library has the potential to store more information than the traditional libraries. The resources of the digital library can easily be read by more number of people.

In the second phase, it is being planned to digitise the university theses and dissertations. The Periyar University also proposes to establish facilities enabling the students in the affiliated colleges to access the database of the digital library through the Internet. Its traditional library however has 22,000 books and subscribing to 147 national and international journals.

Many of the more than 25,000 *granthas* in the libraries of Sri Sringeri Math date back a few centuries. The *granthas* are available in the form of ancient *tala patras* (palm leaf manuscripts), *kadatas* (a form of manuscript made from a long piece of cloth, conditioned by smearing on it powdered tamarind seeds and charcoal, and then folded into pages), paper manuscripts, and printed books. The subjects/ topics they deal with include Vaidika Dharma, philosophy, logic linguistics, science, mathematics, medicine, stories from the *puranas* and *itihasas,* literature, arts and many other subjects, and are in many Indian languages such as Sanskrit, Kannada, Telugu, Tamil, Malayalam and Marathi. However, it is not uncommon to find transcripted books - that is, the language of the text of the book and the script in which it is written are different. An example is Bhaskaracharya's *Lilavati,* the Sanskrit *slokas* or verses (containing mathematical problems) of which are written in Telugu script.

The objective of the project is to create a universal, free-to-read, digital library on the Internet that can be accessed by students and scholars alike. In addition to the books which provide explicit knowledge, the Advaita Sarada Project has set a goal of providing tacit knowledge by making it possible for the seekers to interact with scholars, experts and teachers. This interaction known as 'socialization' in modern knowledge management terms will help students gain a correct understanding of *granthas.*

In addition to the above, informed *Tippani* (annotation)

will be written and created at the book level and at the section/ chapter level. These annotations will guide the student about contents of the book, its relative importance in the gamut of literature available on the subject of study, profile of the author, pre-requisites for studying the book, and also suggest related and advanced books on the subject.

The *granthas* are scanned using a high performance scanner, and its pages stored as images in a powerful computer system, known as the knowledge server, using a modern Database Management System (DBMS). The DBMS has the capability to store images, audio and video recordings as well as texts (words and sentences that can be understood by computers and hence can be processed, that is, indexed, searched, located and retrieved). DBMS also has the capability to serve hundreds of users simultaneously with the information they want, without interfering with one another.

In order to design a knowledge base that can be represented and stored in modern DBMS, it is necessary to conceptualize the knowledge base, which in this case consists of *granthas*, audio and video recordings. A model is a mental picture of the concept; therefore, the knowledge base model is a mental picture of it.

While modeling a knowledge base consisting of various entities associated with the knowledge base under discussion are:

- ★ Books (*granthas*) in various physical forms (palm leaf manuscript, paper manuscript, *kadata*, printed books etc);
- ★ Authors, who are associated with the *grantha* as its creators, or as persons who have written commentaries on it, or as those who have edited and brought out a critical edition of it.

These entities about which one wants to know are

known as *'Objects'* in computational terminology. Examples of a few more objects are: taxonomy, which represents a hierarchical categorization of various subjects (or disciplines of study); sub divisions of a *grantha* into sections/chapters (eg: *kandas, parvas, prakaranas or adhyayas*).

Details that needed about various objects are known as the '*Attributes*' of those 'objects'. It certainly does not want to know every detail about an 'object' - only those details that are relevant for the purpose. For example, in the case of books, one may need to know its name, author, language, subject etc. Similarly, about an author, his name, period and a brief profile of him is needed.

All 'objects' that share common properties and that exhibit similar behaviour are classified together into what are called *'Classes'*. Therefore, 'classes' consist of 'objects' that are similar and an 'object' becomes an example of a 'class'. Bhaskaracharya's book on Mathematics, *Lilavati,* is thus an example of a 'class' called 'Book' and Bhaskaracharya is an example of a 'class' called 'Author'. 'Objects' of a 'class' may be interrelated with other 'objects' in another 'class'.

## 15. PHYSICAL RESEARCH LABORATORY DIGITAL INITIATIVE

The Physical Research Laboratory, Ahmedabad owes its existence to Dr Vikram A Sarabhai and his deep interest in scientific research, his initiative and his outstanding powers of organisation and management. It was founded following an agreement between the Ahmedabad Education Society and the Karmakshetra Educational Foundation in November 1947. At present PRL has grown and is spread to four campuses : PRL - main campus, PRL -Thaltej, PRL - Mt Abu and Udaiput Solar Observatory (USO) at Udaipur.

To meet its objectives, the PRL Library has embarked

on major initiative to meet user needs, improve access to the collection and to resources beyond our own collection. It is our aim to develop and manage the collection for the benefit of our users today and for posterity, and to ensure that we function efficiently and effectively as a unified Library. Library users and potential Library users everywhere are becoming more aware of what it is possible to do with computers and networks, although they are most of the time naware of the costs or timescales that would be required to turn the possible technologynhanced world into the actual world.

The Library houses 10 PCs (including 2 multimedia) on a network with a server dedicated to the Library, two barcode scanners, one CD-writer, one HP scanner, one laser printer and two deskjet color printers. LIBSYS package is being used for various Library functions like acquisition, cataloging, circulation, serials management, etc. Reports from each module can be taken to assist in managing the various functions of the Library. Other Equipment. Library also houses a photocopying machine with pass-word facility.

PRL Library has a rich collection of about 45,000 documents including the bound volumes. A staff of 3 professionals serve about 400 users. Services of the library include circulation (approx. issue 3600/year), ILL (500/year), internet searches carried out ( 84 / year), and photocopying service. At present, the library is equipped with 6 PCs for the staff and 4 PCs for the users to consult the OPAC. The library is connected through LAN (Novell Netware). LIBSYS software package is being used for acquisition, processing and retrieving the document information.

There are various kinds of data being used by the scientists regularly. For instance preprints (preprint is an article before it is printed in a journal), technical reports.

The publications of PRL scientists can be made available full-text in multiple formats preferably in PS format (PostScript format). (Multiple formats will also make the document available to a user who is using 'Word'). Another collection, referred quite often is Ph D theses submitted by the students carrying out doctoral study at PRL. Nowadays, full-texts of these are already available in PS format with the students. This database of PRL Publications can be made available on the Web too. The main goal in developing DL is to provide the researchers at PRL, opportunities for accessing and using variety of information in highly flexible manner.

## 16. TIFR DIGITAL LIBRARY INITIATIVE

The TIFR online public access catalog provides access to several standard international publications and journals such as IEEE and Springer. This resource is also involved in the process of providing digital access to materials, e-books. It uses Dublin Core metadata for this purpose.

The Tata Institute of Fundamental Research was founded in 1945 as a centre for pursuit of fundamental research in mathematics, theoretical physics, nuclear physics, cosmic rays. It slowly encompassed subjects like astronomy/astrophysics, molecular biology and computer science, as well. The library, which was established almost simultaneously with its parent organization, not only functions as a depository but also serves an information dissemination centre for scientists. As a national centre, it also caters to the needs of scientists of other organizations.

The Library presently has a collection of more than 138,000 volumes. It currently subscribes to around 650 printed journals and has access to over 3000 e-journals. Library has a large collection of bound volumes of journals, some dating back to 1820s. In addition to these, the library also has theses, newspapers, maps, etc. Besides, the library is equipped with modern resources such as online databases, offline databases, audio-visual materials in the form of CDs, Audio and Video Tapes, etc. Collection of the library is housed mainly in three stack rooms - Journals Stack, Books Stack and Extension Area. While Book Stack and Journals Stack house books and bound volumes of currently subscribed journals respectively, the Extension Area stocks bound volumes of discontinued journals, some less used books and very old bound volumes of journals. Loose Issues of journals are kept in pigeonholes in the main library and recent issues of journals are displayed on the flap of pigeonholes. The library also has a special collection of Manuscripts of Prof. Harish Chandra and Prof. C.P. Ramanujan and original Drawings of Dr. Homi Bhabha.

## 17. TRADITIONAL KNOWLEDGE DIGITAL LIBRARY

Traditional Knowledge Digital Library (TKDL) is a joint venture of the National Institute of Science Communication and Information Resources (NISCAIR) and Department of Indian Systems of Medicine and Homeopathy (ISM&H) which gives focus to preservation of community knowledge resources. It also is supposed to give legitimacy to the existing traditional knowledge and enable protection of such information. There are interesting digital library initiatives in India

India has possessed a rich traditional knowledge of ways and means practiced to treat diseases afflicting people since the time immemorial. This knowledge has generally been passed down by word of mouth from generation to generation. A part of this knowledge has been described in ancient classical and other literature, often inaccessible to the common man. Documentation of this existing knowledge, available in public domain, on various traditional systems of medicine has become imperative to safeguard the sovereignty of this traditional knowledge and to protect it from being misused by obtaining patents on non-original innovations, and this has been a matter of national concern. India fought successfully for the revocation of turmeric and basmati patents granted by United States Patent and Trademark Office (US PTO) and neem patent granted by European Patent Office (EPO). As a sequel to this, in 1999, the Department of Ayurveda, Yoga & Naturopathy, Unani, Siddha and Homoeopathy-AYUSH, erstwhile Department of Indian System of Medicine and Homoeopathy- ISM&H) constituted an inter-disciplinary Task Force, for preparing an approach paper on establishing a Traditional Knowledge Digital Library (TKDL).

The project TKDL involves documentation of the knowledge available in public domain on traditional knowledge from the existing literature related to Ayurveda, Unani and Siddha, in digitized format in five international languages which are English, German, French, Japanese and Spanish. Traditional Knowledge Resource Classification (TKRC), an innovative structured classification system for the purpose of systematic arrangement, dissemination and retrieval has been evolved for about 10,500 subgroups against one group in International Patent Classification (IPC), i.e. *AK61K35/78* related to medicinal plants.

Presentation on Traditional Knowledge Resource Classification (TKRC) at IPC Union led to the creation of WIPO-TK Task Force consisting of USPTO, EPO, JPO, China and India by (IPC) Union for enhancing the sub-groups in IPC for classifying the TK related subject matter and considering the linking of TKRC with IPC. In February 2002, Committee of Experts recommended : (i) inclusion of 200 subgroups on TK against earlier single group on medicinal plants, (ii) linking of TKRC to IPC and (iii) continuation of work on biodiversity, TK and TCE. Thus, a new main group was included in IPC i.e. AK61K 36/00 with approx. 200 subgroups covering different categories of plants

Traditional Knowledge Digital Library is based on Ayurveda which is one of the oldest systems of medicine (2500 B.C.), and *Google search results* for which shows about 4,100,000 references/citations/documents, whereas references/citations/documents for TKDL established in 2003, are about 11,000,000 i.e more than two and a half times than Ayurveda on which TKDL is based.Similarly, Traditional Knowledge Resource Classification recognized in February 2002 is based on International Patent Classification System (1971). Google search results show about 1,730,000 references/citations/documents for IPC and 11, 900,000 citations for TKRC which is more than seven times to that for IPC.

# 3 International Information Networks

## 1. ONLINE COMPUTER LIBRARY CENTER (OCLC)

Founded in 1967, OCLC is a nonprofit, membership, computer library service and research organization dedicated to the public purposes of furthering access to the world's information and reducing information costs. More than 45,000 libraries in 84 countries and territories around the world use OCLC services to locate, acquire, catalog, lend and preserve library materials. Its objectives are establish, maintain and operate a computerized library network and to promote the evolution of library use, of libraries themselves and of librarianship, and to provide processes and products for the benefit of library users and libraries, including such objectives as increasing availability of library resources to individual library patrons and reducing the rate-of-rise of library per-unit costs, all for the fundamental public purpose of furthering ease of access to and use of the ever-expanding body of worldwide scientific, literary and educational knowledge and information. It is a unique cooperative venture, giving your library access to a wide range of services and databases, including WorldCat. Together OCLC member libraries make up the world's largest consortium.

OCLC's first offices were in the Main Library on the

campus of The Ohio State University (OSU), and its first computer room was housed in the OSU Research Center. It was from these academic roots that Frederick G. Kilgour, OCLC's first president, oversaw the growth of OCLC from a regional computer system for 54 Ohio colleges into an international network.

In 1977, the Ohio members of OCLC adopted changes in the governance structure that enabled libraries outside Ohio to become members and participate in the election of the Board of Trustees; the Ohio College Library Center became OCLC, Inc. In 1981, the legal name of the corporation became OCLC Online Computer Library Center, Inc. Today, OCLC serves more than 45,000 libraries of all types in the U.S. and 84 countries and territories around the world.

Researchers, students, faculty, scholars, professional librarians and other information seekers use OCLC services to obtain bibliographic, abstract and full-text information when and where they need it. CLC and its member libraries cooperatively produce and maintain WorldCat—the OCLC Online Union Catalog. Membership in OCLC is a unique cooperative venture, giving your library access to a wide range of services and databases, including WorldCat. Together OCLC member libraries make up the world's largest consortium.

**Products Services and eContent**

OCLC offers full-service online cataloging, simple copy cataloging, MARC record collections, offline cataloging, customized OCLC cataloging from your materials vendor, automated copy cataloging for materials purchased and custom cataloging services. It also administers the Dewey Decimal Classification system, the most widely used library classification system in the world.

### Collection Management

It offers collection development services to meet collection goals. Assess the strengths and gaps of collection with targeted analysis tools. Serve culturally diverse community with easy-to-order, shelf-ready collections of non-English materials.

### Digital Collection and Preservation

OCLC's digitization, microfilm and archival services are designed to protect and share collections. Managees special collections, or turn to the skilled staff at our preservation centers.

### EContent

Offers enhance your collections with eBooks from netLibrary, full-text electronic journals and a variety of online reference databases.

### Reference

Through FirstSearch, OCLC offer online access to full-text documents, abstracts, indices and WorldCat, the world's most powerful bibliographic database. It is also a partner with the Library of Congress to provide a comprehensive virtual reference service.

### 1. Cataloguing and Metadata

Cataloguing and Metadata Services include Connexion CatExpress Dewey services Custom cataloging Batch processing PromptCat Cataloging partners program WorldCat Collection Sets GovDoc CJK Cataloging Arabic Cataloging CatME Z39.50 Cataloging Collection Management Digital Collection and Preservation eContent Reference Resource Sharing and ILL Services for Groups

### Connexion

**Integrated online cataloging :** OCLC's flagship cataloging service. Connexion's flexible suite of tools aligns your bibliographic and authority record activities with WorldCat and the OCLC Authority File.

**CatExpress**

**Simple copy cataloging :** CatExpress is a Web-based tool for cataloging popular materials via an easy-to-learn interface, perfect for lower volumes and catalogers with less experience.

**Dewey Services**

**Dewey Decimal Classification :** The most widely used library classification system in the world. Order the new DDC22 print edition or subscribe to WebDewey, the online version that's continually updated.

**Custom Cataloging**

**Comprehensive technical services :** Improve access to materials and save library time, money and effort. Customized, expert solutions for your most difficult cataloging, conversion and authority control challenges.

**Batch Processing**

**Records and holdings maintenance :** Add, change or cancel large numbers of records or holdings—locally and in WorldCat—with a variety of offline options.

**PromptCat**

**Automated copy cataloging :** Save staff time and be ready to shelve materials faster. Materials ordered through participating material partners arrive with complete MARC records and your holdings set in WorldCat.

**Cataloging Partners**

**Custom OCLC cataloging from material vendors:** Receive high-quality, full MARC records for every title you order from participating vendors. Order materials and MARC records from one source, with one invoice, at a surprisingly low cost.

**WorldCat Collection Sets**

**MARC record collections :** Pre-packaged sets of full catalog records for microform, non-microform and electronic content purchased from vendors, ready to load into your local system.

**GovDoc**

**Government document records** : For federal depository institutions, delivery of up-to-date records for the government documents your library holds.

**CJK Cataloging**

**Software for cataloging in Chinese, Japanese and Korean** using vernacular characters. Ideal for libraries supporting Asian studies or communities.

**Arabic Cataloging**

**Cataloging software for Arabic-language materials:** This Windows-based application lets you catalog in basic and extended Arabic character sets.

**CatME**

**Cataloging software :** Create and edit new records and bibliographic information online or offline. Produce and update records in batch mode, and export records to local systems.

**Z39.50 Cataloging Service**

**Z39.50 access to WorldCat** : Search and retrieve MARC records from WorldCat using your Z39.50-compliant local system.

**WorldCat**

The power behind OCLC cataloging solutions is WorldCat,

the authoritative source of cataloging records built by librarians.

**Now available:** Connexion client version 1.10

Version 1.10 includes changes for set up options, editing records, a new macro recorder, and more. Learn more and download the client.

### DDC 22

Dewey Decimal Classification 22 is now available in print (and online). One can order it at any time using the new Dewey Web Store. Learn more about the print version and the robust WebDewey online alternative.

The July 2003 edition of the OCLC Newsletter also offers a detailed look at DDC22; view the article online, or download the full issue (2.2MB PDF).

### Watch WorldCat grow!

A new online counter lets you see the newest records added to WorldCat. The page, which refreshes every eight seconds, gives a glimpse at the variety of materials represented in WorldCat, the world's most comprehensive bibliographic database.

## 2. COLLECTION MANAGEMENT

OCLC helps in analyzing collection to identify gaps and overlaps so that one can plan more effectively for the future and enhance collections with non-English materials or electronic resources.

### Language Sets

**Non-English collections :** Preselected sets of non-English materials are delivered ready to shelve. It's a fast, affordable way to serve a multicultural community. Now available in 12 languages.

### NetLibrary

**Electronic books (eBooks) :** Full-text digital books, journals, newspapers and other published works in hundreds of subject areas. NetLibrary launched the eBook category and remains the worldwide leader.

### Collection Analysis

**Collection analysis and assessment :** Coming in early 2005, the OCLC Collection Analysis service will provide libraries and library groups with WorldCat-based collection management tools accessed via the OCLC FirstSearch service.

### Electronic Collections Online

**Electronic journals :** Easy Web access to thousands of full-text academic and professional journals from more than 70 publishers.

### WorldCat

As your collection changes and grows, WorldCat evolves with it. Libraries use WorldCat, the world's most comprehensive bibliographic database, to analyze and augment their collections.

### New Services

Six South Asian languages added to Language Sets

Serve your Indian, Pakistani and Bangladeshi communities with shelf-ready collections in six languages: Bengali, Gujarati, Hindi, Panjabi, Tamil and Urdu. Each set offers a mix of fiction and non-fiction titles for adults or children. Ordering Language Sets is easier than ever using the online store.

### eBooks: 58,000 titles now available

NetLibrary, OCLC's eBook division, recent celebrated surpassing the 58,000-title milestone. Nearly 2,000 new eBook titles are added in one month , from some of the world's leading publishers. Learn more about NetLibrary eBooks.

## 3. DIGITAL COLLECTION AND PRESERVATION

Preserve and manage your digital collections with microfilming, digitizing and archiving services. Learn more about best practices and funding, and discover outsourcing opportunities that let you manage your digital collection's life cycle as successfully as you do your print collection.

### CONTENTdm

Digital collection management for special collections. Build and manage a digital collection on your own with CONTENTdm, an affordable, scalable solution that's easy to use.

### Olive

**Digital collection management for newspapers :** A solution for digitizing and managing historical newspapers that preserves cultural context while providing powerful indexing and searching.

### Preservation Services

**Custom, expert preservation :** Let OCLC preserve a collection for you with film, digitization and other services performed by skilled teams with the newest technology.

### Digital Archive

**Storage, access and retrieval of digital assets :** Capture Web pages and other digital-only assets and maintain them for tomorrow in the Digital Archive. You choose how information is harvested and how your users find it.

### Education and Planning

**Comprehensive front-end help :** We understand the challenges of planning for and developing digital collections. From grant-writing assistance to technology training, OCLC is a resource center designed around your needs.

### Why OCLC?

**OCLC is uniquely qualified to assist :** As a library technology leader, OCLC understands the challenges faced by community members when planning for and developing digital collections. The value and benefit of shared resources—through cataloging and now through digitization and archiving—drives everything we do.

### WorldCat

WorldCat is the world's largest bibliographic database. It makes easy to catalog the digital assets in WorldCat, so libraries and users worldwide can benefit from such unique collection.

### eContent

These Web-based digital resources occupy no shelf space, but offer patrons a wealth of full-text content. Choose from the world's largest collection of eBook titles and a suite of reference databases that connect users with thousands of abstracts, journal articles and more.

### NetLibrary

**Electronic books (eBooks) :** Full-text digital books, journals, newspapers and other published works in hundreds of subject areas. NetLibrary launched the eBook category and remains the worldwide leader.

### Electronic Collections Online

**Electronic journals :** Easy Web access to thousands of full-text academic and professional journals from more than 70 publishers.

### PAIS International

**Public affairs database :** An unparalleled resource for users who research public policy and world affairs. Accessible through FirstSearch, it covers politics, human rights, health, energy, science and many other topics.

## OCLC Databases

In addition to the hundreds of third-party databases accessible through FirstSearch, a number of databases are owned and managed by OCLC—and many are included with the FirstSearch Base Package.

### WorldCat

Records for nearly all OCLC eContent resources are included in WorldCat, the world's most comprehensive bibliographic database.

### Reference

Reference services that tap dozens of leading databases and leverage your library's own assets more effectively. These online services help your users with accuracy, speed and convenience.

### FirstSearch

**Online reference :** Powerful and highly customizable, FirstSearch is a key reference tool for any library, and the most intuitive access available to the WorldCat bibliographic database. Your patrons will marvel at how quickly they locate the right resources.

### QuestionPoint

**Virtual reference :** Add this Web-based tool to your library's Web site and give users access to quality online reference assistance at any time. QuestionPoint is brought to you by the Library of Congress and OCLC.

### PAIS International

**Public affairs database :** An unparalleled resource for users who research public policy and world affairs. Accessible through FirstSearch, it covers politics, human rights, health, energy, science and many other topics.

## OCLC Databases

In addition to the dozens of third-party databases accessible through FirstSearch, a number of databases are owned and managed by OCLC—and many are included with the FirstSearch Base Package.

### WorldCat

The power behind FirstSearch is WorldCat, the most comprehensive bibliographic database anywhere.

### Resource Sharing and ILL

Create, track and send integrated Interlibrary Loan requests via the Web to participating libraries and document suppliers. ILLiad, our management system, helps you streamline your resource sharing.

### OCLC Interlibrary Loan

**Resoource sharing solutions :** Resources your users need for borrowing and lending. Regionally or globally, OCLC ILL lets you share your collection and offers convenient access to materials at thousands of participating libraries.

### ILLiad

**Interlibrary Loan management software :** Reduce resource-sharing paperwork and let your users track their own loan requests with software that consolidates all ILL functions in one place.

### Union List

**Holdings for serials and more :** Greatly improve users' access to serials and similar materials while lowering your borrowing costs. Union List gives you access to shared holdings information via more than 200 groups and other online resources.

## WorldCat

Our Interlibrary Loan service is faciliated by WorldCat, the world's most comprehensive bibliographic database.

## Services for Groups

With OCLC Services for Groups, your library consortium can have its own union catalog in WorldCat that offers a single, unified view of your collections. Eliminate duplicate spending. Gain maximum use of your most valuable materials by sharing resources. And do it economically. Using a unique modular approach, OCLC builds a custom solution based on search tools and infrastructure you've already put in place, so implementation is accelerated and the end result is completely familiar.

## What's included and who can join

OCLC Services for Groups include a centralized union catalog, unlimited access to cataloging and resource sharing, plus a customized FirstSearch interface. OCLC hosts the solution while you maintain control over all operations. Every library in your group and subgroups—regardless of size, type or current OCLC membership status—can participate in the group catalog.

## Group catalog is already started

Many library groups already have millions of holdings in WorldCat, so OCLC can get you set up with a union catalog quickly. Rollout is fast, because every library that uses WorldCat already has the necessary infrastructure in place. Your group will provide users ready access to all its resources, and will be taking full advantage of investments already made in other OCLC services—such as cataloging, resource sharing and reference.

### The added benefit of WorldCat

When group's catalog has its foundation in WorldCat, the world's largest bibliographic database, your users get the advantage of high-quality indexing, access to their own libraries' holdings and to the holdings of libraries worldwide.

### Encourages users to start searching locally

OCLC creates group catalog from holdings set in WorldCat, including only those resources held by the libraries in your group. Users can start with local resources first, then expand outward to regional, consortium-wide and worldwide listings in WorldCat. For circulation and item availability information, materials can link at the record level to the home catalogs of all participating libraries.

### Your savings begin at once

One can start saving immediately, without having to finance new hardware, software or staff training. Hosted by OCLC, these group services continue to make good financial sense for the long term. When each member library has access to all the holdings within the group, user satisfaction increases and libraries will lower acquisition costs by increasing opportunities for resource sharing. And with unlimited access and subscription-based purchase, you can continue to expand your capabilities while managing your budget with predictable pricing.

## 2. CONSORTIUM OF UNIVERSITY RESEARCH LIBRARIES ) CURL)

CURL was established in 1983 to promote co-operation between academic research libraries in Great Britain and Ireland. The rich holdings of the CURL libraries are represented by catalogue records of varying types and quality, and there is a need to take the manual records, which are limited to local use, and make them universally available through electronic databases. This process is known in the library world as retrospective conversion.

When the CURL Strategic Directions for 2000-2004 were published, there were 21 university libraries in full membership of the Consortium. By March 2002 the number of full members had risen to 25, including 22 university libraries, as well as the British Library, the National Library of Scotland and the National Library of Wales. The change in the three national libraries' status from associate to full member, together with the British Library's commitment to working in close collaboration with the HE sector, has greatly increased CURL' s potential for improving information resources and service provision for research and research-led learning and teaching across the British Isles.

Other factors have led to a significant change in the information and library environment since 2002. To name only a few, by July 2002, all UK CURL libraries had experienced close working collaboration with other CURL and non-CURL libraries through participation in the highly successful UK-wide Research Support Libraries Programme (RSLP). 2002 was also the year when the Consortium actively participated in the debates generated by the Research Support Library Group (RSLG), including the implications of the electronic media on the national research infrastructure. The expected resulting establishment of the Research Libraries

Network represents a significant shift in the landscape for CURL.

Given the importance of these developments, both internal and external, CURL believes that, rather than wait until 2004, it must review its mission and strategic goals now. Within this updated framework, CURL can seize the opportunities created by this new environment and work towards enhancing library and information provision for the research community as a whole.

CURL's mission is to increase the ability of research libraries to share resources for the benefit of the local, national and international research community. CURL will make a difference for researchers by helping to build the Distributed and Hybrid Research Library of the future. Researchers, wherever in the world and whatever their disciplines, will be able to:

Search, locate and request all resources, whatever their format, easily and quickly from the desktop

Have quick and easy access to an increasing amount of electronic resources, both born-digital and digitized

Have physical access to manuscripts, archives or printed items that have not been digitized and cannot be moved, wherever these are held

Have other printed items from outside their own institutions delivered to them efficiently

CURL is committed to:

Provide strong leadership to find research-centred solutions to common problems

Influence change and provide a seedbed for innovative projects and services

Provide practical tools for finding information

Engage its membership to improve support for researchers

Foster synergies through strategic alliances and collaborative partnerships that will benefit research support in the UK, Ireland and worldwide

Help to shape the wider debate at national and international levels

## Databases

The Consortium of University Research Libraries (CURL) has established a database for bibliographic records. This record retrieval service offers UKMARC records at competitive rates. The database currently contains some 38 million records, and the number is growing constantly. The records include those from member libraries and also from LC (Roman script monograph records 1968- and CJK records) and from the BNB (1985-). As libraries progress their retrospective conversion programmes the number of records for older material and for non book material is increasing. The records are of good quality and CURL has established Bibliographic Standards for contributors and records are flagged to indicate standard.

The service is open to any non-profit organization. There is a flat-rate for searching and no other charges. A month's free trial is available if required. Access is subject to signing licence agreements.

## Other Database links and projects

MARC21 Project

National Online Public-Access Catalogue (COPAC)

CURL feasibility study of Z39.50 technology

CURL Database Project: A Feasibility Study for a National Programme of Retrospective Conversion of Catalogue Records

CURL Minimum Standards for Bibliographic Records

National Union Catalogue Feasibility Study

## MARC21 Project

In August 2002, CURL appointed Nicholas Syrotiuk to be its MARC21 Officer. The MARC21 Officer is based in Manchester, working alongside the MIMAS COPAC team. The brief of the MARC21 Officer is to write the specification for the new database structures that will be put in place in July 2003 in order to effect the transition of the CURL Database to MARC21.

### Test Database

With efforts at MIMAS, a MARC 21 database system consisting of data-handling programs, a database and a Z39.50 target was made open to testing by CURL cataloguers on 19 May 03. This test database has benefited from the work done by MIMAS on the inclusion of both MARC-8 and Unicode UTF-8 encoded records, which means that the database already enables the searching, retrieval and display of some non-Roman script. Testing came to an end on 20 June 03.

MIMAS has been invited to prepare a costed proposal, to be submitted first to the RD&D SG and then to the Board in the Autumn 03, that will concentrate on the development of a web interface and of a clustering system for the display of search results.

Meanwhile, some collaboration will be taking place between CURL and RLG. Durham, as the principal CURL user of the Eureka MARC export facility, has agreed to act as the tester of the new RLG interface and to share its finding with MIMAS by the end of 03, in line with RLG's own timeframe and testing. The point of the exercise is to find out to what extent the software developed by RLG can be adapted to the CURL MARC 21 database.

### 'Interim' Database

An interim version of the CURL database, containing MARC21 records, was released on 28 July 03. Given that it will be several months before the new CURL MARC 21 gets big enough to become useful, MARC 21 versions of recently loaded catalogues have been preserved in a form which is compatible with the existing CURL UKMARC database. It has now been made possible to release this 'Interim' version of the CURL database for access via Z39.50. (Telnet access will continue to be to the UKMARC database only).

At present the MARC21content is only from a small number of CURL libraries, though this will grow as we progress with the reloading schedule. The remainder is held in UKMARC.

### Stage 2 of the MARC21 Project

After the completion of the indexes for the new database, outlined in the original MARC21 specification, we enter stage 2 of the MARC21 project. MIMAS's proposal to develop a clustering mechanism for the new MARC21 database has now been approved by the CURL Board. From January 2004, MIMAS will be working on a new algorithm for delivery in June 2004. MIMAS has underlined its commitment to deliver a service modelled closely on the consultation with CURL staff in the autumn of 2002, especially with regard to defining a primary cluster member according to local priorities. MIMAS has also noted that the clustering mechanism would be compatible with Members' proprietary Z-clients.

### Strategic aims

For the next three years CURL will pursue five main strategic aims:

### National Strategies for Research Support

CURL will actively contribute to the development and implementation of appropriately funded national strategies aimed at coordinating the provision of research information and generating sustainable solutions to the information needs of the research communities. This objective will be at the heart of CURL's activity in a number of areas, including resource management and discovery, digitisation and scholarly communications. CURL will also seek to make a significant contribution to the success of the Research Libraries Network, the new body recommended by the Research Support Libraries Group.

## Collaborative Resource Management

In the light of the widely recognised fact that no research library can cater for all the needs of its researchers, CURL will continue to explore, test and implement procedures enabling research information providers to engage in deep collaboration with one another in all areas of resource management. This will involve furthering the collection mapping agenda and developing strategies aimed at facilitating the sharing of responsibilities in the areas of acquisition, preservation, digitisation and retention, e.g. as initiated by the CURL-CoFoR project.

## Resource Discovery

CURL will adopt a two-pronged strategy to further the development of electronic resource discovery tools in the light of recent and future technological developments.

It will (a) continue to enhance existing activities, such as the CURL record retrieval database and the COPAC resource discovery service, and to contribute to the development of the Archives Hub and the e-prints SHERPA project; (b) revisit the whole resource discovery landscape with a view to identifying innovative, inclusive and sustainable solutions, in particular, in terms of models (types of data, technology, quality control) and services. CURL will also actively contribute to other national initiatives, in particular, Full Disclosure.

## Digital Content Creation and Curation

CURL will develop and implement a digitisation strategy aimed at facilitating digitisation and digital preservation work at institutional level within a coherent and coordinated national framework. In order to do this, it will identify what is already being done by other organisations and what needs to be done by CURL, on its own or in collaboration with other bodies, particularly in the areas of repositories for born-digital content, digitisation of library material, preservation and long-term access of digital content.

## Communication & Working Methods

CURL will develop and implement a communication strategy and working methods within the Consortium aimed at providing a framework for greater engagement from the Members in order to increase consortial debate, networking and co-operation. It will also seek to provide a framework conducive to appropriate involvement across sectors and domains, as well as to the development of strategic alliances and collaborative partnerships with other stakeholders and sister organisations both in the UK, Ireland and worldwide.

## CURL Projects and Services

### *Ongoing Projects*

**Archives Hub :** The Archives Hub is a collaborative service which provides a single point of access to descriptions of archive collections held in universities and colleges throughout the United Kingdom. Over 60 institutions are contributing high-quality information to the Hub, which will cover over 20,000 archives by July 2003. The website is free to use and contains information relevant to a wide range of research areas. The service is funded by the Joint Information Systems Committee (JISC) and is overseen by CURL. MIMAS runs the service at the University of Manchester and development work on the Archives Hub software is undertaken by the Cheshire Development Team at the University of Liverpool.

**Britain in Print :** The Britain in Print project involves the participation of eight CURL libraries as well as that of the Edinburgh Royal College of Physicians and the Mitchell Library in Glasgow. All ten libraries have significant collections of pre-1700 British books which are not yet catalogued in electronic form and the aim of the project is to enhance electronic access to this wealth of heritage material for the benefit of the general public.

This work will also embrace the creation of a subject-based interpretative resource which will add value to the discovery information on COPAC by identifying key materials of importance to special interest groups, in particular school-age learners, local history groups, genealogical societies, life-long learners.

**CURL-CoFoR**

A CURL project to promote collaborative collection management. CoFoR (Collaboration For Research) is a new CURL initiative, set up to provide its members and other research libraries with practical tools (templates, guidelines and recommendations) for collaborative acquisition and retention. It will also give special attention to techniques for serial deduplication and to the mapping of relationships between research activity and library provision.

The 21-month project builds on work already carried out by the RSLP COCOREES project (Collaborative Collection Management for Russian and East European Studies) and by the CURL Task Force on Resource Management. The service offered by the COCOREES database, with its large set of collection descriptions and massive finding list for Russian and East European serials will be maintained.

## Monograph Inter-lending Project

**Project Brief :** The purpose of this one-year project is to explore further and take forward the principal recommendation made in the report "Monograph Inter-lending for the Higher Education Research Community", which was jointly commissioned by CURL and the British Library in 2003.

The report recommends the adoption and implementation of a 'BLDSC Plus' option that would involve the British Library forming a consortium with a range of partner libraries willing to provide monograph inter-lending services to defined service standards and charges.

The project will aim:

(a) To scope the prior implementation phase for BLDSC Plus, as recommended by the Report, including making specific recommendations on the following issues: governance mechanisms; criteria and terms of conditions for participation in the scheme; specification of service levels; pricing and payment policy and mechanisms; IT specifications; future funding requirements; relationship of the service to the soon to be created Research Libraries Network (RLN).

(b) To discuss and agree the prior implementation scoping recommendations with:

— the key organisations involved, including the British Library, the other national libraries, CURL, the RLN and a sample of research librarians (including CURL librarians);

— with the wider information community via a broad cross-sectoral consultation exercise, with a view to gaining commitment to the new scheme from as broad a base as possible;

(c) To prepare an implementation plan for the agreed scheme, by making specific recommendations on the following: membership and terms of reference of the scheme's Management Board; identification of partner libraries; a detailed and timed work plan for implementation.

(d) To liaise closely with the CURL Resource Management Task Force on progress with implementation.

## Access to CURL Libraries

The Libraries in membership of CURL (both full members and associate members) recognise their obligations as the major research libraries of the UK and Ireland in the support of research both at a national and international level.

Their combined holdings represent a major resource in the support of research.

The CURL member libraries are committed to:

* Making their holdings available (in the case of full members) through COPAC nationally and internationally
* Providing access to their collections to all *bona fide* researchers

Access is defined as:

Access to print collections, special collections and archives and other material for consultation purposes during normal library opening hours

* It may not include access to electronic material and computer networks where the conditions of site licences do not permit this

Some CURL libraries may offer services to external researchers on payment of a fee. Each member library of CURL will publish on its web site details of opening hours, a description of its special collections and archives, requirements for access (e.g. proof of identity) and details of any charged services.

Researchers intending to apply for access to a CURL library are urged to consult that library's web site before making a visit. Contact details and a summary of the requirements for access to each library can be found at

All of these libraries welcome visits by academic staff or graduate students from other universities who are undertaking research for which the collections in the library to be visited will be valuable. In some cases prior arrangement is necessary by writing or telephoning, in order that the host library staff may be able to notify you if there is any difficulty about access to the collection you require on the day of your visit. On arrival at the library you wish to visit, please indicate that you are a visitor from another CURL institution, showing any form of identification that the host library may require.

Further information about all of the libraries listed here (collections, opening hours, etc.) may be obtained on the World Wide Web. There are links to the pages of each library included below.

- ★ University of Aberdeen Directorate of Information Systems & Services
- ★ University of Birmingham Information Services
- ★ University of Bristol Information Services
- ★ British Library
- ★ Cambridge University Library
- ★ Durham University Library
- ★ Edinburgh University Library
- ★ Glasgow University Library
- ★ Imperial College London Library

* John Rylands University Library of Manchester
* King's College London Information Services & Systems
* Leeds University Library
* University of Liverpool Library
* University of London Library
* Library of The London School of Economics and Political Science (LSE)
* National Library of Scotland
* National Library of Wales
* Newcastle University Library
* University of Nottingham Information Services
* University of Oxford Libraries
* School of Advanced Study
* The University of Sheffield Library
* University of Southampton Libraries
* Trinity College Library Dublin
* UCL (University College London) Library Services
* University of Warwick Library
* Wellcome Library for the History and Understanding of Medicine

## 3. LIBRARY INFORMATION NETWORKS RESEARCH (RLG)

RLG is an international, not-for-profit membership organization of over 150 universities, libraries, archives, historical societies and other institutions with collections for research and learning. Founded in 1974 by The New York Public Library and Columbia, Harvard, and Yale universities, RLG provides solutions to the challenges presented by information access and management in the digital era.

RLG is governed and run by its members, staff and board

of directors. It is headquartered in Mountain View, California. It supports researchers and learners worldwide by expanding access to research materials held in libraries, archives, and museums.

RLG works with and for its member organizations enhancing their ability to provide research resources. RLG designs and delivers innovative information discovery services, organizes collaborative programs, and takes an active role in creating and promoting relevant standards and practices. As a result, RLG offers a variety of information resources useful to institutions and individuals.

## Mission & Goals

RLG is a not-for-profit membership corporation of universities, archives, historical societies, museums, and other institutions devoted to improving access to information that supports research and learning.

RLG exists to support its members in containing costs, improving local services, and contributing to the world's collective access to scholarly materials. The mechanisms applied in pursuit of these goals take many shapes but have one thing in common—cooperative action.

RLG has been working with research collections and their communities for nearly three decades. Work underway addresses three primary goals shared by RLG's international membership:

— The fullest online access to research resources
— Effective, global resource sharing on new models
— Enduring access to resources through digital preservation

## Organization

In the early 1970s, three US universities and the New York Public Library created a new kind of practical resource-sharing consortium, which incorporated in 1975 as The Research Libraries Group, Inc. (RLG). Since then, RLG has grown to include virtually every type of cultural memory institution—universities, national libraries, archives, historical societies, museums—all with remarkable collections for research and learning. Given our increasingly comprehensive membership mix, we use "RLG" to identify the organization and our projects and products. RLG has offices in Mountain View, California, approximately seven miles south of Stanford University (where our data center is housed) and in New York City.

RLG staff, numbering approximately 90, are organized into the following departments:

— General Administration
— Member Programs and Initiatives
— Integrated Information Services
— (Technology) Development
— Customer and Operations Support
— Finance and Administration

**Projects**

How do institutions of research and learning provide online access to information about their collections, share the actual materials, and ensure access over the long term? RLG has been helping its international members solve these problems over the past three decades.

**Projects by Goal**

The three large and interlocking goals listed here have guided a wide range of current and past efforts. The lists they link to demonstrate that one project can advance more than one goal. Members and staff seek projects that are results-oriented and respond to shared institutional objectives.

Expanded Online Access to Research Resources

Global Resource Sharing

Digital Preservation & Ensured Long-term Access

**Expanded Online Access to Research Resources**

Bringing information about materials for research and learning onto the Internet is both a primary RLG goal and a defining strength of the organization. This page indexes both current projects and past work to increase online access through new databases, enabling standards, and shared expertise. More results are demonstrated in **Products & Services:**

**Global Resource Sharing**

RLG was born from the will of major research institutions to share their collections with each other's scholars and students in new and cost-effective ways. In this arena, the SHARES partnership of RLG members has been the driving force for innovative protocols, technology, and partnerships.

**Digital Preservation & Ensured Long-term Access**

**Guides & Tools :** RLG projects have produced a number of guides and tools useful both to members and to the larger community. Additional printed reports and symposium proceedings, as well as resources like *RLG DigiNews,* are under Publications.

Description Guidelines for RLG Cultural Materials

Digital Preservation Needs and Requirements in RLG Member Institutions

EAD Best Practice Guidelines

EAD Conversion Service

Guides to Quality in Visual Resource Imaging

Guidelines for Microfilming to Support Digitization (pdf)

Preparing Digital Surrogates for RLG Cultural Materials

Preservation Metadata and the OAIS Information Model (pdf)

Preserving Digital Information (pdf)

Tools for Digital Imaging

Trusted Digital Repositories—Attributes & Responsibilities (pdf)

Trusted Digital Repositories—Draft (pdf)

**Products & Services**

RLG's complementary databases support access to research collections around the world. Its consortial partnership and Windows®-based software set the standard for cost-effective, peer-to-peer interlibrary loan. Any institution can take advantage of the wealth of online data available from RLG to meet local reference and cataloging needs. It also encourages to join in expanding these unique resources with contributions of an institution's records through file transfers or online record creation in RLG catalogs. Everyone is welcome and encouraged to make use of RedLightGreen (redlightgreen.com), a free site that mines the RLG Union Catalog to give any Web user a better, faster research tool.

***Free Use at Accredited Schools of Library & Information Science***

There is a provision of free searches of a variety of RLG databases to ALA-accredited schools of library and information science in North America and to recognized schools on other continents. This access is limited to use for instructional purposes. As part of the special arrangement, OCLC does not charge for network connections.

This program includes:

The AMICO Library™ from RLG

RLG Archival Resources

RLG Cultural Materials

English Short Title Catalogue

Hand Press Book Database

SCIPIO: Art and Rare Book Sales Catalogs

RLG Union Catalog

Authority Files (LC/NACO & LC/SACO)

Access is through RLG's Eureka® searching interface or the special digital objects interface used for The AMICO Library and RLG Cultural Materials.

With SCIPIO, the RLG Union Catalog, and the Authority Files one students can *also* use the RLIN21™searching interface. This enables them to locate and export records in MARC format for cataloging and other collection management activities.

To arrange free instructional access for faculty and students, determine which databases want to use in your courses and then contact the RLG Information Center. Short-term access to other RLG databases besides the ones listed here may also be arranged.

**Online Databases**

RLG'c Web-accessible databases contain a wealth of information and resources: Traditional library materials, including books, journals, music, and maps; indexes to archival collections; art and rare book auction catalogs; even digital images of works of art and cultural artifacts.

Which database for which kinds of research? Index to each database for features, sample records, and more:

RLG Union Catalog

The AMICO Library™from RLG

Anthropological Index, Royal Anthropological Institute

Anthropological Literature

Anthropology Plus

RLG Archival Resources

Avery Index to Architectural Periodicals
Bibliography of the History of Art
Chicano Database
RLG Cultural Materials
English Short Title Catalogue (ESTC)
FRANCIS
Hand Press Book Database
Handbook of Latin American Studies
History of Science, Technology, and Medicine
Index to Foreign Legal Periodicals
Index to Hispanic Legislation (World Law Index, Part 1)
Index to 19th-Century American Art Periodicals
Inside Information Plus
Russian Academy of Sciences Bibliographies
SCIPIO: Art and Rare Book Sales Catalogs
Authority Files

**Resource Sharing & Interlending**

Effective, global resource sharing is central to RLG's mission. For this, our members' SHARES partnership and RLG's cutting-edge, distributed ILL management software are essential.

**SHARES**

This program for a partnership of RLG members fosters expedited request and delivery, powerful supporting software, and ongoing improvements. SHARES participants save thousands of dollars annually in reduced lending charges and overhead.

**ILL Manager**

RLG's Windows®-based, state-of-the-art software eliminates

dependence on multiple legacy systems for interlibrary loan, reduces operating costs, streamlines workflows, and empowers your library patrons.

**Record creation**

RLG's RLIN21™Windows®-based software enables to do record creation directly in the RLG Union Catalog—as well as in the SCIPIO database and the LC/NACO Authority File.

**Record supply**

One can take advantage of the wealth of cataloging already done by RLG members and contributors as copy for its systems. We offer record supply through a Z39.50 connection that lets you use your own local system to search and retrieve records, or through its specially designed RLIN21 Web interface.

**Marcadia® cataloging**

Marcadia is a fully automated and customizable cataloging service that lets one set the highest standards for copy from the RLG Union Catalog.

Creating Records in the RLG Union Catalog with RLIN21™

Creating Records in the SCIPIO Database with RLIN21™

Creating Records in the LC/NACO Authority File with RLIN21™

Record Supply Through a Z39.50 Connection

Record Supply Through the RLIN21™Web Interface

Marcadia® Cataloging Service from Backstage Library Works

Freely Available Databases

The RLG Resources gives access to records of books, journal titles, manuscripts and archival material, music scores, maps, government publications, audiovisual material, art, and rare book auction catalogues and computer files. The material is contributed by over 200 research libraries, archives and museums, public and corporate libraries and learned societies. The RLG Resources include: - the RLG union catalogue for books (RLIN), artifacts and electronic material: Citation Resources (CitaDel), which includes a number of databases and covers mostly journal articles, but includes sales catalogues (SCIPIO) as well as the English Short Title Catalogue.

The RLG individual databases listed below do not require a password if you are accessing on campus or accessing via dial-up but DO need a password if accessing off-campus via an alternative ISP

**Anthropology Plus :** brings together into one resource the highly respected Anthropological Literature from Harvard University and Anthropological Index, Royal Anthropological Institute from the UK. Anthropology Plus provides extensive worldwide indexing of journal articles, reports, commentaries, edited works, and obituaries in the fields of social, cultural, physical, biological, and linguistic anthropology, ethnology, archaeology, folklore, material culture, and interdisciplinary studies. The index offers excellent coverage of all core periodicals in the field in addition to local and lesser-known journals. Coverage is from the late 19th century to the present

**RLG's Archival Resources** : provide centralized access for searching and retrieval of archival finding aids that have been encoded using SGML [Standard General Markup Language] and the emerging standard for Encoded Archival Description (EAD). The finding aids are indexed centrally at RLG but are supported in a distributed environment. Some reside on a server at RLG, others are located on other servers around the world. Archival Resources also includes access to RLG's AMC (Archival and Mixed Collections) file. AMC provides researchers with timely and comprehensive access to brief, high-level information for nearly half a million collections of manuscripts and archives, and has greatly enhanced the dissemination of information about the holdings in repositories around the world.

**Index to Periodical Literature** : The only comprehensive American index to the current periodical literature of architecture and design. The Avery surveys more than 2000 US and foreign journals, 75 percent of which are not indexed in any other source. It covers not only the international scholarly and popular literature, but also the publications of professional associations, US state and regional periodicals, and major serial publications in the architecture and design of Europe, Asia, Latin America, and Australia.

**Art History Bibliography** : The most comprehensive and up-to-date art history bibliography available, this file covers European and American art from late antiquity to the present, indexing art-related books, conference proceedings, dissertations, exhibition and dealer's catalogs, and articles in more than 2,500 periodicals from 1973 to the present.

This file covers Mexican-American topics and the broader Latino experience of Puerto Ricans, Cuban Americans, and Central American immigrants; it indexes all types of materials including journal articles, books, and newspaper articles published from the 1960s to the present, with selective coverage dating back to the early 1900s.

Descriptions and holdings information for letterpress materials printed in England or its dependencies (in any language) or in English (anywhere in the world) from 1473 to 1800.

**Humanities & Social Sciences :** An index to multilingual, multidisciplinary information in the humanities, social sciences, economics, religion, the history of art, and literature from 1984 to the present.

Scholarly evaluations of books, book chapters, articles, and conference papers in the field of Latin American studies published worldwide from 1990 to the present, indexed by the Hispanic Division, Library of Congress.

The definitive international bibliography for the history of science, technology, and medicine and its influence on culture from pre-history to the present. Journal articles, conference proceedings, books, book reviews, and dissertations from 1975 to the present are indexed in this file, which combines the Isis Current Bibliography of the History of Science, Current Bibliography in the History of Technology, the Bibliografia Italiana di Storia della Scienza and the Welcome Library for the History and Understanding of Medicine.

The only online index to art periodicals that were published in the United States during the 19th century. Since entire journal contents are indexed — articles, art notes, illustrations, stories, poems, and advertisements — the index is a valuable source of information on popular culture and industry, as well as artists and illustrators, painting, sculpture, drawing, photography, architecture and design, exhibitions and sales, decoration, and collecting.

This file cites and abstracts books, manuscripts, dissertations, and articles from more than 19,000 periodicals covering Slavic studies and social sciences published primarily in Russia, the republics of the former Soviet Union and countries in Eastern Europe from 1986 to the present. Records are provided by INION: the Institute of Scientific Information on Social Sciences, Russian Academy of Sciences.

**RLG Cultural Materials :** is a collaborative effort from RLG member institutions, bringing together primary source materials in high-quality digital form. It contains maps, photographs, objects, documents, art, sound, and motion. Archives, libraries, and museums from around the world are making their treasured collections available through RLG Cultural Materials. The content reflects the richness of the human experience through time, high-quality digital versions of ancient maps, medieval manuscripts, handwritten letters, drawings, paintings, sound recordings, books, and moving images? from prestigious memory institutions. Bringing these exceptional materials together encourages new kinds of multidisciplinary research. This database has separate password

**The RLG Serials File** : is a comprehensive database of primarily textual material such as journals, magazines, periodicals, newspapers, monographic series, some conference proceedings, annuals, yearbooks, annual reports, looseleaf, and electronic journals. Some formats and materials issued serially such as maps and computer files may be included.

## 4. INTERNATIONAL NUCLEAR INFORMATION SYSTEM (INIS)

INIS, the International Nuclear Information System is the world´s leading information system on the peaceful uses of nuclear science and technology. INIS is operated by the International Atomic Energy Agency (IAEA) in collaboration with its Member States and co-operating international organizations. The IAEA, based in Vienna, Austria, is an autonomous organization within the United Nations System.

The IAEA is the world´s center of cooperation in the nuclear field. It was set up as the world´s "Atoms for Peace" organization in 1957 within the United Nations family. The Agency works with its Member States and multiple partners worldwide to promote safe, secure and peaceful nuclear technologies. The IAEA was created in response to the deep fears and expectations resulting from the discovery of nuclear energy. Its fortunes are uniquely geared to this controversial technology that can be used either as a weapon or as a practical and useful tool.

The Agency's genesis was US President Eisenhower's "Atoms for Peace" address to the General Assembly of the United Nations on 8 December 1953. These ideas helped to shape the IAEA Statute, which 81 nations unanimously approved in October 1956. The Statute outlines the three pillars of the Agency's work - nuclear verification and security, safety and technology transfer. In the years following the Agency's creation, the political and technical climate had changed so much that by 1958 it had become politically impracticable for the IAEA to begin work on some of the main tasks foreseen in its Statute. But in the aftermath of the 1962 Cuban missile crisis, the USA and the USSR began seeking common ground in nuclear arms control.

The 1970s showed that the NPT would be accepted by almost all of the key industrial countries and by the vast majority of developing countries. At the same time the prospects for nuclear power improved dramatically. The technology had matured and was commercially available, and the oil crisis of 1973 enhanced the attraction of the nuclear energy option. The IAEA's functions became distinctly more important. But the pendulum was soon to swing back. The first surge of worldwide enthusiasm for nuclear power lasted barely two decades. By the early 1980s, the demand for new nuclear power plants had declined sharply in most Western countries, and it shrank nearly to zero in these countries after the 1986 Chernobyl accident.

In 1988 the IAEA and UN Food and Agricultural Organization joined forces with other agencies to eradicate

New World Screwworm - which spreads a deadly livestock disease. The radiation-based technology to eradicate the worm was developed at the Agency's Seibersdorf Laboratory.

In the early 1990s, the end of the Cold War and the consequent improvement in international security virtually eliminated the danger of a global nuclear conflict. Broad adherence to regional treaties underscored the nuclear weapon free status of Latin America, Africa and South East Asia, as well as the South Pacific. The threat of proliferation in some successor States of the former Soviet Union was averted; in Iraq and the DPRK the threat was contained.

In recent years, the Agency's work has taken on some urgent added dimensions. Among them are countermeasures against the threat of nuclear terrorism, the focus of a new multi-faceted Agency action plan. The IAEA works for the safe, secure and peaceful uses of nuclear science and technology. Its key roles contribute to international peace and security, and to the World's Millennium Goals for social, economic and environmental development.

INIS provides a comprehensive information reference service for literature on the peaceful applications of nuclear science and technology. To do this, INIS processes most of the world's scientific and technical literature that falls within its subject scope and maintains a database which currently contains over 2.7 million bibliographic references, making it the world's most comprehensive information source on the peaceful applications of nuclear science and technology.

The INIS Database is a bibliographic database compiled from the data submitted by INIS Members. All of the bibliographic references found in INIS Database have been selected, abstracted and indexed in English by INIS Members according to agreed rules and standards.

The subject scope of the INIS Database was developed to respond to the information needs of the international community in the areas of the IAEA´s interests and activities covering the peaceful uses of nuclear science and technology. There are central areas to the scope such as nuclear reactors, reactor safety, nuclear fusion, applications of radiation and radioisotopes in medicine, agriculture, industry and pest control as well as related fields such as nuclear chemistry, nuclear physics and materials science. Legal and social aspects associated with nuclear energy are also covered. And, from 1992, the economic and environmental aspects of all non-nuclear energy sources are included in the scope. Additionally, INIS also maintains a unique collection of full text non-conventional (grey) literature that would be difficult to obtain elsewhere.

The collection and the preparation of input and the dissemination of output to users are decentralized within INIS. Only the data processing and output production are centralized in the INIS Secretariat. International co-operation is an INIS distinguishable characteristic and its most valuable asset. INIS is maintained by 138 Members. 116 Member Countries and 22 International Organizations contribute their own literature to build the Database. INIS represents a wealth of experience and an extensive pool of knowledge in the nuclear fields. The first INIS output products, the printed Atomindex and associated magnetic tapes, were issued in April 1970. The system has since grown into one of the most successful and comprehensive information systems.

The Secretariat function of INIS is vested in the IAEA and is carried out by the INIS & Nuclear Knowledge Management Section. The IAEA Secretariat is headquartered at the Vienna International Centre in Vienna, Austria. Operational liaison and regional offices are located in Geneva,

Switzerland; New York, USA; Toronto, Canada; and Tokyo, Japan. The IAEA runs or supports research centers and scientific laboratories in Vienna and Seibersdorf, Austria; Monaco; and Trieste, Italy. See Offices and Contacts.

The IAEA Secretariat is a team of 2200 multi-disciplinary professional and support staff from more than 90 countries. The Agency is led by Director General Mohamed ElBaradei and six Deputy Directors General who head the major departments. See IAEA Staff.

IAEA programmes and budgets are set through decisions of its policymaking bodies - the 35-member Board of Governors and the General Conference of all Member States. Reports on IAEA activities are submitted periodically or as cases warrant to the UN Security Council and UN General Assembly. See Policy Bodies.

IAEA financial resources include the regular budget and voluntary contributions. The Regular Budget for 2006 amounts to Euro 273 619 000. The target for voluntary contributions to the Technical Co-operation Fund for 2006 is $77.5 million.

## INIS Membership

Membership to INIS is open to countries who are members of the IAEA, to United Nations organizations and to other subject-oriented international or intergovernmental organizations with whom the IAEA has relations. urrently, 116 countries and 22 international organizations participate in INIS. To join INIS, a formal request needs to be made by the appropriate authority to the Director General of the IAEA expressing the wish to participate in INIS and undertaking to supply input regularly to the System. Every INIS Member is represented in the System by a Liaison Officer officially appointed by the national authority, or the executive head, in the case of an international organization. Read more...

## Benefits of Membership

Provides access to comprehensive and extensive pool of knowledge in the Nuclear fields Increases the visibility of national literature Helps in establishing and improving the National INIS Centres Transfers modern information technology and know how to its Member States

A co-operative system with a large member base allows INIS to have the most comprehensive collection of documents on nuclear related areas, ensuring completeness and broad geographic coverage not found elsewhere.

## INIS Policy/Advisory Groups

INIS is a co-operative system and participating members play a key role in the INIS System. Each participating member country and international organization is represented in the System by a *Liaison Officer* officially appointed by the national authority, or the executive head in the case of an international organization.

The Liaison Officers are instrumental in deciding the path along which INIS evolves and grows by :

Providing the Secretariat with advice on matters relating to the administration, operation, and development of INIS.

Undertaking the responsibility for organizing the collection and the preparation of input from their country or international organization.

Being responsible for the dissemination of INIS products through their information services and for encouraging their utilization.

Regular communication takes place by correspondence and through Biennial Consultative Meetings of the INIS Liaison Officers.

INIS also receives advice from the *INIS Advisory Committee* which reports to the Director General of the IAEA.

This committee includes producers, users, and administrators of information organizations, has a broad geographical distribution and represents the interests of developing countries. The operation of INIS is reviewed at times of major change in the System or at intervals of not more than four years by this committee. Major policy and budgetary matters are referred to this committee.

## Partners

INIS recognizes the benefits of collaboration and co-operation with international partners in the information industry, to fulfill the need for timely exchange of global information, broaden the information resources and encourage the developments in information processing and standardization.

## OECD/NEA

As a part of the co-operative arrangement between IAEA and OECD/NEA, the OECD/NEA provides its computer programs to IAEA Member States that are not OECD Members. The liaison function between OECD/NEA, IAEA and Member States is vested in the INIS Secretariat.

The agreement takes the following forms:

Assisting new organizations to participate in the Computer Program Service;

Publicizing OECD/NEA benchmarks, conferences and seminars to these and other organizations; nominating their scientists to attend and channeling the participation forms to OECD/NEA.

## Energy Technology Data Exchange (ETDE)

A major international partner for INIS in the areas of data processing standards and authorities is the International Energy Agency´s (IEA), Energy Technology Data Exchange (ETDE).

INIS and ETDE are both international information

systems that were established to facilitate information sharing among their member countries. INIS focuses on the peaceful uses of nuclear energy; ETDE focuses on all aspects of energy. All ETDE member countries are also members of INIS. Because of this membership duality for ETDE countries, the Exchange adopted INIS standards for information exchange, with some minor modifications to accommodate ETDE's broader subject scope.

In 1994, the two organizations formalized a longstanding relationship by signing a Memorandum of Understanding (MOU). As a result of the MOU, INIS and ETDE have formed a Joint Technical Committee (JCT) to facilitate cooperation on issues of interest to both organizations. The MOU identifies specific areas for future cooperation, with a special emphasis on database development and the assurance of data integrity. Goals for technical cooperation include shared authorities, standards and publications.

This partnership benefits both organizations by ensuring simplification of formatting & inputting rules and most importantly it introduces cost savings for inputting centres as well as central processing

**INIS Database**

Leading information source for *scientific literature published worldwide on the peaceful applications of nuclear science and technology* dating back to 1970;

Since 1992, the INIS Database also includes the economic and environmental aspects of all non-nuclear energy sources.

Over 2.7 million scientific and technical bibliographic references have been indexed & abstracted in English according to agreed rules and standards.

**Comprehensive international coverage by INIS Members**

The Database only contains validated, high quality references.

**Testimonials**

**Subject Scope Literature Coverage :** Nuclear engineering and technology, nuclear safety and radiation protection, application of nuclear and isotopic techniques, sciences relevant to nuclear research and other applications, physics, chemistry, legal aspects, safeguards and non-proliferation and environmental and economic aspects of nuclear & non-nuclear energy sources. The INIS Database contains bibliographic citations and abstracts for journal articles, R&D reports, conference papers, books, patents, theses, laws, regulations and standards. Access to the INIS Database is available to individuals and institutions in INIS Member States and co-operating international organizations

**INIS Non-conventional literature (NCL)**

An outstanding feature of INIS is the easy access to the full text of non-conventional - NCL or grey literature.

Literature reported to INIS Database falls into two categories, conventional and non-conventional

Conventional literature is commercially available through normal distribution channels, such as books and journals.

Non-conventional literature (NCL, also called ´grey literature´) comprises scientific and technical reports, patent documents, conference papers and theses, which are not readily available through commercial channels.

**Availability**

The full text INIS NCL collection includes about 650,000 full text documents from 1970 to the present.

It is available in the following formats:

NCL on CD-ROM (from 1997 onwards)

Document Delivery (ad hoc orders)

NCL on CD-ROM (from 1997 onwards)

The full text documents reported in INIS Atomindex Volume/Update 28/01 (1997) and onwards are available on CD-ROMs. The CD-ROMs can be purchased on a subscription basis for • 40 per disc. Each CD-ROM contains approximately 150 Reports. The number of CD-ROMs produced in one year depends on the volume of input from INIS Centres. The total number of CD-ROMs produced from 1997 to the present is 312 CDs.

Each CD-ROM comes with retrieval software in both English and French. The documents are arranged by Reference Number (RN) or Report Number (RP) as listed in the INIS Atomindex or the INIS Database. Each CD-ROM is serialized by the first and last RN. Results of a query on the INIS Database on CD-ROM can be linked to the NCL CD-ROMs for rapid viewing of the full text.

Copies of individual documents found in the INIS NCL collection can be ordered from the INIS & NKM Section or from some of the National INIS Centres. Currently, INIS has arrangements with 60 INIS National Centres to provide document delivery services to users within their national boundaries. All requests for individual reports produced since 1997 (beginning with Volume 28) are referred to these Centres if they exist in the country of the requester.

Requesters in countries where no such service is available, and requests for reports published prior to 1997, can be referred to the INIS & NKM Section.

The following document delivery service is offered:

**Electronic delivery (Adobe Acrobat PDF format)**

All reports published after 1997 are available electronically in

Acrobat PDF format. Some reports published prior to 1997 can also be delivered electronically depending on the size of the report or analytic requested. Contact us for details. When requesting documents, the order should specify the Reference Number (RN), or Accession Number (AN) in the INIS bibliographic database; the Report Number (RP) and/or the title. All orders require prepayment. The cost is Euro 7 per document (Euro 3.5 for developing countries). For fast delivery please use a credit card (VISA or MASTERCARD), a cheque or a deposit account. Bank transfers are accepted but take longer to process.

## INIS Reference Series

The INIS Reference Series defines the rules, standards, formats, codes and authority lists on which the International Nuclear Information System is based. The series is an essential tool for users of the system, whether they be cataloguers, indexers, abstractors or searchers. It consists of current manuals published by the IAEA from 1969 to the present. Over the years most manuals have been revised or merged and further revisions will be issued in the future.

All the manuals may be purchased worldwide without restriction. The manuals are available in print and on diazo microfiche at 24X reduction.

## Marketing and Promotion

Marketing and promotion of INIS is done jointly by the INIS Secretariat in Vienna and the Member States. INIS Marketing and promotion is carried out through:

- ★ Promotion and marketing at IAEA and other nuclear conferences, meetings, symposia and exhibitions with online and/or CD-ROM demonstrations;
- ★ Publishing articles in professional journals;
- ★ INIS advertising in professional journals;

* Provision of promotional materials to hosts;
* Preparation and distribution of booklets, fact sheets, demo CDs, video film and other promotional tools;
* INIS entries published in directories world-wide.

The INIS Member States are responsible for establishing and carrying out promotional activities throughout the applicable boundaries/confines so that all persons who can derive benefit from INIS are made aware of its potential and of the information services that can be derived from it. The INIS Secretariat assists by providing general promotional and informational materials about INIS and its Database.

## Training

It is very important for the quality of INIS output products to ensure a common understanding of the INIS standards and rules by the staff of all inputting centers of INIS Members. For this reason, the INIS Training Program plays a significant role in INIS activity.

All aspects of INIS operations are thoroughly considered in the training events organized by the IAEA for INIS members, including selection criteria, abstracting, descriptive cataloging, indexing, retrieval, marketing and promotion. The training events are aimed at assisting INIS Members in training personnel newly involved in input preparation and utilization of output products.

Through the IAEA program of Technical Co-operation, the INIS Secretariat provides assistance to developing countries participating in INIS in their establishment and operation of information systems on nuclear energy. The Technical Co-operation Program includes Regional Training and Fellowships and Scientific Visits.

The INIS Training Program has evolved over the years to ensure increased effectiveness and efficiency and also to take advantage of training techniques and approaches available as a result of new electronic technologies.

Until 1997, training was primarily achieved through classroom sessions and scientific visits. In June 1997, INIS took a step towards providing new means of learning by introducing the PC-based Training Package which was distributed on CD-ROM to INIS Centres for their use in individualized, self-paced learning. In 2000, INIS went a step further in its effort to enlarge, improve and equalize its training program with the launch of the INIS Distance Learning Program on the Internet.

The INIS Training Program is designed to meet a number of objectives which include:

- ★ Establishment and improvement of a national information infrastructure
- ★ Transfer of modern information technology
- ★ Fostering exchange of scientific and technical information
- ★ High quality and coverage of the INIS Database
- ★ Maximum utilization of INIS output products
- ★ Responsiveness to country needs

Currently the INIS Training Program comprises the following :

### *1. INIS Training Seminars*

INIS Training Seminars are generally held on "even" years usually in Vienna. The seminars are funded and staffed by INIS and emphasize INIS input skills and use of INIS output products.

### *2. INIS Distance Learning Program*

The INIS Distance Learning Program provides comprehensive instructions about input preparation in two courses : Bibliographic Description and Subject Analysis. The program is available free, both on-line and off-line, for individualized, self-paced study addressed to the staff of the INIS Centres.

### *3. Technical Co-operation Training*

Through the IAEA program of Technical Co-operation, the INIS Secretariat provides assistance to developing countries participating in INIS in their establishment and operation of information systems on nuclear energy. INIS works in conjunction with the IAEA Technical Co-operation Department to organize regional training for Member States. Individual training, in the form of fellowships and scientific visits, is also organized jointly by INIS and Technical Co-operation Department.

#### Regional Training

Regional Training is sponsored by the IAEA Technical Co-operation Department in conjunction with INIS. It is generally related to Technical Co-operation Projects and is hosted by a Member State in the Region.

#### Fellowships and Scientific Visits

Fellowships and scientific visits are sponsored by the IAEA Technical Co-operation Department in conjunction with INIS. A Fellowship is designed for junior staff members in Member States, generally has a two to three month duration in a single geographic area, and constitutes on-the-job training. A Scientific Visit on the other hand, is designed for senior staff in a Member State and has a duration of one to three weeks in more than one location.

#### OECD/NEA Data Bank Computer Program Services

As a part of the co-operative arrangement between IAEA and OECD/NEA, the OECD/NEA provides its computer programs to IAEA Member States that are not OECD

Members. The liaison function between OECD/NEA, IAEA and Member States is vested in the INIS Secretariat.

The agreement takes the following forms:

Assisting new organizations to participate in the Computer Program Service;

Publicizing OECD/NEA benchmarks, conferences and seminars to these and other organizations; nominating their scientists to attend and channeling the participation forms to OECD/NEA.

NEA Computer Program Service ?

The NEA Data Bank operates a computer program service related to nuclear energy applications. The software library collects programs, compiles and verifies them in an appropriate computer environment, ensuring that the computer program package is complete and adequately documented. This collection of material contains more than 2000 documented packages and group cross-section data sets. The subject categories primarily represented in the NEA's program collection are as follows :

Nuclear models and cross section calculations;

Spectrum calculations, generation of multi-group cross-sections, lattice and cell problems;

Static design studies of reactors;

Fuel management and reactor economics;

Kinetics, coupled neutronics, hydrodynamics;

Radiological safety and accident analysis;

Steady state and transient heat transfer, hydrodynamics, thermodynamics;

Structural analysis, stress distributions;

Samma heating and shield design;

General mathematics and computing system routines;

Environmental impact of nuclear activities, waste management;

Material properties and behavior under irradiation, fuel behavior;

Integral experiments databases for program validation.

Programs available are listed in a regular electronic newsletter, in the Computer Program Abstracts on the Web and on CD-ROM.

Upon request, computer programs are distributed on CD-ROM, diskette and via electronic transfer. In cases, where a program has been tested and is included in the NEA's master files, a copy of the program package file can be supplied quickly. However, if the program must first be obtained from the author and then tested before it can be sent out, waiting times may become lengthy. The NEA may in such cases be able to suggest a code that is comparable to the one requested and that can be made available at once.

The NEA Data Bank Computer Program Service is based at Issy-les-Moulineaux (France) and serves scientific users authorized by Member States and belonging to over 500 organizations: national laboratories, universities and safety authorities. The NEA Data Bank services are financed by contributions from the Data Bank's Member States, and no direct service charge is made to users.

### Participation in the Service

To participate in the NEA Computer Program Service, an official request must be made by the appropriate national authority to the Director General of the IAEA expressing the wish to participate in the Service. Every participant is represented in the Service by a Liaison Officer officially appointed by the national authority.

All requests for programs must be sent to the NEA

Computer Program Service, through a Liaison Officer. Where no Liaison Officer for an institute has been appointed, or in case of difficulty please contact the OECD/NEA Computer Program Service

**Services in other Countries**

The INIS Database is available on the Internet, through the IAEA and other hosts and on CD-ROM. Similarly, the INIS NCL is available on CD-ROM, Microfiche and as ad-hoc requests. Apart from these products, each Member State offers a variety of individualized services based on INIS Products.

**Alert Services**

Additionally, some INIS Member States offer SDI services for their users, based on INIS products. Selective dissemination of information (SDI) refers to those alert services where individual searches are performed against individual interest profiles, in an automatic way.

**Document Delivery Services**

Currently, INIS has arrangements with 60 INIS National Centres to provide full texts of INIS non-conventional literature, where available, to users within their national boundaries. All requests for individual reports produced since 1997 (beginning with Volume 28) are referred to these Centres if they exist in the country of the requester. Requesters in countries where no such service is available, as well as requests for reports published prior to 1997, can be referred to the Knowledge Preservation Group.

**Organizational Profile**

**IAEA Mission & Programmes :** The IAEA's mission is guided by the interests and needs of Member States, strategic plans and the vision embodied in the IAEA Statute. Three main pillars - or areas of work - underpin the IAEA's mission:

Safety and Security; Science and Technology; and Safeguards and Verification. See Our Work.

## 5. INTERNATIONAL FEDERATION FOR INFORMATION PROCESSING (IFIP)

IFIP is a non-governmental, non-profit umbrella organization for national societies working in the field of information processing. It was established in 1960 under the auspices of UNESCO as an aftermath of the first World Computer Congress held in Paris in 1959. Today, IFIP has several types of Members and maintains friendly connections to specialized agencies of the UN system and non-governmental organizations. Technical work, which is the heart of IFIP's activity, is managed by a series of Technical Committees.

IFIP traces its roots to the very first major international conference on computers and computing which was held in Paris in 1959 under the auspices of UNESCO. Representatives of the main computer societies active in computing got together at that meeting to explore ways of building on the achievements of the conference. As a result thirteen national computer societies agreed to found in 1960 an international federation and named it IFIP - the International Federation for Information Processing.

IFIP's principal aims were and are to foster international cooperation, to stimulate research, development and applications and to encourage education and the dissemination and exchange of information on all aspects of computing and communication.

IFIP's creation was well timed. In the 1960s there began a veritable explosion in the growth of the computer industry and in the application of its products. Within the life-span of IFIP information technology (as it is widely known today) has become a potent instrument affecting people in everything from their education and work to their leisure and in their homes. It is a powerful tool in science and engineering, in commerce and industry, in education and administration and in entertainment.

## Mission

IFIP's mission is to be the leading, truly international, apolitical organization which encourages and assists in the development, exploitation and application of Information Technology for the benefit of all people.

## Principal Elements

* To stimulate, encourage and participate in research, development and application of Information Technology (IT) and to foster international co-operation in these activities.
* To provide a meeting place where national IT Societies can discuss and plan courses of action on issues in our field which are of international significance and thereby to forge increasingly strong links between them and with IFIP.
* To promote international co-operation directly and through national IT Societies in a free environment between individuals, national and international governmental bodies and kindred scientific and professional organizations.
* To pay special attention to the needs of developing countries and to assist them in appropriate ways to secure the optimum benefit from the application of IT.
* To promote professionalism, incorporating high standards of ethics and conduct, among all IT practitioners.
* To provide a forum for assessing the social consequences of IT applications; to campaign for the safe and beneficial

development and use of IT and the protection of people from abuse through its improper application.

* To foster and facilitate co-operation between academics, the IT industry and governmental bodies and to seek to represent the interest of users.
* To provide a vehicle for work on the international aspects of IT development and application including the necessary preparatory work for the generation of international standards.
* To contribute to the formulation of the education and training needed by IT practitioners, users and the public at large.

**Organisation**

Today IFIP has 46 organizations as Full Members, 4 Corresponding Members and 10 Affiliate Members, representing countries from all regions of the world. A General Assembly of all its Members and TC Chairs takes place annually and has overall responsibility for all of IFIP's strategy, finance and activities. It elects a President, four Vice-Presidents, a Treasurer, a Secretary and eight Trustees who together form the IFIP Council.

IFIP's flagship event is its World Computer Congress, currently held biannually. The 18th IFIP World Computer Congress was held in Toulouse, France, from 23 to 26 August 2004 (www.wcc2004.org).

The nature of these Congresses has changed substantially over the years. They are no longer of the all-singing and - dancing variety addressing every conceivable facet of our field. Instead they consist of a number of independent conferences, each dealing with a major specialised subject. These run in parallel so that some more general keynote addresses can be attended by all participants who can also share in social and other acitivities.

In addition there are major international conferences organised by our Technical Committees. These include events dealing with Production Engineering, Security, Computers in Education and Human Computer Interaction.

## Technical Activities

At the heart of IFIP lie its Technical Committees that, between them, count on the active participation of some two thousand people world-wide. There are twelve such Committees. Each Technical committee is, in effect, a management team responsible for a given field of activity and for the work of from three to nine Working Groups, a total of 80. These Groups work in a variety of ways to share experience and to develop their specialised knowledge. These include open conferences, smaller working conferences, seminars and tutorials, circulated papers and, increasingly, as befits our subject, electronic conferencing and e-mail.

## Publications

Many. IFIP events are linked to publications and there are annually some 30 to 40 IFIP books. A vital element of IFIP's communication with its Members and with all who participate in our work is the IFIP Newsletter. This is published quarterly in both hard copy and electronic form.

## Relationships

IFIP enjoys friendly cooperation with a number of international organisations. First among these is UNESCO with which IFIP maintains a formal consultative relationship. UNESCO has commissioned from IFIP several projects and supports the participation of some people from developing countries in IFIP events. IFIP is a Scientific Associate of ICSU (International Council of Scientific Unions).

There are four international federations with which IFIP

collaborates. These are IFAC (International Federation of Automatic Control), near neighbours of ours in Laxenburg, IMACS (International Association for Mathematics and Computers in Simulation), IFORS (International Federation of Operational Research Societies) and IMEKO (International Measurement Confederation).

### IFIP Secretariat

The administrative hub of IFIP is our secretariat at Laxenburg, near Vienna. The Head of the IFIP Secretariat is Eduard Dundler, who with the assistance of Brigitte Brauneis and Marion Smith is responsible for the wide range of tasks vital to the operation of such a far-flung international body. Good communication and information are essential and our secretariat provides a comprehensive service using up-to-date technology.

### Institutional membership

Issues related to IFIP membership are treated in the IFIP Statutes and Bylaws [http://www.ifip.org/s&b.htm], in particular Article 3 of the Statutes and Section 2 of the Bylaws.

IFIP Full Members vary from country to country - there are National Computer Societies, Academies of Sciences, Institutes and Agencies. The most important aspect is that the applicant organization should be representative of the national potential and activities in the field of informatics and information processing. A list of all IFIP Member organizations is available at http://www.ifip.org/members.htm

The application procedure for IFIP membership is described in Section 2 of the Bylaws. A formal Letter of Application should be sent to the IFIP President (c/o the address of the IFIP Secretariat). Such a letter should be accompanied by the following documents: the constitution of the organization, a list of financial resources, the names and titles of its officers, number of members and a brief outline of its history. These documents should be in English and are intended for review by the IFIP Admissions Committee. It is very desirable that an electronic copy (an attachment or reference to an URL) of these documents is provided. The Admissions Committee will prepare and submit its recommendations to the IFIP General Assembly, which has the mandate to decide on the admission of new Members. The IFIP General Assembly will decide on the scale of annual dues. A new Member is classified according to the scale of assessment for the apportionment of expenses of the United Nations.

There are 2 other categories of affiliation that could be considered by applicants - Corresponding Member and Associate Member. These categories, however, do not foresee voting rights.

International organizations, professional or governmental, having interest in information processing and willingness to cooperate and coordinate its activities with IFIP may become IFIP Affiliate members.

**Individuals interested to join IFIP activities**

All IT professional and practitioners interested in IFIP work may contact the respective national IFIP Member Computer Society. A list of all IFIP Member organizations is available at http://www.ifip.org/members.htm . Information about IFIP Technical Committees (TCs) and Working Groups (WGs) can be found at http://www.ifip.org/bulletin/bulltcs/b_tcs.htm . IFIP Member societies nominate their representatives to the 12 IFIP TCs. WGs consist of technical experts selected and assigned without consideration of nationality. WG membership is not restricted to those who belong to an IFIP Member society. Individuals who are interested to join a specific WG should submit an application (with a c.v. including professional data) to the respective WG Chair.

## 6. THE PAN AFRICAN DEVELOPMENT INFORMATION SYSTEM [PADIS]

The Pan African Development Information System (PADIS) is a co-operative regional development information system created in January 1980 under the aegis of the United Nations Economic Commission for Africa (ECA) in Addis, Ababa, Ethiopia.

In its decision 48/453 of 21 December 1993 on "Strengthening development information systems for regional cooperation and Africa" the United Nations General Assembly agreed to ensure adequate staffing and resources to the United Nations Economic Commission for Africa to permit the delivery of UNECA's subprogramme activities on information systems development. The decision stipulated that the resources would begin with the programme budget for 1994- 1995.

This decision was a very important one for the continuation of PADIS, whose activities are comprised by UNECA's subprogramme on statistics and information systems development. Since March 1992 when its funding from UNDP came to an end, PADIS financial resources have been very tenuous. The decision of the General Assembly ensures the commitment of the United Nations to include activities on behalf of information systems development in Africa within the resource structure of the United Nations regular programme budget.

The overall objective of PADIS is the promotion of development information management in the Africa region. Central to this objective is the operation of a regional information system in Africa which will serve as a conduit for information and data for development, centered around national, subregional and regional networks to which all members will voluntarily contribute information and share their information management techniques.

The immediate objectives of PADIS are the following:

* To assist African states, subregional and regional organizations in building capacities for collection, storage and utilization of data on development through advisory services, training and user services;
* To promote the improvement of information infrastructure in African member States, especially through the adoption of information technology in Africa as a tool for improvement information management and exchange on behalf of development;
* To promote the creation of databases in fields of importance to development in the region;
* To promote the utilization of common norms and standards of information handling in the Region in order to ensure compatibility and to facilitate information exchange;
* To establish a system which will improve access to both published and unpublished documents produced in Africa on questions relating to scientific and technological aspects, economic, and social aspects of development;
* To train information specialists at national, subregional and regional levels in order to upgrade skills and introduce improved methods of information handling.

What are its activities? PADIS undertakes the following activities:

Delivery of advisory services to African States and institutions on aspects of development of information and documentation systems, e.g. needs assessment, formulation of information plans and policies, design of national/sectoral information systems, choice of information technologies and strengthening of information centres;

Training staff of national, subregional and institutional participating centres as well as information policy makers and other system users through workshops, seminars and short courses in information system methodologies, computerized documentation techniques, information systems policy and management and statistical data base management and utilization;

Creation and maintenance of bibliographic, referral and numerical data bases; Provision of user services, including printed outputs from data bases, newsletters, selective dissemination of information, current awareness profiles and retrospective searches, question/answer service, hardcopy and microfiche document delivery, data bases on magnetic media and consolidating and repackaging of information.

**Structure of PADIS**

PADIS is part of the United Nations System. It presently receives financial and/or technical support from the United Nations regular budget for the ECA, from African member States of the ECA, the International Development Research Centre (IDRC) and the Governments of Germany and the Netherlands. The head of PADIS reports to the Executive Secretary of the ECA. The Regional Technical Committee for PADIS, which was established by resolution 498 of the ECA Conference of Ministers (1984), is responsible for establishing overall policy for PADIS as well as overseeing all aspects of its implementation. It reports biennially to the ECA Conference of Ministers Responsible for Planning and Development. Members of the Committee are the Executive Secretary of the ECA (who serves as chairman ex-officio), five high-level experts in telecommunications, documentation, library, information or computer science from the five ECA subregions who represent their respective subregions; representatives of OAU, UNESCO and UNDP and up to three other specialists from disciplines relative to the programme. Subregional Technical Committees monitor the implementation of the project within their respective subregions.

**Areas of Emphasis**

Since 1990 PADIS has been placing increasing emphasis on the following two areas:

Electronic networking as a tool to link information services in Africa From 1990-1993 PADIS implemented a pilot project in electronic networking in Africa, linking some 18 African institutions in a FIDOnet-based network. It also set up a bulletin board on networking and African development and an electronic conference on information technology in Africa. As a result of its success with this pilot project, it is now beginning the implementation of a much larger three-year project funded by International Development Research Centre entitled, "Building Capacities for Electronic Communication in Africa." Through this project, it hopes to install electronic networks in 24 African countries.

Informatics Policies Among its activities in these areas have been the promotion of the adoption of informatics policies by African States. It introduced this issue to the ECA Conference of Ministers responsible for Planning and Economic Development in 1992 and secured a resolution (732, XXVII) on this topic calling for African States to adopt policies related to the acquisition and utilization of appropriate information technology. In 1988 it held a Regional Seminar on informatics policies, and in 1993 it is conducting in-depth studies of the informatics policy instruments in place in 10 African countries. It has worked closely with the ECA Strategic Programme for African Management on its Agenda for Improving Public Administration in Africa, to secure the exclusion of a chapter on information technology there.

### PADIS' Information System and Network

PADIS comprises both an information system and a network.The Information System. PADIS' information system is comprised of five in-house databases that derive from information produced in or originating from Africa. These include: The PADIS networkThe PADIS network consists of 39 national participating centres, which receive advisory services, training and PADIS data bases and input data into the system for exchange with other countries in the region, subregional and regional institutional participating centres.Four subregional centres have been or are in the process of being established. Institutional participating centres include 43 institutions specialized in particular development fields.

National participating centres are government-designated institutions which perform the function of assisting national development planning by providing ready access to information required by policy makers, planners and others engaged in national socio-economic development efforts. Once operational, the subregional centres will provide on-site training for member countries, enable the sharing of expensive resources (equipment and personnel), deliver advisory services to member states and institutional participating centres, serve as subregional information clearinghouses and as links for the transfer of information between national participating centres and PADIS.

Institutional participating centres are the subject-oriented African subregional nodes in the PADIS network. Presently 44 in number, they comprise subregional and regional institutions responsible for coordination of information collection, classification and dissemination and development of tools and methodology in their special subjects of focus. These include ECA-sponsored subregional and regional institutions as well as other institutions in the region which have concluded agreements with PADIS to promote the harmonization and standardization of documentation and information systems in the Region. They include the Association of African Universities, the African Regional Organization for Standardization, the Africa Regional Centre for Technology and the Council for the Development of Economic and Social Research in Africa.

Activities of the institutional participating centres are co-ordinated through the Standing Committee on the Harmonization of Documentation and Information Systems in Africa which meets annually in Addis Ababa. How to access PADIS' services There are many ways in which a user can avail themselves of PADIS services. To start with, individuals or institutions can subscribe, free of charge, to the PADIS Newsletter, issued quarterly in English, French and Arabic, to keep abreast of the activities and services of PADIS.

## PADISNET

Under a grant from IDRC, PADIS has initiated a pilot project in information technology that will improve utilization of its data bases and facilitate communications on development information in the Africa region. Entitled PADISNET, the project will electronically link selected nodes of the PADIS network. Nodes will use modem communication to send messages, request data base searches, exchange information over bulletin boards and participate in electronic conferences on issues related to development information. PADIS will act as a gateway for the network to access external data bases and international networks. The project will also experiment with online access to PADIS data bases and will test the applicability of recent information technology, including the use of optical storage media (CD-ROM and optical erasable disks), scanners and facsimile transmission.

PADIS' Publications DEVINDEX-Africa is produced three times yearly from the PAD-DEV data base. Past volumes (15 in all) have included special national editions of materials from Botswana, Togo, Guinea and Niger. Microfiche or photocopies of all regional documents listed in DEVINDEX are available upon request at a nominal charge. Subscriptions to DEVINDEX are available upon request. The printed output of the PADIS-TCDC data base is the Directory of African Experts. Queries of the data base are invited for replies to specific information problems, e.g. if an institution or organization requires the name of possible consultants living in a specific country and specializing in a particular field. The ECA Statistical Yearbook, issued in four annual volumes corresponding to the ECA Subregions of Central, East and Southern, North and West Africa, is the printed output of the PADIS-STAT data base. Copies or subscriptions are available by writing to the ECA Statistics Division, P O Box 3001, Addis Ababa.

**Selective Dissemination of Information [SDI]**

PADIS operates a Selective Dissemination of Information Service (SDI) by which individuals or institutions can request to be kept regularly informed of references to written materials in their fields of interest. Regular searches are made of PAD-DEV as well as the data bases from other international and bilateral organizations available at PADIS and sent to subscribers. Enrolment in SDI is available by filling out a form available upon request from PADIS.

## Question/Answer Service

PADIS will send a custom printed reply to requests for information on topics relating to African development on the basis of searches of any of the data bases, - bibliographic, statistical or referral - at its disposal. Requests may be sent to PADIS by any means available, including letter, telephone, telex, cable, facsimile or e-mail.

PADIS participating centres may request the downloading of data bases, and installation where necessary, on magnetic media including tape and diskette. Files may also be sent electronically to centres with the necessary equipment.

Advisory services, training and fellowships Members of the PADIS network may request these services from PADIS in fields relating to PADIS' immediate objectives listed above. PADIS services in these areas are also available to non-governmental organizations as well as institutions outside the Africa region on a fee for service basis. Further details are available by writing to PADIS.

## 7. INSPEC

Inspec is the leading English-language bibliographic information service providing access to the world's scientific and technical literature in physics, electrical engineering, electronics, communications, control engineering, computers and computing, information technology, production, manufacturing and mechanical engineering.

Inspec was formed in 1967, based on the *Science Abstracts* service which had been provided by the Institution of Electrical Engineers since 1898. (A complete history of *Science Abstracts* is provided on our Centenary Website, electronic access to the backfile of Science Abstracts from 1898 to 1968 is now also available as the Inspec Archive). Though based in the UK, its sales are worldwide with over 80 per cent exported. The Inspec database, which lies at the centre of this service, dates back to 1969 and has a long-standing reputation for database quality.

The Inspec database began its life in 1969. Given the limited power and memory size of the mainframe computers of the 1960s, it is not surprising that validation and the use of authority files was then fairly rudimentary. However, as the power and memory size of computers increased and software engineering became more sophisticated, validation techniques improved. The quality of the data going into the Inspec database currently is consequently much higher than it was 25 years ago. Over the years, there have also been changes of standards and practices in bibliographic and subject descriptions. It was in order to improve the appearance, retrievability and value of the Inspec database that Inspec, in the mid-1980s, embarked on a project to upgrade the database to meet the highest current standards, as far as possible.

Inspec is one of the most respected databases in the information business, and this reputation is due largely to the quality of the indexing. To ensure knowledgeable, consistent indexing, Inspec's indexers are subject specialists. In addition, the scope of the indexing has grown since the inception of the file to include not only the usual Thesaurus Term and Classification Code indexes, but also the Uncontrolled Index Terms, Treatment codes, Chemical Substance Indexing, Numerical Data Indexing and Astronomical Object Indexing (a sample record showing most of these is available).

Inspec prides itself not only on the provision of rigorous indexing, but also on the quality and integrity of all the data. Extensive computer validation procedures are used to ensure that the database is nearly error-free. For many fields, the entries are checked against an authority file. Fields such as Thesaurus Terms, Classification, Journal Names, Author Affiliation,

Language, and Country of Publication all have authority files. For fields where it is not possible to create an authority file, field size and format checks are made. For instance in fields which contain a date, only valid dates are allowed. In the Author Name field, the format of the data is checked to ensure that the surname comes first, followed by the initials, e.g. Smith, T.H. For free text fields such as the title and abstract, spelling checks are used.

The project required 3.5 man years of software development and more than 2 years of computer time. When the project was completed in 1989, every single record of the database (3.25 million) was brought up to current day quality standards and re-archived on to WORM optical disks. When the reprocessed data was re-loaded on to online systems, the database was renamed Inspec2.

In the 1970s, however, computer validation techniques were less rigorous than today's standards, so that the early years of the database contained a higher percentage of errors. Also, with the growth of science, many changes and additions were made to the Classification and the Thesaurus. Therefore, in the mid 1980's Inspec embarked on an enormous project (The Database Upgrade Project) to bring the whole Database up to modern quality standards.

Since the completion of the Database Upgrade Project in 1989, to ensure that the database is of the highest quality and to take care of the very few errors that now occur, Inspec has introduced a Correction facility.

Inspec won the EUROLUG Product Award in 1993 in recognition of the major quality enhancements that have been made to the database.

The following illustrates the work undertaken for some key fields of the database (a sample record showing these fields is available):

### Spelling Correction

Since February 1984 all the words in the Title, Abstract and Free Indexing fields have been matched against a dictionary. For the upgrade, automatic spelling correction was used and this corrected, on average, one word in every 25 records.

### Classification

Between 1969 and 1988, there were five distinct versions of the classification scheme used over the years for the Inspec database. Since the approach of the classification scheme for all these had been fairly similar, it was possible to reclassify all material, using automatic mapping procedures, to appropriate codes in the then current (1988) classification scheme. In the few cases where it was not possible to reclassify at the most specific place in the scheme, automatic re-classification was made at a broader level.

### Controlled Terms

Since 1973 Controlled Indexing Terms have been assigned from the Inspec Thesaurus. The earlier (1969-1972) records were re-indexed, using automatic mapping procedures, to equivalent terms in the 1973 Thesaurus. The changes since then are listed in the current Thesaurus, providing date of introduction and prior term information for new terms.

### Journal Description Inspec

It holds standard journal information in an authority file. A set of journal fields was copied into each journal paper record on the database from this file. This meant that in addition to the abbreviated title, ISSNs and CODEN, the full journal title was added to each record.

### Country Names

Country Names were validated for the following fields: Affiliation or Corporate Source, Abbreviated Journal Title,

Place of Publication for Monographs, and Conference Location. In addition a single standardised country of publication field was added to all records.

**Language**

Incorrect entries in the language field from the early years of the database were corrected using a set of automatic mappings.

Inspec assists engineers, scientists and others in their research, to locate relevant journal articles, conference papers and other documents. In addition, the database may be used for:

Current Awareness

New Product Information

Technological Forecasting

Competitive Intelligence

Patent-Related Searching

**Database Content**

Over 3850 scientific and technical journals and some 2200 conference proceedings, as well as numerous books, reports and dissertations are scanned each year by Inspec staff for relevant articles to abstract and index for inclusion in the Database. Of the 3850 journals 1600 are indexed cover-to-cover. The Database now contains over 8 million bibliographic records and is growing at the rate of over 450,000 records each year. Copies of source documents are available from Inspec's preferred Document Delivery Service.

**Subject Coverage**

Although Inspec provides a comprehensive index to the literature in physics, electrical/electronic engineering, computing, control engineering, information technology, production, manufacturing and mechanical engineering, it also has significant coverage in areas such as materials science, oceanography, nuclear engineering, geophysics, biomedical engineering and biophysics. The full scope of subject coverage is given in the Inspec Classification.

In order to ensure the highest quality standards, Inspec has a correction service which provides tape customers, including the online systems, with complete replacement records for any records that have been found to contain an error. Reports of possible errors come both from Inspec staff and from customers of the various Inspec services. Ten correction files have been issued since this service was introduced in 1992.

**Products & Services**

The Institution provides a range of publications and information services in many areas of engineering and technology. Information for members.

Inspec bibliographic database covers nearly 4,000 scientific journals, 2,000 conferences, plus books, reports and dissertations in the fields of physics, electrical and electronic engineering, computing, IT, and manufacturing

IEE Wiring Regulations BS 7671 and associated publications can be purchased online. You will also find cable colour changes, Building Regulations Part P, Test Certificates, EAS and Model Forms of Contract

IET Digital Library provides access to technical articles from journals such as IEE Proceedings, and Electronics Letters , plus Conference Publications and magazines. You can freely browse the table of contents, article abstracts, or search

Magazines including the Institution's flagship publication 'Engineering and Technology', the new magazine for teenagers Flipside, plus 7 professional magazines are available online, or as print subscriptions

Books and Conferences Publications including seminar digests and IEE Wiring Regulations and associated publications are available in print via the web shop

Library & Archives provide access to the latest technical, marketing and company news, plus extensive historical collections. Members can use the online catalogue, specialist search services, and much more

**Members**

A member of the Institution of Engineering and Technology can access full-text magazine articles via the relevant engineering community Industry Sector. Members purchasing books, conference publications and IEE Wiring Regulations, or subscribing to print magazines and journals can also enjoy special discounts.

**Career Manager**

Career Manager is an on-line professional development tool designed to encourage career progression to a higher level enabling focused career management, defined learning and targeted professional goals. Create your own competency profile, carry out an assessment, record your evidence and demonstrate your continued professional development using this advanced on-line tool.

The Inspec Database is published by the Institution of Engineering and Technology.

Inspec information is available in a wide range of products:

**Electronic format :** Online database for remote access, pay-as-you go and subscription pricing Inspec Ondisc (CD-ROM)

Inspec Archive - Electronic Access to Science Abstracts 1898 to 1968 Inspec Web

Site licences and direct data services for in-house & remote access information systems

Inspec Specialised Databases. Three subject oriented databases in the areas of photonics, biomedical technology, and information and communication technology.

**Current awareness**

A range of services, including new online products, which offer specialised subject areas to meet the needs of specific individuals and research groups

**Abstracts Journals**

3 titles giving comprehensive coverage of all **Inspec** subject areas

**User Aids**

Inspec Thesaurus

Inspec Classification

Inspec List of Journals

**Related products and services**

Customised Inspec searches available through the Institution's search service attached to the Institution's Library

Document Delivery Service - publications indexed by Inspec are warehoused for this service

IEL - the IEEE/IET Electronic Library - the full text of publications of the IEEE and the Institution of Engineering and Technology with Inspec indexing

Electronic Materials Information Service (EMIS) - giving data and background text on the properties and technology of semiconductors

Which of these best meets your requirements will depend on the frequency with which you expect to use Inspec, whether you are providing access for one or two specialists in a small organisation, or for hundreds in a large one, the complementary databases that you require alongside Inspec, and so on:

Which Inspec Product or Service? is a summary guide to help you choose the best service for your organisation

Table of Inspec Database Products gives a list of vendors offering the Inspec database and details of their services including pricing options.

**Inspec Archive**

**Key Features :** Fully searchable electronic access to over 70 years of international scientific and technical literature in physics, electrical engineering, electronics, computing and control engineering: gives easier access to a wealth of knowledge gathered since 1898

Elimination of the need to keep aging print volumes: saves on storage costs, your time and frees-up library shelving

High-quality English-language records with value-added indexing plus modern indexing: allows for simple searches across consistently indexed records

Complements the main Inspec database: extends coverage from 1898 to date Access through many Vendors Flexible pricing options

As library space becomes a premium, print copies of early abstracts journals are becoming scarce. To overcome this, Inspec digitised the entire collection of Science Abstracts Journals (back to volume one) dating from 1898 to 1968. The Science Abstracts Journals were the precursor to the Inspec database. The subject coverage is:

***All aspects of physics (originally published as Physics Abstracts)***

Electrical and electronic engineering (introduced as a separate journal in 1903, and originally published as Electrical and Electronic Abstracts)

Computing and control engineering (introduced as a separate journal in 1966, and published initially as Control Abstracts, later renamed to Computer and Control Abstracts)

An XML archival backfile has been produced containing:

Over 873,700 records

Tables, graphs and figures from the original source document in many cases

The original value-added indexing and classifications

Enhancements in the form of the nearest equivalent current Inspec Thesaurus Terms and Inspec Classification Codes

Conference proceedings, books, journals, reports and dissertations (List of Journals covered by the Inspec Archive)

Longer abstracts than today varying in length from half a page to several pages including diagrams and complex mathematical proof because hard copy originals were less accessible

**Benefits**

The fully searchable electronic Inspec Archive is far more usable, flexible, durable and more readily available than the 176 volumes (and over 140000 pages) of the printed Science Abstracts Journals. Imagine the time and shelf space that will be saved. It has never been easier to locate references to historic research or engineering breakthroughs from hundreds of scientists and engineers such as Albert Einstein, Guglielmo Marconi, Max Planck, Ernest Rutherford, Marie Curie. Not only does the Inspec Archive give access to the work of famous scientists, it also gives access to the often forgotten works (sometimes known as "Sleeping Beauties") that may be of use in assessing the validity of current patents. An idea suggested decades ago that did not develop then, may be of relevance today.

The Inspec archive will be of use to everyone but especially:

Academics

Biographers

Patent examiners

Scientific researchers and engineers

**History of Science Abstracts**

The first issue of Science Abstracts in January 1898 covered 100 scientific and engineering periodicals, contained 110 abstracts divided into 10 sections, and thus provided a comprehensive record of the principle papers published in Europe and America. For a history of Science Abstracts, published at its centenary in 1998, see the Inspec Centenary Website. Famous Science Abstracts editors include Arthur C Clarke who worked on Physics Abstracts in 1949.

**Document Delivery**

All **Inspec** information services help engineers, scientists, librarians and information scientists to identify relevant papers. Infotrieve, **Inspec's** preferred document delivery service offers two of the world's most prestigious collections of literature in electrical engineering, computer sciences and the physical sciences:

the **Inspec** Collection (from 1994 - present)

the IEE Collection

Infotrieve also obtains non-collection materials from a wide range of sources including its own in-house collections, and external sources such as academic and government libraries, specialised document suppliers and publishers around the world.

Requests for articles may be sent by phone, fax, and E-mail. Delivery will be made the way you choose, fax, Ariel® fax, E-mail, overnight express or mail and costs $10.75 plus copyright royalties for most articles. Other documents may be individually priced.

Copies of journal articles, technical reports, books, standards, U.S. patents, foreign patents, dissertations, conference papers, obscure or specialised publications, and more.

Infotrieve also obtains non-collection materials from a wide range of sources including its own in-house collections, and external sources such as academic and government libraries, specialised document suppliers and publishers around the world.

Requests for articles may be sent by phone, fax, and E-mail. Delivery will be made the way you choose, fax, Ariel® fax, E-mail, overnight express or mail and costs $10.75 plus copyright royalties for most articles. Other documents may be individually priced.

### Documentation

**Search Aids :** The Inspec Classification, Thesaurus and List of Journals are available as the Inspec Search Aids CD-ROM or other electronic versions.

### Other Documentation

Various other free documentation is also available, either in print (from the Inspec Helpdesk) or in electronic form (on this server):

List of Astronomical Catalogue Designations

Chemical and Numerical Indexing Guides

User Notes & Quick Reference Cards

Inspec Ondisc Documentation

List of journals and classification codes in biophysics and biomedical technology

List of journals covered by the Inspec Archive (Alphabetically)

List of journals covered by the Inspec Archive (By country)

## Training

To help broaden r knowledge of the Inspec database and improve your searching techniques, Inspec provides:

**Documentation :** A range of vendor-specific search guides and other publications to assist search effectiveness

## Training sessions

Seminars and workshops held throughout the world (see information on workshops in the Americas and in the rest of the world)

**Helpdesks** Helpdesks in the UK, Hong Kong and USA where expert staff can answer questions concerning search techniques, database content, coverage, etc., and advise about products and pricing.

Advanced applications of Inspec in statistical analysis and competitive intelligence.

When you register, please provide your name, organization, address, telephone number, fax, e-mail, the search software you currently use to access Inspec, your main areas of work in science and technology, and the workshop you wish to attend. Please indicate whether you want your name and address to be listed on an attendee roster to be handed out the day of the workshop.

Demonstrations illustrating key search elements, such as the extensive thesaurus, hierarchical classification and bibliographic fields, and All that is required is a room with an overhead projector, a PC with PowerPoint software and PCs with an access to the Inspec Database for demo and hands-on sessions.

Supporting material is provided, which includes an Online Training Seminar Workbook based on the PowerPoint presentation, an Online Database brochure and a set of hands-on exercises.

Would any university which is interested in hosting an Inspec training session please contact one of our database trainers via the Inspec Helpdesk.

## Joint Seminars

Joint Seminars are organised in co-operation with Inspec Vendors and in some cases also with Agents/Distributors.

These half-day events are designed to keep you up to date with the latest features introduced by the Vendors and to discuss with them any software or administrative problems or issues, as well as to develop your searching skills on the Inspec Database.

The Vendor's introductory presentation is followed by an overview of the Inspec Database content and a description of the main subject and bibliographic search fields implemented by the specific Vendor. Demonstrations illustrating the key search elements are included and, where facilities allow, a hands-on session is also encouraged.

Supporting material is provided, which includes an Online Training Seminar Workbook based on the PowerPoint presentation, an Online Database brochure and a set of hands-on exercises.

The joint sessions can be offered to Academic Consortia or to Corporate or Government Organisations

## In-House Training for Corporate & Government Organisations

In-house database training can be arranged for as few as six participants. The training is free of charge and can be customised to suit your search needs and levels of skill.

All that is required is a room with an overhead projector, a PC with PowerPoint software and PCs with an access to the Inspec Database for demo and hands-on sessions.

Supporting material is provided, which includes an Online Training Seminar Workbook based on a PowerPoint presentation, an Online Database brochure and a set of hands-on exercises.

A typical session includes an overview of the Database, demonstrations illustrating key search elements, such as the extensive thesaurus, hierarchical classification and bibliographic fields, and a practical hands-on session where possible

## 8. INFORMATION FOR ALL PROGRAM (IFAP)

The Information for All Programme is an intergovernmental programme, created in 2000. Through IFAP, Governments of the world have pledged to harness the new opportunities of the information age to create equitable societies through better access to information. The challenge the world faces is to ensure equitable access for all people to seize these new opportunities. Information is central to development. Information is essential for survival and sustainability. Information is the pathway to understanding and peace. The Information for All Programme is UNESCO's response to the challenges and opportunities of the Information Society.

The Information for All Programme is closely integrated with UNESCO's regular programme, especially in the area of communication and information. IFAP works closely with other intergovernmental organizations and international NGOs, particularly those with expertise in information management and preservation, for example the International Federation of Library Associations and Institutions (IFLA) and the International Council on Archives (ICA).

At the beginning of 2006, more than 50 IFAP National Committees exist, providing a focus at the country level as well as an opportunity to interpret and mobilize the IFAP vision for local communities.

Numerous activities have been carried out in the past by UNESCO with a view to defining its place in the information society, particularly within the framework of the former General Information Programme (PGI) and the Intergovernmental Informatics Programme (IIP).

The information revolution has resulted in an overlap of the two programmes which have been increasingly concentrating their activities in two main areas: firstly on content for the information society, and secondly on actions necessary to build "infostructure" for this evolving society through training, the establishment of information policies and the promotion of networking.

As of 1 January 2001, the Information for All Programme has been replaced the General information Programme and the Intergovernmental informatics Programme, according to Decision 3.6.1 taken at the 160th session of UNESCO's Executive Board.

Decisions leading to the creation of the Information for All Programme:

**1997 :** 29th General Conference Resolution invites the Director-General "to convene the statutory meetings of the PGI Intergovernmental Council and the IIP Intergovernmental Committee, as well as those of their Bureaux, as joint meetings, in order to release funds for concrete activities in MemberStates and to establish the synergies necessary to adapt UNESCO's activities to the challenges of the information highways, thus enabling the 30th session of the General Conference to take a well-informed decision about a possible merger of these two intergovernmental programmes or any other appropriate solution." (Resolution 29 C/Resolution 28 (Paragraph 2.C.(f)).

**1999 :** 30th General Conference approves Resolution 36 "New programme merging the General Information

Programme (PGI) and the Intergovernmental Informatics Programme (IIP)"(30 C/Resolution 36)

**2000 :** 60th session of the Executives Board adopts decisions 3.6.1 on the "Replacement of the General Information Programme (PGI) and the Intergovernmental Informatics Programme (IIP) by a new intergovernmental programme" (160 EX/Decision 3.6.1)

A central concern of UNESCO is the disparity between developed and developing countries. Countries are often characterised as "north" and "south" depending on their economic situations, but in recent years, a new divide between them has emerged - the digital divide.

IFAP exists to be an advocate for all people on the wrong side of the information divide, whether they be in developed or developing countries. Of special concern are the needs of women, youth and the elderly, as well as persons with disabilities.

The Information for All Programme seeks to:

1. promote international reflection and debate on the ethical, legal and societal challenges of the information society;
2. promote and widen access to information in the public domain through the organization, digitization and preservation of information;
3. support training, continuing education and lifelong learning in the fields of communication, information and informatics;
4. support the production of local content and foster the availability of indigenous knowledge through basic literacy and ICT literacy training;
5. promote the use of international standards and best practices in communication, information and informatics in UNESCO's fields of competence; and

6. promote information and knowledge networking at local, national, regional and international levels.

The Programme is guided in its planning and implementation by an Intergovernmental Council comprising 26 UNESCO Member States that are elected by UNESCO's General Conference. The functioning of the Council is financed by UNESCO's regular budget.

* Functions
* Composition
* Bureau
* Rules of procedure
* Statutes
* Meetings

**Functions**

Within the framework of the decisions of the General Conference concerning the Information for All Programme, the Council shall guide its planning and implementation. This shall, in particular, include:

1. considering proposals on the development and adaptation of the Information for All Programme;
2. recommending the broad lines of action that the Information for All Programme could take;
3. reviewing and assessing achievements and defining the basic areas requiring increased international co-operation;
4. promoting participation of Member States in the Information for All Programme;
5. supporting all fund raising efforts for the implementation of the Information for All Programme.

The IFAP Bureau consists of eight Member States nominated by the governing Council. It meets twice a year to appraise, select and approve projects as well as to hold thematic debates on issues of importance for the Programme.

The Bureau is composed of a Chairperson, three Vice-Chairpersons, three other members and a Rapporteur.

**Information Literacy**

Information literacy and lifelong learning have been described as the beacons of the Information Society, illuminating the courses to development, prosperity and freedom. Information literacy empowers people in all walks of life to seek, evaluate, use and create information effectively to achieve their personal, social, occupational and educational goals. It is a basic human right in a digital world and promotes social inclusion in all nations.

Information literacy enables people to interpret and make informed judgments as users of information sources, as well as to become producers of information in their own right. Information literate people are able to access information about their health, their environment, their education and work, empowering them to make critical decisions about their lives, e.g. in taking more responsibility for their own health and education.

In a digital world, information literacy requires users to have the skills to use information and communication technologies and their applications to access and create information. For example, the ability to navigate in cyberspace and negotiate hypertext multimedia documents requires both the technical skills to use the Internet as well as the literacy skills to interpret the information.

IFAP seeks to raise awareness of the importance of information literacy for all and to support projects enhancing information literacy skills.

## Ethical, legal and societal implications of ICTs

IFAP helps increasing global awareness on the ethical, legal and societal aspects of the application of ICTs.

The international debate on infoethics addresses the ethical, legal and societal aspects of the application of ICTs. Ethical principles for the Information Society derive from the Universal Declaration of Human Rights and include the right to freedom of expression, universal access to information, particularly in the public domain, the right to education and the right to participate in cultural life.

One of the most challenging ethical issues is the inequity of access to ICTs between countries, and between urban and rural communities within countries. In 2003, UNESCO adopted a framework for addressing this and other challenging ethical issues with the Recommendation concerning the Promotion and Use of Multilingualism and Universal Access to Cyberspace. This provides guidance to countries seeking access for their people to the new opportunities arising from the Internet.

Along with the benefits of a digitally connected world come the threats of misuse and abuse. Already countries are building mechanisms to protect their people against these risks, for example to ensure the safety of children on the Internet, but clearly a lot more needs to be done to address the ethical implications of the Information Society. In collaboration with its partner institutions, IFAP seeks to do so.

## Preservation of Information

IFAP plays a key role in promoting awareness of the importance of preserving information.

Universal access to information is an essential element of a Knowledge Society. Throughout history, libraries and archives have been the guardians of the documentary heritage of humankind. Although in past centuries the materials used for writing underwent very few changes, the last two centuries have seen the recurrent emergence of new media, ranging from photography to digital formats.

Access to and dissemination of information relies, however, on the stability of documents and the retrievability of their content. Paradoxically, technical developments often result in greater instability and shorter lifespans of documents. For example, the clay tablets of Mesopotamia can last further millennia, but audiovisual documents will only survive for decades, and the life of digital objects, on average, will not exceed ten years. In addition, natural disasters and wars frequently destroy entire archival and library collections. The preservation of the world's legacy of knowledge is a prerequisite for universal access and will greatly impact the extent to which Knowledge Societies develop.

IFAP has a key part to play in promoting awareness of the importance of preserving information. It can assist by supporting the development of preservation standards and management tools, and by strengthening the role of libraries and archives and the librarians and archivists who work in these institutions. A special focus is on standards for the preservation of digitally born materials; a Charter on the Preservation of Digital Heritage was adopted by the 32nd session of the General Conference in 2003.

## Funding

No Programme can be successful without adequate financial support. IFAP needs complementary funding if it is to achieve the objectives that have been set. Much needs to be done to raise additional extra-budgetary funds.

While the functioning of the IFAP Council is supported by UNESCO's regular budget, all programme work, including pilot projects, relies on funds from voluntary contributions by donor countries.

These contributions are held in the IFAP Special Account, which is administered in accordance with the financial regulations of UNESCO, with the Director-General regularly reporting on its functioning to the Executive Board.IFAP also administers a Funds-in-Trust (FIT) scheme, whereby donors can nominate specific projects, countries or regions they wish to support.

A key focus for the work of the Council is to secure ongoing funding for its programmes and projects. Up until the end of 2005, the Council has been able to fund some 37 pilot projects. These play a critically important role in raising awareness within countries of the benefits of Knowledge Societies. The Council encourages Governments to expand their financial support so that IFAP can continue to support this extremely important activity.

### 9. IFLA NET

IFLANET (The International Federation of Library Associations and Institutions) is the leading international body representing the interests of library and information services and their users. It is the global voice of the library and information profession.

Initiated in 1993, IFLANET and its services are designed to improve communication within IFLA and to provide a 24/7 virtual presence for the organization, which only meets as a whole once a year at its General Conference. IFLANET is administered by the IFLA HQ and hosted by the Institut de l'Information Scientifique et Technique (INIST), France.

The National Library of Canada has made a continuing and significant commitment to supporting library development and networking through its participation in the International

Federation of Library Associations and Institutions (IFLA), notably by hosting the Universal Dataflow and Telecommunications (UDT) Core Programme of IFLA and most recently, in its support of the electronic services of IFLANET.

The UDT Core Programme seeks to facilitate the international and national exchange of electronic data by providing the library community with pragmatic approaches to resource sharing. The programme monitors and promotes the use of relevant standards, relevant technologies, and relevant policy issues in an effort to overcome barriers to the electronic transfer of data in library fields.

The effort to create a global information infrastructure — of which the Internet is often described as the prelude — is progressing at an astounding rate. It has revolutionized human communication, allowing geographically dispersed individuals and organizations to form "virtual communities" and "virtual organizations" devoid of the constraints of physical location.

Because of the far-reaching effects of this new environment, many libraries, businesses, private and governmental organizations and institutions are devoting considerable resources to ensuring that their own internal information infrastructures are in place — that the necessary skills, technology, policies, and procedures exist to take advantage of this rapidly expanding environment.

**IFLANET Development**

Since 1993, in an effort to improve personal and professional communication between IFLA HQ, its membership, and the international library community, UDT has been working toward the establishment of an electronic information infrastructure, called IFLANET, to provide enhanced communication and information exchange for the international library community.

Three principles guide the UDT effort in providing IFLANET electronic services:

**The goal :** to educate members around the world in the benefits and challenges of networking and other information technologies, while raising the profile of libraries and IFLA globally.

**The utility of the service :** to provide exemplary electronic information services to the international library community based on content that IFLA can provide — organizational information, research papers, conference proceedings, directories and current awareness services, and other types of electronic publications.

**The challenge :** sowing the seeds for a "virtual IFLA" through the development of sustainable electronic services, maintaining current awareness of technological and policy changes, and creating a fertile ground for the new services to members and non-members alike.

The IFLANET service is being hosted by the National Library of Canada on the DEC Alpha InfoServer, while the content is being maintained through the UDT Core Programme, IFLA Headquarters and the various units of IFLA.

Internet mailing lists have proved themselves an important and popular means for special interest groups to communicate among themselves and with others. Electronic mail access to IFLA personnel, services and information is the cornerstone of IFLANET.

IFLA-L, the mailing list devoted to IFLA communications and the general exchange of information among international librarians, was first initiated at the 1994 IFLA conference in Cuba and proved to be a great success. IFLA-L now has over 600 subscribers. Other IFLANET moderated lists include:

LIBJOBS-a mailing list used by almost 2 000 subscribers to locate employment opportunities in library and information science;

DIGLIB-where over 1 300 subscribers share information about digital library research and developments.

Other IFLANET-supported mailing lists assist in facilitating communications between specialized groups within IFLA. IFLANET continues to utilize electronic mail communications to distribute organizational information and to facilitate resource-sharing. In 1996, IFLANET will explore the delivery of WWW-based documents through electronic mail to reach an even wider and more diverse audience.

**IFLANET WWW Service**

IFLANET began the full operation of a World Wide Web service in March 1995. Within a very short time, the IFLANET WWW service has become a primary resource for library and information science on the Internet. Some recent IFLANET statistics are an indicator of the popularity of the service:

In an average week, almost 10 000 documents were provided through the IFLANET service to more than 4 500 users. These numbers continue to increase each month as the service provides even more information to librarians and becomes more widely known. Available documents include newsletters, technical reports, bibliographies, organizational information, conference proceedings, and software.

Users from nearly every country in the world with electronic mail connectivity have been able to access IFLANET services and documents. Individuals in more than 65 countries have accessed the IFLANET WWW service-Argentina, Australia, Austria, Belgium, Botswana, Brazil, Canada, Chile, China, Colombia, Costa Rica, Croatia, Czech Republic, Denmark, Dominican Republic, Ecuador, Egypt, Estonia,

Finland, France, Germany, Great Britain, Greece, Hong Kong, Hungary, Iceland, India, Indonesia, Iran, Ireland, Israel, Italy, Jamaica, Japan, South Korea, Kuwait, Latvia, Lithuania, Luxembourg, Malaysia, Mexico, Netherlands, New Zealand, Norway, Papua New Guinea, Peru, Poland, Portugal, Romania, Russian Federation, Saudi-Arabia, Singapore, Slovak Republic, Slovenia, South Africa, Spain, Sweden, Switzerland, Taiwan, Thailand, Turkey, United Arab Emirates, USA, Uruguay, and Venezuela!

Thousands of items, ranging from the UDT Newsletter or information about IFLA services to software or conference proceedings, are downloaded each week from IFLANET. It provides specialized lists of resources to librarians on topics such as digital libraries, copyright and intellectual property, global information infrastructure projects, information policy, electronic text archives, cataloguing of electronic documents, resource-sharing and interlibrary loan, and even a list of library-related quotations!

The Governing Board is responsible for the managerial and professional direction of IFLA within guidelines approved by Council. The Board consists of the President, the President-elect, 10 directly elected Members (by postal and/or electronic ballot, every 2 years) and 9 indirectly elected members of the Professional Committee (by the professional groups through the sections and divisions); up to 3 Members may be co-opted.

The Executive Committee has executive responsibility delegated by the Governing Board to oversee the direction of IFLA between meetings of this Board within the policies established by the Board. The Committee consists of the President, President-elect, the Treasures, the Chair of the Professional Committee, 2 members of the Governing Board, elected every 2 years by members of the Board from among its elected members, and IFLA's Secretary General, ex-officio.

**Professional Committee**

It is the duty of the Professional Committee to ensure coordination of the work of all the IFLA units responsible for professional activities, policies and programmes. The Committee consists of a chair, elected by the outgoing Committee, an officer of each of IFLA's 8 Divisions plus 3 members of the Governing Board, elected by that Board from among its members.

IFLA's Executive Board, at its meeting in Bangkok, Thailand in August 1999, decided that:

1. IFLANET is officially recognised as the primary and exclusive vehicle for electronic communications within IFLA and the repository of all online IFLA-related information regardless of language.
2. Individual IFLA unit Web sites are prohibited, and any in existence at that date would be migrated to IFLANET. [Note: For this purpose "IFLA Unit" is defined as any Division, Section, Discussion Group, Core Activity, Regional Office and any comparable unit which might be established in the future].
3. IFLA Conference sites shall be hosted on IFLANET. Arrangements may be made with Conference organizers to cooperate on various aspects of their creation, including some pointers to external sites (for example; on-line registration, hotel information, etc.). However, the main Conference site shall reside on the IFLANET server.
4. Consortia of members in a country or language group [but which are not IFLA units as defined above] may establish a site making use of some IFLA material that they translate. However, such sites can only be created if

it is made clear that they are not official IFLA sites and if they do not carry the IFLA logo.

The Executive Board believes that a single IFLA Website:

1. allows IFLA units to focus their energies on content, rather than the minutiae of running a Web site
2. ensures a regular update schedule of all materials
3. ensures that materials conform to IFLANET's brand or "look-and-feel", thus providing IFLA with a unified corporate look and a clearly identifiable network presence
4. allows materials to be easily modified to reflect any future changes to that "look-and-feel"
5. ensures that all materials are identifiable as authoritative IFLA documents
6. allows materials to be mirrored on official IFLANET mirror sites
7. permits all documents to be retrieved using an IFLANET site search tool
8. ensures that all documents are part of IFLANET's long-term archive
9. provides users with consistent user support
10. allows materials to be included in any IFLANET initiatives designed to keep the Web site in step with network advances (e.g., eventual conversion to XML).
11. guarantees continuous support, because the responsibility for IFLANET resides with IFLA. In contrast, Sections, Divisions, and other IFLA units can shift from person to person and institution to institution over time.

## Preparing Documents for Publication on IFLANET

Information Coordinators and other contributors should follow the following procedures and guidelines when preparing documents for, or submitting changes to IFLANET.

Supported electronic file types

IFLANET can accept documents in the following formats only:

MS-Word / Excel /PowerPoint (do not convert to ASCII text) PostScript and Encapsulated PostScript Adobe Acrobat PDF files

IFLANET cannot accept files in desktop publishing formats (i.e., PageMaker, Quark XPress, InDesign) or in other proprietary formats. Information Coordinators wishing to supply database information to IFLANET are requested to contact IFLANET Administration directly.

If graphics are embedded in a document, they should be made available as separate files. File formats should be GIF, JPG, JPEG, TIF or TIFF. Proprietary graphics formats such as Corel cannot be converted by IFLANET Administration.

If materials are to be compressed for transfer, please use common compression formats (WINZip preferred).

**Required administrative metadata**

To help identify materials sent for publication on IFLANET, all texts should include the following administrative metadata:

author(s)/organization name(s)

Information Coordinator's name

IFLA Unit or other affiliation

descriptive document title

email address

mailing address/phone number

**HTML (Hypertext Markup Language) Support**

Information Coordinator's and other contributors should not do their own HTML mark up. In practice, it is very difficult to maintain consistency across IFLANET when many individuals engage in HTML coding independently. It takes more time to modify documents received in HTML format, than to mark them up in their entirety. Please send only supported electronic formats.

### Supplying information about document structure and placement

To facilitate HTML mark up and placement of documents on IFLANET, Information Coordinators and other contributors must provide information about their documents' structures and proper location. While standard templates are used on IFLANET, information about a document's structure is required to construct it appropriately (a simple way of providing structure information is to send a paper version, if available, along with the electronic text).

### Databases

Database projects, which can be resource intensive, will be dealt with on a case-by-case basis. Please contact IFLANET Administration directly to discuss the possibility of creating databases of materials.

### Non-electronic submissions

Information Coordinators should submit their documents in electronic format where possible. In cases where this is not possible (e.g., lost files, non-Roman characters), paper documents will be scanned and converted to PDF for delivery through IFLANET. Please ensure that paper versions are of high quality or they will not be able to be scanned well enough for inclusion on IFLANET.

**Note:** IFLANET personnel will not re-key or OCR paper documents.

### Sending files to IFLANET Administration

The following methods are acceptable for sending files to IFLANET Administration.

## Electronic Mail Attachments

Simply attach the document to a notification message and send it to: Please provide URLs and filenames when referencing documents and pages on IFLANET.

## CD-ROM, DVD-ROM

Electronic files can be sent to IFLANET on CD-ROM or DVD-ROM using the IFLANET postal address in The Hague, clearly labeled as to their contents. An index file describing the contents of the CDs should also be included.

## The Future of IFLANET

IFLANET uses a combination of networking and communications technologies to provide IFLA with an unprecedented opportunity to deliver information services to members and non-members alike. But many members of IFLA do not yet have access to Internet mail or the WWW service. IFLANET plans include the exploration and expansion of services to these users as well.

IFLANET will continue to provide users with low-level connectivity, the ability to deliver IFLANET documents through electronic mail (for example, by means of the WebMail service in Ireland) and by exploring the provision of similar services locally. The technical and economic feasibility of other potential means for expanded delivery mechanisms is also being explored. These mechanisms include fax-on-demand, fax-back, print-on-demand, CD-ROM distribution, and MIME-based services.

Important goals for IFLANET are to ensure that the service provides current and valuable content, is sustainable, responsive to its user community, and accessible to the widest possible range of users.

All members of IFLA and librarians around the world

are being encouraged to participate in the "virtual IFLA" to use the electronic discussion lists and to provide it with the content that enriches and enhances it. With IFLANET, the International Federation of Library Associations and Institutions has entered a new era one in which networked communication allows it to be constantly in touch with its membership and to have a constant presence in the international library community. Through IFLANET, and the leadership and support of the National Library of Canada, IFLA makes an invaluable contribution to the development of libraries and librarianship around the world.

## 10. MEDLINE (MEDICAL LITERATURE ANALYSIS AND RETRIEVAL SYSTEM ONLINE)

MEDLINE (Medical Literature Analysis and Retrieval System Online) is the U.S. National Library of Medicine's (NLM) premier bibliographic database that contains over 15 million references to journal articles in life sciences with a concentration on biomedicine. A distinctive feature of MEDLINE is that the records are indexed with NLM's Medical Subject Headings.

The majority of journals are selected for MEDLINE based on the recommendation of the Literature Selection Technical Review Committee (LSTRC), an NIH-chartered advisory committee of external experts analogous to the committees that review NIH grant applications. Some additional journals and newsletters are selected based on NLM-initiated reviews, e.g., history of medicine, health services research, AIDS, toxicology and environmental health, molecular biology, and complementary medicine, that are special priorities for NLM or other NIH components. These reviews generally also involve consultation with an array of NIH and outside experts or, in some cases, external organizations with which NLM has special collaborative arrangements.

MEDLINE is the primary component of PubMed, part of the Entrez series of databases provided by NLM's National Center for Biotechnology Information (NCBI). MEDLINE may also be searched via the NLM Gateway. The time coveragei s generally 1950 to the present, with some older material. Currently, citations from approximately 5,000 worldwide journals in 37 languages; 60 languages for older journals. Citations for MEDLINE are created by the NLM, international partners, and collaborating organizations. Since 2005, between 2,000-4,000 completed references are added each day Tuesday through Saturday; over 623,000 total added in 2006. Updates are suspended for several weeks during November and December as NLM makes the transition to a new year of Medical Subject Headings (MeSH) vocabulary used to index the articles.

The subjects covered in the MEDLINE are biomedicine and health, broadly defined to encompass those areas of the life sciences, behavioral sciences, chemical sciences, and bioengineering needed by health professionals and others engaged in basic research and clinical care, public health, health policy development, or related educational activities. MEDLINE also covers life sciences vital to biomedical practitioners, researchers, and educators, including aspects of biology, environmental science, marine biology, plant and animal science as well as biophysics and chemistry. Increased coverage of life sciences began in 2000.

The majority of the publications covered in MEDLINE are scholarly journals; a small number of newspapers, magazines, and newsletters considered useful to particular segments of NLM's broad user community are also included. For citations added during 2000-2005: about 47% are for cited articles published in the U.S., about 90% are published in English, and about 79% have English abstracts written by authors of the articles.

MEDLINE is the primary component of PubMed (http://pubmed.gov); a link to PubMed is found on the NLM home page at http://www.nlm.nih.gov. The result of a MEDLINE/PubMed search is a list of citations (including authors, title, source, and often an abstract) to journal articles and an indication of free electronic full-text availability. Searching is free of charge and does not require registration. MEDLINE in PubMed may also be searched using the NLM Gateway, a single Web interface that searches multiple NLM retrieval systems.

A growing number of MEDLINE citations contain a link to the free full text of the article archived in PubMed Central or to other sites. You can also link from many MEDLINE references to the Web site of the publisher or other full text provider to request or view the full article, depending upon the publisher's access requirements. For articles not freely available on the web, the "Loansome Doc®" feature in PubMed provides an easy way to place an electronic order through the National Network of Libraries of Medicine® (NN/LM®) for the full-text copy of an article cited in MEDLINE. Registration is required and local fees may apply for this service.

Services/products providing access to MEDLINE data are also developed and made available by organizations that lease the database from NLM. Access to various MEDLINE services is often available from medical libraries, many public libraries, and commercial sources.

MedlinePlus is a service offered by the NLM, provides consumer-oriented health information. Health consumers are encouraged to discuss search results with their health care provider.

Related NLM Fact Sheets as given on the web at http://www.nlm.nih.gov are:

- ★ Copyright Information & Downloading
- ★ Journal Selection for MEDLINE
- ★ Loansome Doc®
- ★ MedlinePlus®
- ★ Medical Subject Headings (MeSH®)
- ★ PubMed®: MEDLINE® Retrieval on the World Wide Web
- ★ What is the Difference Between MEDLINE® and PubMed®?
- ★ NLM Gateway
- ★ Errata, Retraction, and Comment Policy
- ★ OLDMEDLINE
- ★ PubMed Central® Overview

**Copyright Information & Downloading National Library of Medicine Data**

Prospective licensees and those considering downloading data for redistribution should obtain opinion from legal counsel for any use planned for the author-generated abstracts in National Library of Medicine (NLM) databases and to ensure compliance with intellectual property laws. NLM cannot provide advice about copyright issues. Some material in the NLM databases is from copyrighted publications of the respective copyright claimants. Users of the NLM databases are solely responsible for compliance with any copyright restrictions and are referred to the publication data appearing in the bibliographic citations, as well as to the copyright notices appearing in the original publications, all of which are hereby incorporated by reference. Those who search NLM databases may download for personal use and may provide others with a single copy of downloaded data.

Some records are submitted electronically by publishers for entry to PubMed. You should consult with legal counsel regarding re-use of PubMed records annotated [PubMed - as supplied by publisher]. Although a signed license agreement is not needed, users must ensure that all downloaded publicly accessible data stored in electronic form for over one year must be in compliance with the following provisions of the NLM license agreement:

a. Users of these data must be provided a clear description of how the product/service was derived, indicating the currency and the source database.

b. At least annually, the data in the downloaded product/service containing searchable MEDLINE-derived data must be corrected to incorporate the corrections NLM has made to these records during the year and in year-end maintenance. NLM data in the product/service must be carefully checked with that maintained on NLM's version of the database at the end of each calendar year and corrections made. This does not apply to products/services containing MEDLINE-derived data which itself is not searchable (e.g., MEDLINE-derived references and abstracts in the bibliography of an electronic textbook). The MEDLINE-derived data should be updated when a new edition of the product is released. In this case, users should be informed that the MEDLINE-derived data may change.

c. Users are advised to consult legal counsel to ensure compliance with intellectual property laws. NLM cannot provide advice about copyright issues.

d. Because NLM goes to considerable effort to assign MeSH terms, it prefers that these be retained as assigned by the indexers.

e. The NLM record (or portion thereof) in the product/service must be labeled so as to identify NLM as the source, except for data derived from LocatorPlus.

f. Trademark symbols must properly be used when referring to the NLM databases, system and products. A product/service using downloaded data must be named in a fashion that clearly distinguishes it from NLM-produced databases accessible at NLM.

## Journal Selection for MEDLINE

MEDLINE, the principal online bibliographic citation database of NLM's MEDLARS® system, is used internationally to provide access to the world's biomedical journal literature. The decision whether or not to index a journal for this service is an important one and is made by the Director of the National Library of Medicine, based on considerations of both scientific policy and scientific quality. The Board of Regents of the Library sets policy for the Library. The Literature Selection Technical Review Committee (LSTRC) has been established to review journal titles and assess the quality of their contents.

There is a rough analogy to the National Institutes of Health's (NIH) decision-making process, with respect to research grant awards. Namely, the relative scientific merit of individual grant applications is determined by Study Sections in the same way journals are evaluated by LSTRC, while the mixture of types of research grants or types of journals is determined independently by Council or Board according to considerations of program relevance. Consonant with this principle, the LSTRC frequently incorporates the review and advice of outside experts in the subject area. As a result of these reviews, currently indexed titles may be dropped and new titles added.

About 5,000 titles are indexed and included in the

MEDLINE database. The LSTRC meets three times a year and considers approximately 140 titles at each meeting. Additional titles are considered in reviews of specialty coverage.

The world-wide users of the MEDLARS indexes are researchers, health care practitioners, educators, administrators, and students whose needs vary considerably. All are important, and the goal of the indexes will not be met by concentrating on one set of users at the expense of another. The content, format, and accepted structure of the journals, designed to meet the needs of these users, also vary greatly. NLM still seeks a practical system to guide our selection of journals that will reflect these different needs and desires. In the meantime, the selection is highly dependent on the judgment of Committee members and the Director. The following critical elements are intended as a general guide so that a consistent set of issues will be considered as the Committee members examine journals in their search for the best and the most appropriate coverage of the biomedical literature.

## Critical Elements

**Scope and coverage:** The journals brought to the Committee for review will contain articles predominantly on core biomedical subjects. Journals whose content is predominantly a subject peripheral or related to biomedicine are occasionally brought to the Committee when they have some biomedical content. In these cases, the Committee's advice is sought not only on the quality of the content but also on the contribution it makes to the coverage of the subjects in question. Generally, such journals will not be indexed if their biomedical content is already adequately covered.

**Quality of content :** Scientific merit of a journal's content is the primary consideration in selecting journals for indexing. The validity, importance, originality, and contribution to the coverage of the field of the overall contents of each title are the key factors considered in recommending a title for indexing, whatever the intended purpose and audience.

**Quality of editorial work :** The journal should demonstrate features that contribute to the objectivity, credibility, and quality of its contents. These features may include information about the methods of selecting articles, especially on the explicit process of external peer review; statements indicating adherence to ethical guidelines; evidence that authors have disclosed financial conflicts of interest; timely correction of errata; explicit responsible retractions as appropriate; and opportunity for comments and dissenting opinion. Neither the advertising content nor commercial sponsorship should raise questions about the objectivity of the published material. Sponsorship by national or international professional societies may be considered.

**Production quality :** Quality of the layout, printing, graphics, and illustrations are all considered in assessing a journal. Though not a requirement for selection, journals of archival importance should be printed on acid-free paper.

**Audience :** MEDLINE is intended primarily for those in the health professions: researchers, practitioners, educators, administrators, and students. The phrase health professionals includes physicians, nurses, dentists, veterinarians, and the many types of allied health professionals in the research and health care delivery systems.

**Types of content :** Journals whose contents consist of one or more of the following types of information will be considered for indexing:

1. Reports of original research
2. Original clinical observations accompanied by analysis and discussion

3. Analysis of philosophical, ethical, or social aspects of the health professions or biomedical sciences
4. Critical reviews
5. Statistical compilations
6. Descriptions of evaluation of methods or procedures
7. Case reports with discussions

All of these forms of information should be included in MEDLINE in order to fulfill the needs of users. However, coverage of a field tends to create a priority approximately parallel to the order in which the types are listed. For example, journals reporting original research are more likely to contain unique contributions to the coverage of a field and therefore are selected more often than those that contain only case reports.

Publications that consist primarily of reprinted articles, reports of association activities, abstracts of the literature, news items or book reviews, will not usually be indexed.

**Foreign language journals :** Criteria for selection are the same as for those written in English. In order to extend the accessibility of the journal's content to a wider potential readership, the majority of published articles in the review issues must contain an English-language abstract before the title will be considered for possible indexing.

**Geographic coverage :** The highest quality and most useful journals are selected without regard for place of publication. In order to provide broad international coverage, special attention is given to research, public health, epidemiology, standards of health care, and indigenous diseases. Journals will generally not be selected for indexing if the contents are subjects already well represented in MEDLINE or that are being published for a local audience.

Interpretation of these criteria will be influenced by the stated purpose of the journal. For purposes of illustration, four broad categories of journals are suggested.

1. Research journals are predominantly devoted to reporting original investigations in the biomedical and health sciences, including research in the basic sciences; clinical trials of therapeutic agents; effectiveness of diagnostic or therapeutic techniques; or studies relating to the behavioral, epidemiological, or educational aspects of medicine.
2. Clinical or practice journals have as their dominant purpose documenting the state of current practice, providing background for those in training, or the continuing education of practitioners. This is done through the publication of case reports, discussions and illustrations of new techniques, evaluations of current practices, and commentaries.
3. Review journals contain the current state of knowledge or practice, integrating recent advances with accepted principles and practice, or summarizing and analyzing the consensus view of controversial issues in knowledge or practice. Review journals provide background information for practitioners and researchers, students and house officers, and others who wish an overview on the current status of a field.
4. General or all-purpose journals contain elements of all the foregoing and frequently contain commentary and analysis of important social, political, and economic issues. They are usually designed for a broad audience and not limited to a specialty.

The International Committee of Medical Journal Editors (ICMJE) has produced and updated the "Uniform

Requirements for Manuscripts (URM) Submitted to Biomedical Journals". Publishers who would like to incorporate the URM into their review and publication process are encouraged to link to www.icmje.org and mention this in their Instructions to Authors section.

The Council of Science Editors (CSE) has produced "Editorial Policy Statements" that cover the responsibilities and rights of editors of peer-reviewed journals. Publishers who would like to incorporate these Statements into their review and publication process are encouraged to link to: http://www.councilscienceeditors.org/services/draft_approved.cfm.

Application Process: Any editors or publishers who would like to have their journal reviewed for possible indexing in MEDLINE should access the new "MEDLINE Review Application Form" at http://wwwcf.nlm.nih.gov/lstrc/lstrcform/med/index.html. This form is required for all journals initially reviewed by the LSTRC for inclusion in MEDLINE.

**Loansome Doc**

Loansome Doc enables PubMed® and NLM Gateway users to order documents found in MEDLINE. It is available to users in the U.S. and internationally. A user can order articles from a list of citations retrieved from PubMed and the NLM Gateway by sending requests to a library for the full-text documents.

**MedlinePlus**

MedlinePlus (http://medlineplus.gov/) is the National Library of Medicine's web site for consumer health information.

The information in MedlinePlus includes:

- ⋆ **Health Topics are the core of MedlinePlus :** Health topics pages link to health information from NIH and other authoritative sources and also include a

MEDLINE/PubMed search, current news items about the topic, and links to related topics.

- **Medical Encyclopedia :** an extensive collection of medical images as well as 4,000 articles about diseases, tests, symptoms, injuries and surgeries
- **Interactive Health Tutorials :** programs that use animated graphics and sound to explain conditions and procedures in easy-to-read language
- Drugs, Supplements, and Herbal Information - prescription and over-the-counter medicines, plus herbs and supplements
- **Current Health News :** late-breaking stories about medicine and health
- **Dictionary :** spellings and definitions of medical terms
- Directories - locations and credentials of doctors, dentists and hospitals
- Other Resources include:
  - *Go Local* - find health services in your home town
  - *Organizations* - a collection of organizations providing health information
  - *Libraries* - consumer health libraries providing services to local residents
  - *Databases* - resources beyond MedlinePlus covering special topics and collections
  - *MEDLINE/PubMed* - search articles published in biomedical journals
  - Special Collections of
    - Easy-to-Read materials
    - Low vision resources
    - Health check tools

### Selection of Links for MedlinePlus?

MedlinePlus is not an exhaustive list of every health web resource. It is a selective list of authoritative health information sources from NIH and other government and professional organizations in the U.S. A link to the guidelines is on the "About MedlinePlus" page. MedlinePlus includes mostly U.S. resources.

### MedlinePlus facts

System - Oracle database and Cold Fusion application

Resources are updated nightly (date on page indicates date of most recent change)

Released October 22, 1998

Includes over 700 topics

For more statistics, see the MedlinePlus Statistics FAQ (http://www.nlm.nih.gov/medlineplus/faq/stats.html)

Medical Subject Headings (MeSH®)

### The Thesaurus

MeSH is the National Library of Medicine's controlled vocabulary thesaurus. It consists of sets of terms naming descriptors in a hierarchical structure that permits searching at various levels of specificity.

MeSH descriptors are arranged in both an alphabetic and a hierarchical structure. At the most general level of the hierarchical structure are very broad headings such as "Anatomy" or "Mental Disorders." More specific headings are found at more narrow levels of the eleven-level hierarchy, such as "Ankle" and "Conduct Disorder." There are 22,997 descriptors in MeSH. In addition to these headings, there are more than 151,000 headings called Supplementary Concept Records (formerly Supplementary Chemical Records) within a separate thesaurus. There are also thousands of cross-references that assist in finding the most appropriate MeSH Heading, for example, Vitamin C *see* Ascorbic Acid. These additional entries include 24,050 printed *see* references and 112,012 other entry points.

### MeSH Applications

The MeSH thesaurus is used by NLM for indexing articles from 4,800 of the world's leading biomedical journals for the MEDLINE/PubMED® database. It is also used for the NLM-produced database that includes cataloging of books, documents, and audiovisuals acquired by the Library. Each bibliographic reference is associated with a set of MeSH terms that describe the content of the item. Similarly, search queries use MeSH vocabulary to find items on a desired topic.

### Establishing and Updating MeSH

The Medical Subject Headings Section staff continually revise and update the MeSH vocabulary. Staff subject specialists are responsible for areas of the health sciences in which they have knowledge and expertise. In addition to receiving suggestions from indexers and others, the staff collect new terms as they appear in the scientific literature or in emerging areas of research; define these terms within the context of existing vocabulary; and recommend their addition to MeSH. Professionals in various disciplines are also consulted regarding broad organizational changes and close coordination is maintained with various specialized vocabularies.

### MeSH Publication

MeSH, in machine-readable form, is provided at no charge via electronic means. The MeSH Website http://www.nlm.nih.gov/mesh is the central access point for additional information about MeSH and for obtaining MeSH in electronic form

## PubMed : MEDLINE Retrieval on the World Wide Web

PubMed (pubmed.gov) is available on the Entrez retrieval system, and was developed by the National Center for Biotechnology Information (NCBI) at the National Library of Medicine (NLM).

### PubMed

- ★ Provides free access to MEDLINE, NLM's database of citations and abstracts in the fields of medicine, nursing, dentistry, veterinary medicine, health care systems, and preclinical sciences.
- ★ Links to many sites providing full text articles and other related resources.
- ★ Provides a Clinical Queries search filters page as well as a Special Queries page.
- ★ Links to related articles for a selected citation.
- ★ Includes automatic e-mailing of search updates, the ability to save records, and filters for search results using "My NCBI".
- ★ Includes a spell checker feature.
- ★ Links to PubChem, NCBI sequence and other molecular biology databases.
- ★ Adds citations Tuesday through Saturday.

In addition to MEDLINE citations, PubMed also contains:

- ★ In-process citations which provide a record for an article before it is indexed with MeSH and added to MEDLINE or converted to out-of-scope status.
- ★ Citations that precede the date that a journal was selected for MEDLINE indexing (when supplied electronically by the publisher).
- ★ Some OLDMEDLINE citations that have not yet been

updated with current vocabulary and converted to MEDLINE status.

- ★ Citations to articles that are out-of-scope (e.g., covering plate tectonics or astrophysics) from certain MEDLINE journals, primarily general science and general chemistry journals, for which the life sciences articles are indexed with MeSH for MEDLINE.
- ★ Some life science journals that submit full text to PubMedCentral® and may not yet have been recommended for inclusion in MEDLINE although they have undergone a review by NLM, and some physics journals that were part of a prototype PubMed in the early to mid-1990's.

## Difference Between MEDLINE and PubMed

MEDLINE is the largest component of PubMed (http://pubmed.gov), the freely accessible online database of biomedical journal citations and abstracts created by the U.S. National Library of Medicine (NLM®). Approximately 5,000 journals published in the United States and more than 80 other countries have been selected and are currently indexed for MEDLINE. A distinctive feature of MEDLINE is that the records are indexed with NLM's controlled vocabulary, the Medical Subject Headings (MeSH®).

In addition to MEDLINE citations, PubMed also contains:

- ★ In-process citations which provide a record for an article before it is indexed with MeSH and added to MEDLINE or converted to out-of-scope status.
- ★ Citations that precede the date that a journal was selected for MEDLINE indexing (when supplied electronically by the publisher).
- ★ Some OLDMEDLINE citations that have not yet been

updated with current vocabulary and converted to MEDLINE status.

* Citations to articles that are out-of-scope (e.g., covering plate tectonics or astrophysics) from certain MEDLINE journals, primarily general science and general chemistry journals, for which the life sciences articles are indexed with MeSH for MEDLINE.
* Some life science journals that submit full text to PubMedCentral® and may not yet have been recommended for inclusion in MEDLINE although they have undergone a review by NLM, and some physics journals that were part of a prototype PubMed in the early to mid-1990's.

One of the ways users can limit their retrieval to MEDLINE citations in PubMed is by selecting MEDLINE from the Subsets menu on the Limits screen.

Other PubMed services include:

* Links to many sites providing full text articles and other related resources
* Clinical queries and Special queries search filters
* Links to see citations to related articles
* Single citation matcher
* The ability to store collections of citations, and save and automatically update searches
* A spell checker
* Filters to group search results

NLM distributes all but approximately 2% of all citations in PubMed to those who formally lease MEDLINE from NLM.

## The NLM Gateway

### Introduction

NLM® Gateway: http://gateway.nlm.nih.gov

Gateway is **"One-stop shopping"** for an increasing number of the information resources of the National Library of Medicine (NLM). It's targeted to the Internet user who comes to NLM not knowing exactly what is here, or how best to search for it. A single interface that searches in multiple retrieval systems, Gateway provides a single address, look, and feel.

### Gateway Characteristics

The user enters one query that is sent automatically to multiple retrieval systems having different characteristics but potentially useful results. Results from the target systems are presented in broad categories (bibliographic resources, consumer health resources, other information resources) rather than by database.

We expect that users will come to Gateway for an overview scan of NLM's resources. Some will find what they need immediately. Others may find that one resource, such as PubMed® or MedlinePlus®, has information they would like to know more about. They may then choose to go straight to that resource for a more focused search.

## Goals

★ Provide "one-stop shopping" for many of NLM's information resources

★ Offer citations, full text, video, audio, and images

★ Link within and across NLM databases on behalf of users

★ Make maximum use of the Unified Medical Language System (UMLS).

**Gateway now Accesses**

- ★ MEDLINE®/PubMed®
- ★ NLM Catalog — catalog information for books, serial titles, audiovisuals
- ★ Bookshelf — full text biomedical books
- ★ TOXLINE® Special — toxicology citations
- ★ DART® — Developmental and Reproductive Toxicology
- ★ Meeting abstracts on HIV/AIDS, health services research, and space life sciences
- ★ MedlinePlus® — consumer health information
- ★ ClinicalTrials.gov — information for the public about clinical trials
- ★ DIRLINE® — Directory of Health Organizations
- ★ Genetics Home Reference™— consumer information for genetic conditions
- ★ Household Products Database
- ★ HSRProj — health services research projects
- ★ OMIM — Online Mendelian Inheritance in Man
- ★ HSDB® — Hazardous Substances Data Bank
- ★ IRIS — Integrated Risk Information System
- ★ ITER — International Toxicity Estimates for Risk
- ★ GENE-TOX — Genetic Toxicology (Mutagenicity)
- ★ CCRIS — Chemical Carcinogenesis Research Information System
- ★ Profiles in Science — archives of several prominent biomedical scientists
- ★ Document delivery through Loansome Doc
- ★ UMLS® Metathesaurus.

## Future Links

★ Images from the History of Medicine

The basic Gateway search interface is simple. It takes advantage of the capabilities of the retrieval systems it links to, for example, the advanced query parser and the Related Articles and LinkOut functions in MEDLINE/PubMed. Users can set preferences to adapt the interface to their needs, such as specifying which elements of a record they wish to see in the display of results. A "locker" is used to store selected results the user wishes to keep across sessions. The user can download, print, or email results.

The design builds on the strength of the intelligent gateway concept: the ability to offer value-added capabilities the user did not know to ask for. In future versions, links within and across databases will be exploited. Searches in clusters of NLM databases (or in *all* databases) will be offered.

## Current Status

The NLM Gateway was released to the public on October 16, 2000. A comprehensively redesigned version was released on April 4, 2005. New versions are released periodically.

Errata, Retraction, Duplicate Publication, Comment, Update and Patient Summary Policy for MEDLINE®

The National Library of Medicine® (NLM) has a long-standing tradition of providing access to information in the biomedical literature through quality programs and services. One of the ways NLM assists users is to add subsequent notices of errata, retractions, republications, duplicate publications and comments (including updates) to citations of articles indexed and available in NLM's online MEDLINE database. Users who search MEDLINE will be informed if they retrieve a citation for an article that has subsequently been retracted, an article that has been found to duplicate another article, an article in which a substantive error has been noted, an article that has been corrected and republished, an article that has generated a separately published commenting article, an original article that has been updated by a subsequent article, or if a summary for patients has been published. NLM updates and links the existing citations to subsequently published errata, retraction notices, comments and similar announcements.

**Errata**

Corrections or corrigenda for previously-published articles are all uniformly considered by NLM to be errata. NLM does not differentiate between errors that originate in the publication process and those that result from errors of scientific logic or methodology, because journal editors do not make this distinction consistently or clearly. Since 1987, when a journal has published a labeled, citable erratum to a previously-published article, NLM has amended its citation to the original article with a bibliographic reference to the erratum notice, in order to alert users and refer them to the source of the erratum information.

In PubMed®, the erratum information typically appears as a text phrase such as:

Erratum in: JAMA. 2004 Nov 24;292(20):2470.

The appearance of the erratum information varies with the display format (Summary, Abstract, etc.) with which a PubMed citation is viewed. In the MEDLINE format, the erratum information appears in the EIN (Erratum in) field.

Errata may be published to correct text or information that appears anywhere within an earlier published article. If the correction involves text or information that is part of the corresponding NLM citation, such as the author, title or abstract, then NLM will update its citation to the corrected form of the text or information, and will indicate in some manner that data within one of the citation fields has been corrected. When appropriate, NLM will retain the ability to retrieve the data via the previous, uncorrected form of the citation.

For example, if an author name has been corrected, NLM will retain the ability to search and retrieve the citation via the originally published, incorrect form of the author name, in addition to the ability to search and retrieve the citation via the corrected form of the author name. A notice about the correction in the citation will show both the incorrect spelling of the name and the corrected form.

If the errata occurred in a portion of the article that is not included in the NLM citation, such as the text, graphs, or tables, only a reference to the published erratum notice will be added to the MEDLINE citation.

A new citation is not generally created by NLM for a brief erratum notice, but a new citation may be created when the erratum notice is published as a substantive article or letter. Such a citation is indexed with the Publication Type PUBLISHED ERRATUM and is linked to the citation for the original article. The reference for the original article appears after the text "Erratum for:" in most PubMed displays, and in the EFR field in the MEDLINE display.

NLM will only acknowledge errata when they are published in citable form: the erratum notice must appear on a numbered page in a subsequent issue of the journal in which the article was originally published. Error notices that are inserted unbound into a journal issue or "tipped" will not be considered part of the permanent bibliographic record. For online journals or online-only content, the erratum notice must be readily discernable in the table of contents of a subsequent issue, and must be associated with identifiable pagination.

NLM does not make changes to citations in response to letters from authors or editors, unless such letters indicate that a substantive published erratum is in press, and galleys or proof sheets are provided that indicate the content and pagination of the forthcoming erratum notice.

**OLDMEDLINE Data**

OLDMEDLINE represents journal article citations from two printed indexes: Cumulated Index Medicus (CIM) and the Current List of Medical Literature (CLML). Created by the National Library of Medicine, these approximately 1,760,000 citations to articles from international biomedical journals cover the fields of medicine, preclinical sciences and allied health sciences from 1950 through 1965. OLDMEDLINE records, most of which are included in the MEDLINE database, can be searched via PubMed® or the NLM Gateway.

**History**

In 1964, NLM began using the computerized MEDLARS® (Medical Literature Analysis and Retrieval System) system as a mechanism for producing Index Medicus® (IM). In 1971, MEDLARS went online with the introduction of MEDLINE®, an interactive searchable database of data from the 1966 Index Medicus forward. The 1964 and 1965 issues of Index Medicus, while available in electronic form, were not included in MEDLINE because of format differences. In the mid-1990s, NLM was assisted in its effort to provide online access to these older citations by the Deutsches Institut fur Medizinische Dokumentation und Information (DIMDI), the International MEDLARS Center in Germany. DIMDI had tapes of the original data from the 1964 and 1965 Cumulative Index Medicus, which they had converted and then supplied to NLM to create OLDMEDLINE in 1996. The citations from the 1960 - 1963 CIM and the 1950 - 1959 Current List of Medical Literature were converted from print copy into machine-readable form.

**OLDMEDLINE Data**

| Date Added | Citations Added | Printed Index |
|---|---|---|
| December 1996 | 153,127 | 1965 CIM |
| | 153,196 | 1964 CIM |
| November 1998 | 233,654 | 1962 - 1963 CIM |
| | 227,897 | 1960 - 1961 CIM |
| July 2000 | 106,301 | 1959 CLML |
| | 113,273 | 1958 CLML |
| May 2002 | 103,427 | 1957 CLML |
| May 2003 | 105,757 | 1956 CLML |
| | 109,778 | 1955 CLML |
| | 107,927 | 1954 CLML |
| | 103,502 | 1953 CLML |
| February 2004 | 89,557 | 1952 CLML |
| | 97,332 | 1951 CLML |
| September 2004 | 55,850 | 53,533 citations from 1950 CLML2,317 citations from 1951 - 1965* |

*In order to load OLDMEDLINE data into PubMed, each citation must be linked to a parent serial record in *LocatorPlus*. Determining the proper link for some of these older citations takes research time which can result in the citations being made available later than the online debut date for the majority of a year's index. Research and user reports also uncover gap issues that NLM adds and citations that are duplicates that NLM deletes; these changes are not reflected in the counts given in the chart.

NLM expects to continue converting citations from its older printed medical indexes to machine-readable form and to add these citations to PubMed's OLDMEDLINE subset as time and resources permit.

**Data Quality**

OLDMEDLINE records have been created using standards

that are different from the data entry standards for MEDLINE records. There are also variations among OLDMEDLINE citations in the data elements (fields) present in the citation as well as in their format, depending on the original source from which the citations were obtained. For details, see the individual MEDLINE/PubMed Data Element (Field) Descriptions.

OLDMEDLINE citations lack the individual and accumulated changes and improvements that have been made to data in other NLM files during annual file maintenance. Certain fields may contain outdated or erroneous data and the data are not cosmetically consistent from year to year (e.g., the use of upper/lower case). The citations basically reflect the contents of the original printed indexes that were produced under policy and procedures of the time. The exceptions to this are that NLM has identified and updated the Journal Title Abbreviation and added the current ISSN. Each OLDMEDLINE citation is linked to a parent serial record in NLM's online catalog LocatorPlus. In addition, beginning with 2005 Year-End Processing, OLDMEDLINE citations with MeSH headings (see MeSH Mapping Project ) are included in the individual and accumulated changes and improvements that are made to the NLM data during annual maintenance, notably changes to the Medical Subject Headings (MeSH®) vocabulary.

**Searching**

Note the following aspects of OLDMEDLINE citations when searching:

**Lack of Abstracts**

When searching OLDMEDLINE citations, it is important to remember that the absence of abstracts affects subject retrieval.

## Original Subject Headings

To distinguish the original subject headings from the printed indexes from current MeSH, all original subjects have been placed in the Other Term [OT] field of OLDMEDLINE records in PubMed. Note the following characteristics of these subject headings:

- ★ Few subject headings (approximately 3 - 5 per citation). See the Sample Record One, below. The 1964 and 1965 citations tend to have more subject headings (approximately 3 - 8 per citation). See the Sample Record Two, below.
- ★ "Check tag" headings (e.g., ANIMALS, CHILD, INFANT) applied inconsistently and should not be used to search.
- ★ Original subject headings have not been updated, and may not match current MeSH vocabulary.
- ★ Subheading practice varied:
  - ★ No subheadings on 1963 - 65 CIM citations and 1950 and 1951 CLML citations.
  - ★ Various subheadings on 1960 - 62 CIM citations and 1952 - 59 CLML citations.
- ★ All headings designated as major topic.

Because these original subject headings are not current MeSH, the subject headings in the [OT] field of OLDMEDLINE citations do not relate to current hierarchical MeSH Tree numbers, and the MeSH search capabilities (i.e., "explosions") that collect indented (more specific) terms are not functional for these data in the OT field.

## MeSH Mapping Project

NLM has begun an OLDMEDLINE OT subject heading-to-MeSH Heading mapping project. This project maps the original subject headings assigned to the citations when they appeared in the print indexes to the current MeSH vocabulary. NLM estimates that approximately 93% of the OLDMEDLINE citations have at least one current MeSH Heading (89% of the original subject headings have been mapped), and will, therefore, be retrieved by PubMed searches that incorporate MeSH headings/explosions. Approximately 73% of the headings and subheadings were a one-for-one match done by machine. The other 16% were mapped after a review by NLM staff. The original subject headings are being retained in the OT field.

Please note that all current MeSH Headings added to OLDMEDLINE records have been added as Major MeSH Headings because 13 of the 15 years of data have only headings under which the citations appeared in the print indexes. However, two years of data, the 1964 and 1965 CIM, contain additional MeSH Headings that do not represent the major point of the article yet are also set to Major status because the original distinction between major and not major had been lost over the years during various conversion efforts and NLM did not have the resources to restore that distinction. Remember, as explained above, that OLDMEDLINE citations have MeSH headings such as the commonly used check tags for Animals, Age groups, etc. applied inconsistently and that the subheading practice varied greatly over the years.

As of late 2006, citations from the OLDMEDLINE print index sources that have had all of their original subject headings mapped to current MeSH carry the status tag [PubMed - indexed for MEDLINE] (see Sample Record Two, below). A search for medline [sb] in PubMed will include these records. Citations that have not had all of their original subject headings mapped to current MeSH will have the status tag [PubMed - OLDMEDLINE] (see Sample Record One, below). A search for oldmedline [sb] will identify these records. Citations digitized in the future from earlier years of the print index CLML will be entered in PubMed with the citation status of [PubMed - OLDMEDLINE] until their original subject headings are completely mapped to current MeSH. Once this mapping is completed, these records will be designated as MEDLINE records and their citation status will become [PubMed - indexed for MEDLINE].

**PMC Overview**

PubMed Central is a free digital archive of biomedical and life sciences journal literature at the U.S. National Institutes of Health (NIH), developed and managed by NIH's National Center for Biotechnology Information (NCBI) in the National Library of Medicine (NLM). With PubMed Central, NLM is taking the lead in preserving and maintaining unrestricted access to the electronic literature, just as it has done for decades with the printed biomedical literature. PubMed Central aims to fill the role of a world class library in the digital age. It is not a journal publisher. NLM believes that giving all users free and unrestricted access to the material in PubMed Central is the best way to ensure the durability and utility of the archive as technology changes over time.

PubMed Central follows in the footsteps of other highly successful and useful services that NCBI has developed for the worldwide scientific community: GenBank, the genetic sequence data repository, and PubMed, the database of citations and abstracts to biomedical and other life science journal literature. GenBank, and the tools provided by NCBI for searching and manipulating its contents, have been a boon to molecular biologists and have helped advance developments in the field. PubMed (which encompasses Medline) is the database of choice, for researchers and clinicians alike, to locate relevant articles and, in many cases, link directly to a publisher's site for the full text.

Participation by publishers in PubMed Central (PMC) is voluntary, although participating journals must meet certain editorial standards. (See the Information for Publishers.) Journals are encouraged to deposit all their content (and not just research papers or other selected material) in PMC so that the archive becomes a true digital counterpart to NLM's extensive collection of print journals. In line with this objective, NLM is digitizing earlier print issues of many of the journals already in PMC. Although immediate free access to all content is most desirable, a journal may delay release of its full text in PMC for some period of time after publication. See the Deposit and Access Policies for more information.

A journal is guaranteed access to a copy of its deposited data upon request, at no cost. PubMed Central does not claim copyright on any material deposited in the archive. Copyright remains with the journal publisher or with individual authors, whichever is applicable.

The value of PubMed Central, in addition to its role as an archive, lies in what can be done when data from diverse sources is stored in a common format in a single repository. GenBank has proven the advantages of collecting DNA sequences in a central repository with a common format. You get more rapid searching, manipulation, and cross-linking of the complete collection, and all the benefits that derive from that. Similarly, with PubMed Central, one can quickly search the entire body of full-text articles and locate relevant material regardless of its source. It also makes it possible to integrate the literature with a variety of other information resources such as sequence databases and other factual databases that are available to scientists, clinicians and everyone else interested in the life sciences. The intentional and serendipitous discoveries that such links might foster excite us and stimulate us to move forward.

Many journals already have online publishing operations and there is a growing tendency to publish material online only, to the exclusion of print. This literature must be preserved in a form that ensures unrestricted access to it over the longer term. This is what NLM has undertaken to do. We invite all journals to join those that have already committed to creating this resource for people all over the world.

# 4 Indian Information Networks

## 1. INFORMATION AND LIBRARY NETWORK (INFLIBNET)

Information and Library Network (INFLIBNET) is regarded as a landmark in the information scenario of higher education. It is the brainchild of Prof. Yashpal, an eminent scientist and the former Chairman of the University Grants Commission. Incepted in the year 1988, INFLIBNET became operational in 1991 and got the status of an autonomous body in 1996.

INFLIBNET is now an Inter-University Centre of the University Grants Commission (UGC) of India. It is a major National Programme initiated by the UGC with its Head Quarters at Gujarat University Campus, Ahmedabad. Initially started as a project under the IUCAA, INFLIBNET is involved in modernizing university libraries in India and connecting them as well as information centres in the country through a nation-wide high speed data network using the state-of-art technologies for the optimum utilization of information. INFLIBNET is set out to be a major player in promoting scholarly communication among academicians and researchers in India.

## Objectives of INFLIBNET

The objectives of INFLIBNET as envisaged in Memorandum of Association are:

To promote and establish communication facilities to improve capability in information transfer and access, that provide support to scholarship, learning, research and academic pursuit through cooperation and involvement of agencies concerned.

To establish **INFLIBNET : Information and Library Network** a computer communication network for linking libraries and information centres in universities, deemed to be universities, colleges, UGC information centres, institutions of national importance and R&D institutions, etc. avoiding duplication of efforts.

## Functions of INFLIBNET

In order to fulfill the broad objectives, INFLIBNET will:

Promote and implement computerization of operations and services in the libraries and information centres of the country, following a uniform standard.

Evolve standards and uniform guidelines in techniques, methods, procedures, computer hardware and software, services and promote their adoption in actual practice by all libraries, in order to facilitate pooling, sharing and exchange of information towards optimal use of resources and facilities.

Evolve a national network interconnecting various libraries and information centres in the country and to improve capability in information handling and service.

Provide reliable access to document collection of libraries by creating on-line union catalogue of serials, theses/ dissertations, books, monographs and non-book materials (manuscripts, audio-visuals, computer data, multimedia, etc.) in various libraries in India.

Provide access to bibliographic information sources with citations, abstracts etc. through indigenously created databases of the Sectoral Information Centres of NISSAT, UGC Information Centres, City Networks and such others and by establishing gateways for on-line accessing of national and international databases held by national and international information networks and centres respectively.

Develop new methods and techniques for archival of valuable information available as manuscripts and information documents in different Indian Languages, in the form of digital images using high density storage media.

Optimize information resource utilization through shared cataloguing, inter-library loan service, catalogue production, collection development and thus avoiding duplication in acquisition to the extent possible.

Enable the users dispersed all over the country, irrespective of location and distance, to have access to information regarding serials, theses/dissertations, books, monographs and non-book materials by locating the sources wherefrom available and to obtain it through the facilities of INFLIBNET and union catalogue of documents.

Create databases of projects, institutions, specialists, etc. for providing on-line information service.

Encourage co-operation among libraries, documentation centres and information centres in the country, so that the resources can be pooled for the benefit of helping the weaker resource centres by stronger ones.

Train and develop human resources in the field of computerized library operations and networking to establish, manage and sustain INFLIBNET.

Facilitate academic communication amongst scientists, engineers, social scientists, academics, faculties, researchers and students through electronic mail, file transfer, computer/audio/video conferencing, etc.

Undertake system design and studies in the field of communications, computer networking, information handling and data management.

Establish appropriate control and monitoring system for the communication network and organize maintenance.

Collaborate with institutions, libraries, information centres and other organizations in India and abroad in the field relevant to the objectives of the Centre.

Create and promote R&D and other facilities and technical positions for realizing the objectives of the Centre.

Generate revenue by providing consultancies and information services.

Do all other such things as may be necessary, incidental or conducive to the attainment of all or any of the above objectives.

## Activities of INFLIBNET

### *Database Development And Management*

Provide reliable access to document collection of libraries i.e. Union Catalogues etc.

Provide access to world wide bibliographical information.

To maintain consistency and quality in databases created by the participating libraries

Evolve standards, uniform guidelines, methods, and procedures, both for data capturing as well as Hardware and Software.

### *Major Activities*

Development, managing and updating of Union databases is one of the major activities of this group. Eight databases have been developed and are continuously growing. Following is the list of databases:

**Books :** Represents holding of participant libraries under the programme

**Theses :** Doctoral theses submitted to various Indian universities till date

**Serial Holdings :** Holdings information of various university libraries about the serial

**Current Serials :** Currently subscribed journals by the universities

**Secondary Serials/CD-ROMs**

**DDC Serials :** Currently subscribed journals by the six universities identified as DDC

**Experts :** Useful data about specialists in various disciplines

**Research Projects :** Information about ongoing projects

**NISSAT Project :** Experts Database (Science & Technology)

Group also proposes to create and develop other databases of national importance viz.

Patents

Manuscripts

Technical Reports

Non-Books Materials

## Standards and Formats required for creation of Databases

**1. Guidelines for Data Capturing a user manual :** To maintain consistency and quality in databases prepared by the libraries and INFLIBNET, INFLIBNET Centre had constituted a taskforce consistency experts in this area. This taskforce has brought out a 100 pages documents entitled GUIDELINES FOR DATA CAPTURING : A USER MANUAL. This documents is prepared based on Common Communication Format (CCF), 1992 edition and same has been given participating libraries for adoption. Taskforce also studies other standard required for this activity and according recommended that the following may also be used

Anglo American Catalogue Rules. Edition 2nd revised

Library of Congress Subject Heading

**2. SOUL Guidelines for Data Capturing: A user manual for books :** This is designed to be a handy manual to create records in SOUL. The user guide lists all bibliographical elements covered in the SOUL, with complete description of each field and subfields. It also provides guidelines as per AACR - 2 as to how to render the information in each field and subfield with examples.

### Creation and Maintenance of Authority File

INFLIBNET is suggesting libraries to use Library of Congress Subject Headings as LCSH as a standard for providing subject headings, INFLIBNET is going create and maintain the authority files of names and subject headings in the machine readable form and it will be linked with the Union Catalog and Library Automation S/w SOUL developed by INFLIBNET.

A few more standards required for the participating libraries and INFLIBNET Centre are being developed.

### Infrastructure

Well equipped laboratory with latest Pentium/RISC computers running on different operating systems like DOS, Windows 95/2000

**Development tools:** CDS/ISIS Ver. 3.08 (DOS version)

**RDBMS:** Databases were loaded on Microsoft SQL Servers on SYBASE Adaptive server.

## Database Research and Development

Creation of union databases of books, serials, theses etc has been one of the major objectives of INFLIBNET and the Database Research and development group has been setup to address the problems involved in the development, maintenance, updating of these union databases. Development of software tools for converting data from one format to another, effective retrieval and managing the databases are the major areas of work undertaken by this group. Future planned activities include research and development of retrieval software for multilingual, multimedia and full text databases. Distribution of databases through the medium of CDROM is also going to become a thrust area for database research and development group.

## Major Activities

Database design, analysis and technical support.

Assisting participating libraries in database development.

Development of utilities for database creation, conversion and maintenance in different formats like CCF and MARC 21 etc.

Development of retrieval software for CD-ROM based bibliographic Databases.

Development of Utility tools for Retrospective conversion of union catalogues.

Development of software tools for Multilingual Database of union catalogues.

Administration (routine jobs like backup, tuning and

implementation of security policies etc) of Union Database servers in the Centre.

Future areas of research and development

Further research and development in the areas of

Retrieval software for CDROM databases

Retrieval software for multilingual databases

Retrieval software for textual and non textual databases

Software for effectively managing union database systems

Retrieval software for union databases

Software for automatic backup, performance tuning

Algorithms for effective searching and sorting and compressing data.

**Infrastructure**

Well-equipped lab with latest Pentium/RISC computers running different operating systems like Windows 95/98/ 2000/XP, LINUX, HP UNIX.

Development tools: Microsoft Visual studio, SDK.

RDBMS: Microsoft ACCESS, Microsoft SQLSERVER 7.0/2000, ORACLE 8i/9i,SYBASE Adaptive Server.

**Library Automation**

The automation of university libraries is a pre-requisite for networking and resource sharing. INFLIBNET Centre, through UGC, has been providing the required support to universities in phases.

Till 1999-2000, 123 universities have been given initial grant of Rs. 6.5 lakhs each to develop infrastructure for automation. By the end of IXth plan period, rest of the universities will also be included. After installation of the systems, further financial support is provided for the first five years to take care of recurring expenditure.

These Libraries on receipt of initial grant sign a Memorandum of Understanding with INFLIBNET. An integrated software for the automation of in-house functions called SOUL has been developed. It has been well received by the University Libraries. SOUL has been installed at 15 Libraries. Many more libraries have shown desire to procure and install SOUL.

Currently libraries funded under the programme are advised to subscribe to one of the following networks, depending on the availability in the respective locations:

ERNET

VSNL

NICNET

Other ISPs

**Wide Area Network**

It is planned to setup a Wide Area Network "UGCNET" linking more than 170 universities and other academic institutes in the country.

**Local Area Network**

INFLIBNET Centre has suggested all the funded universities to set up LANs using HUB/SWITCH and CAT V cables within their libraries for successful installation of SOUL software. Since SOUL is based on client/server architecture, It is essential that the server and all other nodes be connected by LAN.

INFLIBNET Centre desires that each university should establish a LAN in it's campus linking all the departments including library. This LAN in turn will be connected to the WAN.

**E- education**

E-Education Group is concerned with the R & D and keeps

abreast with latest technological changes in the area of computer technology. This group was established sometime in August 2001 and is responsible to implement Web-Based Training (WBT) to technocrats and Professionals. Various e-learning training courses will be launched with the help of HRD group of the Centre. This group will provide the necessary tools and technologies to deliver the e-learning courses.

This group is promoting R & D activities in area of e-learning. One of the major objective of this group is to collaborate with Universities/colleges for setting / managing e-learning lab for various training/e- courses. Consultancy is provided for starting the e-learning activities and also to selecting the H/W, Software combinations etc. Guidelines and suggestions for effective and optimized use, administration, maintenance and timely starting the Web-Based Training are also can be obtained from the Group.

**Major Activities**

The Group is concerned with all the technical and non-technical issues related to e-learning in general and Web Based Training in particular.

Plan, evaluate, implementation, review of e-learning policies, models, soft wares and technology.

Setting up e-learning Lab at INFLIBNET premises. Development of retrieval software for CD-ROM based bibliographic Databases.

Exploring various options regarding e-learning.

Preparation of analysis, and minimum critical resources.

Development of various disaster scenarios and formulation of a framework for the plan coverage.

Assessment, preparation and recommendation of system requirements for e-learning set up.

Analysis of proposals from Techno-major (e-learning vendors) and recommendations for selection of the solution.

Discussions with technocrats on technical and feasibility issues.

Planning, preparation and recommendations for e-learning preparation work and infrastructure for the set up.

Preparation of road map for e-learning activities for the coming next few years.

### Further area of research and development

Implementing e-Learning at all levels at INFLIBNET.

Collaboration with subject-matter-expert from colleges/ universities for contents to be made available free to academic communities from content sever at INFLIBNET

Setting up and starting e-learning software R & D facility equipped with state-of-the art technology at the centre.

Providing consultancy and Guidance to the R & D Institutions/ universities / colleges wishing to work with INFLIBNET.

Design and Development of e-learning Model.

Knowledge Management techniques and sharing, manage knowledge with other national organizations.

Exploring technology to implementing Digital Library (DL) and Knowledge Management (KM).

### Human Resource Development

To enhance the skills of University Library staff for implementation of INFLIBNET Programme, following training courses are conducted.

### One month Training Programme

This is mainly meant for operational staff of libraries. They are given exhaustive training on application of computers to library and information services. Eighteen such programmes were held covering most of the universities, and around 350 persons have been trained.

### On-site Training

Staff from INFLIBNET Centre visited 31 universities, and conducted training for the library staff members for a week initiating automation process.

### ILMS Training

Ten Librarians from different universities spent a week at INFLIBNET to solve their problems in using ILMS.

### SOUL Training

Soul was installed at 66 Libraries and onsite training of one week to the library staff was provided at each site.

### CALIBER

It is an annual convention held every year in collaboration with a university in different region on a theme related to library automation. Nine such conventions have been held so far.

### Works Resource Sharing through Network

**Workshops :** Six workshops for senior level staff viz, University Librarians and Deputy Librarians were conducted.

### Networking of University Libraries

**Present Networking Environment :** Currently libraries funded under the programme are advised to subscribe to one of the following networks, depending on the availability in the respective locations:

ERNET

VSNL

NICNET

Other ISPs

**Wide Area Network**

It is planned to setup a Wide Area Network "UGCNET" linking more than 170 universities and other academic institutes in the country.

**Local Area Network**

INFLIBNET Centre has suggested all the funded universities to set up LANs using HUB/SWITCH and CAT V cables within their libraries for successful installation of SOUL software. Since SOUL is based on client/server architecture, It is essential that the server and all other nodes be connected by LAN.

INFLIBNET Centre desires that each university should establish a LAN in it's campus linking all the departments including library. This LAN in turn will be connected to the WAN.

**Library Management Software**

For the automation of in-house functions of participating university libraries, INFLIBNET Centre has developed a user friendly state of the art GUI based software named ' SOUL' Software for University Libraries. This is based on Client/ Server Architecture. It uses an robust RDBMS as back end tool. This works on Windows and Windows NT environment with a number of new features.

**Library Software Management**

**Utility Software :** Following utility software developed at the Centre are available to the universities on request.

To search the data from union databases (OPAC).

Catalogue card generation.

Duplicate checking of records.

Customized software for Books, Theses, Serials.

Data Conversion from Dbase, Foxpro and text file to

ISO-2709 format.

Major objective of this group is to develop software for Library automation and other supporting tools for library automation. This group is also involved in supporting all other activities of the center by providing adequate software help time to time. The mission of this group is to provide technological support to all activities of the center with software developments using latest technologies and available development tools.

## Major Activities

Development, managing and updating of Union databases is one of the major activities of this group. Eight databases have been developed and are continuously growing. Following is the list of databases:

## Development of SOUL

Incorporation of Various Bibliographic standards in SOUL Constant Update of Current version based on user requirements Trouble Shooting and Customer support for SOUL users.

## Future Plans

Development of fully web based library management system. Incorporation of Multilingual Interface (To be developed by Database R & D Group) in SOUL. Incorporation of Data Conversion Utilities (To be developed by Database R & D Group) for conversion of Various Bibliographic format including MARC and CCF in to SOUL. Development of MARC 21 based database creation tool.

## Infrastructure

Working Platforms of this group:

**Operating Systems :** Windows 95,Windows 98,Windows NT 4.0, Windows 2000

**RDBMS :** MSSQL Server 6.5,MS SQL Server 7.0, MS SQL Server 2000, Sybase 11.5,Oracle 9i

**Development Tools :** PowerBuilder 6.0, Microsoft Visual Studio 6.0,Microsoft Visual Studio. Net (beta), Oracle Internet developer suite.

### Web Development

Organization of vast information present on the Centre's website and making the website a resource gateway and a knowledge hub, to the user community is one of the main objectives of the INFLIBNET Centre. The web development group setup in promoting the access to the information in the field of research and academic pursuit by using latest web technologies is working towards in implementing this objective. The major areas of work undertaken by this group are to select, organize and present the quality resources of the Centre in a meaningful way that will be useful for the user community.

### Major Activities

INFLIBNET Site design and updating.

Promoting the website of the centre and provide a complete tracking reports of users accessing the website.

Maintenance of various web services running at the site.

Identifying the Hardware, Software requirements in improving the Centre's Infrastructure with the latest available technologies.

To install and provide support for the available software at the Centre and advice the participating libraries with regard to hardware and software requirement.

Bringing out SOUL software CD's for all the versions i.e. SOUL network version, SOUL Standalone version & SOUL Demo version.

**Future areas of development**

Setting up an Intranet for managing the internal information of the Centre.

**Infrastructure**

Well equipped with Pentium-IV systems running windows 98/2000 and Linux operating systems. The web server is hosted on a Pentium-IV system and is likely to switch over to a rack-mount machine. There is one CD writer to burn the SOUL software CD's.

This group has been created for promoting R & D activities in area of Networking and Quality management. Major responsibility of this group is to manage, maintain and timely update the campus wide Network. One of the major objective of this group is to coordinate with UGC-NETWORK, the proposed wide area network connecting all academic institutions under University Grants Commission for setting/managing data centre for various databases of INFLIBNET, Indian universities, Information Centres. This group is working progressively for implementing Total Quality Control (TQC) for in-house developed software. Training / workshop in the area of network management, security design and state-of-the-art technologies for library professionals across the country is being initiated by the group. Consultancy work in the area of networking, network security of universities/ colleges library is also going to become thrust area of this group.

**Major Activities**

LAN/WAN Setup and maintenance at INFLIBNET.

Assisting Universities/colleges for Campus LAN.

Design network security policy.

Network Traffic management.

Network resources allocation to the other groups.

System administration, configuration and tuning.

Database administration and tuning.

Disaster recovery plan for e-resources.

System maintenance at Centre.

Testing and Quality control of software developed at the centre.

Guidelines, suggestions and standards to all development groups for maintaining quality.

**Future areas of research and development**

Further research and development in the areas of upgrading Local Area Network (LAN) with FC backbone, Layer-2, Layer-3 switches.

Collaboration with UGC-NETWORK for setting / managing data centre for various databases of INFLIBNET, Indian universities and Information Centers.

Setting up network R & D and quality control Lab. equipped with state-of-the-art technology at the Centre.

Offering consultancy service to the universities / colleges for computer sing the libraries including H/W, Local Area Network (LAN).

Designing the Network security and disaster recovery plan for data servers.

Knowledge sharing with different national and international organization.

Promoting Linux operating system in universities.

Insuring implementation of different standards for software development and management.

Software testing using advanced software available in the market.

### Infrastructure

Well-equipped server lab. with P3 and P4 Servers running on Windows NT/ 2000 Advance Server. Separate mail server is running on Linux. Network is protected by firewall running on Linux. Centre has 128 kbps-leased lines Internet connectivity. Currently LAN at Centre is based on Radio Modem, CISCO 2610 router, hubs. New high End RISC server is being added to the existing infrastructure.

## 2. INFONET

Indian Universities constitute one of the largest higher education systems in the world. With 325 universities/ institutions, 15000 affiliated colleges, 100.00 lakh students and 4.27 lakh teachers; it is a great challenge to ensure effective coordination and communication.

Fast changing curricula and frequent introducing of new subjects impose a great demand on the system in general. Indian Universities need to be given the required thrust to entire the third millennium with a leading edge.

Technology is a driving force in the contemporary education systems. University Grant Commission has launched an ambitious programme to bring about a qualitative change in the academic infrastructure, especially for higher education. Under this initiative UGC is modernizing the University Campuses with State-of-the-art campus wide networks and setting up its own nationwide communication network named UGC-Infonet.

ERNET India, scientific society under the Ministry of Communications and Information Technology, in partnership with the University Grants Commission is setting up UGC-Infonet. Under this programme it is proposed to use information and communication Technology (ICT) and Internet to transform learning environment from a monodimensional one to a multi-dimensional one. UGC-Infonet will be a boon to the higher education systems in several ways:

UGC-Infonet will become a vehicle for distance learning to facilitate spread of quality education all over the country.

UGC-Infonet will be a tool to distribute education material and journals to the remotest of areas.

UGC-Infonet will be a resource for researchers and scholars for tapping the most up-to-date information.

UGC-Infonet will form a medium for collaboration among teachers and students, not only within the country but also all over the world.

UGC-Infonet will be an Intranet for University Automation.

UGC-Infonet will encompass entire University Systems for most efficient utilization of precious network resources.

UGC-Infonet will establish a channel for Globalization of Education and facilitate the universities in marketing their services and developments.

**Intranet for Universities**

Availability of Reliable and Stable network infrastructure will facilitate increased usage of computers in the University Campuses. Campus Management will be more efficient and student friendly. Interlinking of the universities will expand the reach of students and faculty to other universities providing them with better avenues for wider horizontal growth.

UGC-Infonet will establish a seamless link between the UGC and the universities. This will help to provide a more accurate and up-to-date picture of the Universities, while at the same time it will enable universities to have timely information about the various schemes of the UGC. Consequently, this will bring a qualitative change in the UGC-Universities interaction. The huge and multifaceted Indian

Education Systems would achieve greatest efficiency through e-governance of UGC.

### Technology Partnership

Information Technology is evolving at a rapid pace worldwide to cater to the need for providing information in any form, at any anywhere. The trend is to set up networks, which are device independent, thus enabling flexibility of access, and also meet the requirements arising out of codependence technologies. Regular technology inputs would be required to upgrade the network infrastructure to ensure delivery of upcoming applications and contents to the education and research community in the country. UGC and ERNET have come together to meet the challengers that may face the education community with respect to real time information.

### Implementation Methodology

The UGC-Infonet will be overlaid on ERNET Infrastructure in a manner so as to provide assured quality of service and optimal utilization of bandwidth resources. The network will be run and managed by ERNET India. The project will be funded by UGC with 100% capital investment and up to 90% of recurring costs. Towards this end, a MoU has been signed between UGC and ERNET India for implementation of UGC-Infonet and also for long-term technology partnership. A joint technical and tariff committee, consisting of leading experts in the country has also been setup to guide and monitor the design, implementation and operations of UGC-Infonet. INFLIBNET, an autonomous IUC of the UGC, would be the nodal agency for coordination of the UGC-Infonet and facilitate linkage between ERNET and the Universities. In the long run, each University will become a hub for the colleges affiliated to it.

## Network Architecture

UGC Infonet is based on open IP platform, employing state-of-the-art technologies like IP or TV, enabling on-line response to queries. Open system architecture will ensure support for current and future applications. Users from educational Institutions would enjoy high data rates while accessing Intranet and Internet resources.

**Main features of the UGC-Infonet are:**

Scaleable Architecture to grow from Universities to affiliated Colleges. Nation-wide Terrestrial Backbone using Fiber Optic links. Integrated Satellite WAN supporting broadband and SCPC VSAT technology. Comprehensive Network Management Systems for overall monitoring of the network, down to each and every device.

Linkage with other Academic and Research Networks all over the world.

Data security and virus protection using firewalls and Intrusion Detection Systems. Dedicated Data Center for Web hosting, e-Journals and Mail Boxes. Mirror sites spread all over the country for content hosting. Broadband Multimedia and Video Channels for Distance Learning.

## Data Center

A data center with large server capacity is being set up for the UGC-Infonet., Content of common interest will be maintained at this data center. Each University will have the option of hosting their website and the journals subscribed through University Consortia.

The data center will be:

dedicated for the UGC-Info Net

comprising of Email, Web, News and Proxy Servers

protected with firewalls and IDS

co-located with Satellite Hub

within single hop access to the Universities over VSAT

hosting a Portal on Higher Education in India

## Electronic Subscription of Journals

With globalization of education and competitive research, demand for journals has increased over the years. Due to insufficient funds, libraries have been force to cut subscriptions of journals.

UGC has turned towards the Internet to cover the gap between demand and supply by way of e-journals that can be subscribed online. Most of the journals are available in electronic form.

UGC is also exploring the possibilities of alliances with publishers for adapting a consortia-based approach for e-subscription of journals. These journals will be available over UGC-Infonet to all the universities. Much of the new research publications are also available on the net as free ware, thereby, making quality information accessible to a wider academic scholar base spread across the country at an affordable price.

## Connectivity Options for the Universities

UGC-Infonet is overlaid on ERNET Infrastructure including a nation wide terrestrial backbone and a complimentary satellite Wide Area Network (WAN). As such ERNET can provide a complete range of connectivity options to the universities depending upon their location and bandwidth requirements. Since terrestrial media offers greater scalability and performance, efforts will be made to connect the universities on terrestrial media. Alternately a Satellite connection will be provided through VSAT.

## Digital Leased Lines

In the localities where telecom network is well developed,

dedicated leased lines will be hired from basic telecom service providers. Such links are primarily for 64 Kbps and 2 Mbps speeds. Since fiber optic connections facilitate better connectivity, efforts will be made to bring the fiber links as near to the universities as possible. Most of the universities have the potential to become hubs of communication for affiliated colleges. Therefore, basic service providers will be locating their terminal within the university premises.

The universities, located within 30 kms of the ERNET PoPs, will be provided with dedicated radio links operating from 64 Kbps to 2 Mbps speeds. These links require line of sight clearance between the network node and the concerned university. Radio links are very reliable and their operational cost includes only maintenance of the equipment and Radio Link a nominal license fee.

**Satellite based Wide Area Network**

ERNET operates a Satellite based Wide Are Network (SATWAN) using C-Band transponder on INSAT-3C. SATWAN hub, located at Bangalore, supports Broadband VSATs with up to 45 Mbps shared bandwidth and Single Channel Per Carrier (SCPC) VSATs capable of providing up to 2 Mbps dedicated bandwidth.

**Broadband VSAT**

Most of the remote universities will be served using Broadband VSATs. These VSATs operate in a shared bandwidth mode for optimal utilization of the precious satellite resources. Since Internet traffic is asymmetric in nature Broadband VSATs are optimized to receive high bandwidth (shared beam of up to 45 Mbps) and relatively smaller capacity for outgoing traffic (shared channel of up to 307 Kbps) from a University.

## SCPC VSATs

Single channel Per Carrier (SCPC) VSATs will be used for establishing dedicated tow-way channels of 64 Kbps to 2 Mbps from Hub. SCPC VSATs are ideal for those universities which are located in remote areas but wish top host their own internet server for providing access to their information through internet all over the world.

## Campus LANs at Universities

Infrastructure at the University campus is also critical to take full advantage of the UGC-Infonet. Campus LAN technology is evolving rapidly and many universities may not have the expertise to setup the most modern and cost effective LANs. ERNET India has participated with many institutions in the planning and implementation of their campus computing facilities. The expertise generated thus will be extended to the Universities so that every university can have a state of the art infrastructure.

## Network Access Center

For maximum benefits of UGC-Infonet, Universities should preferably set up a campus wide network and ensure uniform access all over the campus. Wherever campus LAN is not in place, it is suggested that the university sets up a network access center, which is open to all students at the university. This will work on lines similar to the terminal in traditional computer centers.

## Network-Trained Manpower

Trained manpower is one of the most critical resources for successful implementation of high-tech programmes like UGC-Infonet. ERNET India has setup a modern training laboratory to train network system managers and users of UGC-Infonet. Technical staff from each of the participating universities will be trained to take maximum advantage of the infrastructure.

### University Grants Commission

The University Grants Commission (UGC) is a statutory organization established by an act of Parliament. This is a national body for the coordination, determination and maintenance of standards of University education. The UGC serves as a vital link between the Union and State Governments and the institutions of higher training. In addition to its role of giving grants to universities and colleges, the UGC also advises Central and State Governments on the measures necessary for the improvement of university education. It also frames regulations on various issues like the minimum standards of instruction and minimum qualifications of teachers, on the advice of subject specialists and academicians with whom it frequently interacts in connection with the formulation, monitoring, and evaluation of programmes.

294 Universities/institutions in the country are directly under the preview of UGC. The universities are uniformly spread all over the country from metropolitan cities to very remote areas.

Implementation and operation of UGC-Infonet will be coordinated by INFLIBENT, an autonomous Inter-University Center of the University Grants Commission of India. INFLIBENT is providing a variety of services to the academic community of the country and is helping libraries in their automation efforts. About 142 University libraries are on the way to computerization.

## 3. DEVELOPING LIBRARY NETWORK (DELNET)

Delnet started as a network of libraries in Delhi in 1988 and was named as Delhi Library Network. It is the first operational library network in India. It was initiated as a project of the India International Centre with the financial and technical assistance by National Information System for Science and Technology (NISSAT), Department of Scientific and Industrial Research, Govt. of India. It was registered as a society in June 1992 under the Societies Registration Act of 1860 and is currently being promoted by the National Informatics Centre (NIC), Planning Commission, Govt. of India and India International Centre, New Delhi.

Delhi is growing as a major centre of information resources in India. These resources cater both to the specialized and the general users. They are located in activities, information and documentation centres, institutional libraries, research libraries, government libraries, public libraries, department libraries besides the libraries of the universities, colleges and schools.

During the recent years, increase in information has led to increase in the demands of the users. It has been noticed that in this area of information explosion, libraries in India are generally ill-equipped to handle and retrieve information effectively, the financial resources and the space requirement for housing library collection are limited in almost all of the libraries. No a single library can afford to house every necessary document even in the area of its interest. Resource sharing, thus assumes great importance at this juncture the option left with the forward looking librarians has been to promote the sharing of resources by automation and networking. With this objective, in January 1988, the India International Centre initiated efforts for the establishment of Delhi Library Network (Now Developing Library Network).

The following are DELNET's main objectives:

* to promote sharing of resources among the libraries by

developing a network of libraries, by collecting, storing and disseminating information and by offering computerized services to the users.

- to offer guidance to the member libraries on cataloguing database services, circulation, acquisition, serials control, online services, selection of hardware and software, etc.
- to coordinate efforts for suitable collection development and reduce unnecessary duplication wherever possible.
- to establish a referral centre, to monitor and/or facilitate catalogue search and maintain a central online union catalogue of books, serials, and non-book materials of all the participating libraries.
- to facilitate and promote delivery of documents manually and mechanically.
- to develop specialist bibliographic database of books, serials and non-book materials.
- to develop a database of projects, specialists and institutions.
- to possess and maintain electronic and mechanical equipment for fast communication of information and delivery of electronic mail.
- to coordinate with other regional, national and international networks for exchange of information and documents.
- to undertake facilitate and provide for the publication of newsletters/journals devoted to networking and sharing of resources.

**Membership**

At present, DELNET has Two Hundred and Forty Three libraries as its members, including both institutional and associate-institutional members: in India 235 and outside India 8.

**Fees Details :** Following are the fees details for its members

*Admission Fee* : Rs.5,000

*Institutional membership* : Rs.7500/- per year (For libraries with 10,000 or more book collection)

*Associate institutional membership* : Rs.10,000/- per year (For libraries with less than 10,000 books)

*Overseas Institutions* : Admission fee : US $100/-

*Annual Membership fee* : US $500/-

The membership is progressively increasing and includes universities, diplomatic missions, college, government department, institutions and public libraries. Some institutions from far off places like Shimla, Bhopal, Punjab, Andhra Pradesh, Lucknow and Pondicherry in India have also joined DELNET as members. DELNET's membership has increased from 103 in Feb'99 to 243 to date (August, 2001).

### DELNET Activities/Services

**1. Promotion of Database Creation :** For effective networking, standard bibliographic data should be available in machine readable form with the libraries. So, efforts were made from the very beginning to promote the standardization of databases in the DELNET libraries. Experts were sent to the libraries to solves day-to-day problems. A panel of experts was seeing maintained for this purpose. Regular meetings of the librarians and computer specialists were organized to discuss mutual problems and the areas of cooperation. Nevertheless, there have been some libraries in Delhi that took keen interest in database creation on their own. But the practice of regular meetings for database creation and resource sharing continue. DELNET provides technical assistance to member libraries in the following areas:

* creation and maintenance of bibliographic databases
* serials controls
* user services
* hardware and software requirements
* union catalogue preparation
* current awareness and SDI services
* authority data compilation
* subject profiles construction
* abstracting services
* inter-library loan and user services
* document transfer/copying facilities
* access to local, national and international databases

**2. Resource Sharing :** DELNET saved foreign exchange worth Rs. 10 million by rationalizing subscriptions to foreign periodicals during 1991, 1992 and 1993 through resource sharing. This was mainly achieved in the fields of physical science, medical science and agricultural sciences. It is hoped that in the years to come, DELNET would be able to save more foreign exchange for India through sharing of periodical resources. In 1991, a courier service was started on contract basis will a private agency for inter library lending among the participating libraries but it was not very effective. Later, DELNET has introduced its own courier service with the financial help of NIC. The service is well used.

**3. Standardization :** A standardization committee of DELNET has been meeting from time to time. The standardization committee takes into account the following areas:

* Communication format for interchanging bibliographic data
* Input output format

* Bibliographic description : Mandatory and optional data elements
* Classification scheme and subject headings
* Thesaurus
* Authority files
* Language scripts into roman script
* Forms of heading
* Identification numbers, codes and abbreviations
* Data input for abstracting and indexing
* Search/command language

It was noticed that colon classification, universal Decimal classification and Dewey Decimal classification were mostly used in Indian libraries and therefore, it would be almost impossible to impose a standard classification scheme on all libraries. It was decided to use Dewey Class Number. As searching by class numbers was done by very few librarians, it was decided that the participating libraries could search by the classification numbers or they could pass on such requests to DELNET central office for necessary action. With regard to the standardization of subject headings and to usage DELNET recommends the use of LCSM. Specialized libraries may use additional thesauri that are available in each major discipline such as social sciences, humanities and science and technology.

**3. Online databases :** DELNET has around twenty databases available online for its users. These are:

* Union Catalogue of Books : UCF
* Union Catalogue of Books : MARC Format
* Union List of Current Periodicals
* Union Catalogue of Periodicals
* Database of Periodic Articles
* Indian Specialists Database

- ★ CD-ROM database
- ★ Union list of Video recordings
- ★ Union List of Sound Recordings
- ★ Union List of Newspapers
- ★ Union List of Serials of Management Libraries
- ★ Union Catalogue of Hindi Books
- ★ Multilingual Books : Sample database
- ★ Urdu Manuscripts Database
- ★ Database of Theses and Dissertations
- ★ DEVINSA Database
- ★ Serials : Petroleum and Natural Gas
- ★ Books in-Print Database
- ★ Jain Database
- ★ Directory of Libraries

## The Other Services

### *ILL Online*

DELNET members can place their inter-library loan requests through our ILL online facility, which is available on the union catalogue of books database. The member requests appear on the main server, which are monitored by DELNET staff at regular intervals and the books are acquired and supplied to the requesting library through the courier. Photocopying charges for journal articles etc. and courier charges for sending books to member libraries outside Delhi are extra.

### *DEL-LISTSERV*

DELNET has created a Listserv service called DEL-LISTSERV to provide the current awareness service to users and allow the member libraries to receive the latest daily information from the INTERNET automatically in the form of electronic mail. The following listservs have been created and are available online through DELNET:

*Net-happenings* : This Listserv appraises the users about the latest new sites along with their web addresses on the INTERNET and has proved to be a major source of information for the users on the INTERNET.

*Med-clips* : This medical clippings listing discusses the various topics of medical interest like AIDI, cancer, etc. and is informative in nature.

*IFLA* : This Listserv allows the users to get the latest information from the International Federation of Library Associations and Institutions, which includes the issues of concern to library and information professionals.

*LIBJOBS* : Through this Listserv, the library professionals are able to find out daily, the jobs/vacancies available throughout the world.

**Book : New Arrivals**

This is a new service through internet giving a list of recent publications in all subjects. The service covers education, management and physical sciences. Other subjects can be introduced on demand.

**Book Reviews from INTERNET**

This is an INTERNET service of reviews of latest published books covering different subjects. The service covers in the field of Arts and Music, INTERNET and military history. From time to time, other subjects will come into this fold.

**Current Contents**

This service gives the current contents of the latest issues of journals. It is particularly useful for rationalization of periodicals and resources sharing in member libraries.

**Index to Hindu**

DELNET has started offering Index to Hindu online to its members. Indexed news items are available on the system covering different periods of the Chennai edition. More updates and archival data is being added into the system regularly.

### Retro-Conversion

DELNET offers retro conversion facilities to the libraries through specialized agencies and also facilitates the use of modern tools such as CO-ROM's and online facilities for retro-conversion.

### Referral Services

DELNET maintains a referral centre that provides reference facilities to participating libraries. The referral centre also looks after the access to the central databases and monitors access to international databases.

### Document Transfer/Copy facilities

DELNET provides the facility for transferring or copying of the documents to its users.

### Training Programmes

DELNET conducts training programmes in the use of DELNET services, software, E-mail, AACR II and LC subject headings, Internet, etc. from time to time. Information about future training programmes is available on request.

### Lectures and Workshops

DELNET organizes lectures by networking specialists working in different parts of the world. The lectures are open to members, specialists and users in general. DELNET also organizes national workshops, seminars and meets on library networking from time to time. DELNET had organized National Annual convention on Library and Information Networking (NACLIN) in 1998 & 1999.

### Newsletter

DELNET publishes a newsletter in order to spread the message and increase the awareness about library networking in India. Through this Newsletter, DELNET communicates to its members the progress, it is making in various fields. The Newsletter is also a forum for communication on the advances, achievements and needs of the libraries and their services.

## 6. INTERNET

**Electronic Mail :** DELNET provides RENNIC Email facility to its member libraries, which is introduced by National Informatics Centre. This gives them access to both national and international E-mail users and also to INTERNET users. DELNET Email reaches the libraries, institutions and individuals in India as well as abroad having E-mail connection. Email is being used not only for communication between institutions but also for inter-library-loan requests.

Subscription rates for E-mails are as follows:

*RENNIC of NIC* : Rs. 2750/- per year for 5 MB data transfer

### Full INTERNET (TCP/IP) connectivity

DELNET is providing full INTERNET SLIP/PPP dial up access at a concessional rate of Rs. 8,500/- per annum for Rs. 500 hours of connect time through NIC to the member libraries. Also the shell account facility for INTERNET access is available for Rs.4,000 per annum for 500 hrs of connect time. A number of DELNET member libraries are already availing these facilities. These rates are subject to change by NIC.

### Web Page

DELNET has a web page (http://www.delnet.nic.in/) on INTERNET. This enables all INTERNET users the world over to know about DELNET and its activities. The web page also includes a list of Member-libraries along with their E-mail addresses. The Web page is being updated from time to time.

### 7. Products

**DELSIS :** A major breakthrough has been achieved by DELNET with the launch of DELSIS, a powerful library networking software. DELSIS (DELNET System for Information Services) is an integrated modular system, which supports DELNET online databases.

It has been developed by DELNET on a Relational Database management System called BASIC plus, a product of Information Dimension Inc. of USA, which has been provided to DELNET courtesy National Informatics Centre, New Delhi. It handles not only the Online Public Access Catalogue (OPAC) but also has the administrative tools for building up the union catalogues on BASISplus. It provides powerful and extensive facilities for online enquiries for books, serials, biographical details about the specialists and supports the cataloguing of books in Indian languages.

### Features of DELSIS

- ★ DELSIS is a user friendly menu driven package
- ★ Its versatile options allow the users to retrieve the information quickly.
- ★ It contains the modules for Online Public Access Catalogue as well as the modules for the creation of databases e.g. addition, deletion, inserting of records etc.
- ★ The Online Public Access Catalogue (OPAC) components of DELSIS can meet the needs of the users, irrespective of whether the user has little computer experience or is familiar with using computers to perform various library tasks.

## DEL-WINDOWS

DELNET has released the DEL-WINDOWS version 1.0 after the successful creation and implementation of DELSIS Unix version. It is an efficient tool for creating and retrieving bibliographic databases and catalogues.

DEL-WINDOWS can convert the simple PC into a powerful management information system. Some of the salient features are:

* It is simple and easy to use. The novice library professionals and end users can interact with the software without any prior training.
* It is user-friendly with adequate windows-menus for data inputting and search capabilities.
* It provides the option for creating the bibliographic records either using ECF or the MARC format.

## DELSEARCH

DELNET has opened a new chapter in the information retrieval procedure by devising a new database access mechanism through DELSEARCH. It is an off-line remote database access system through E-mail. It is the first of its kind and is the most economical and user-friendly remote database access system. It helps institutions, information specialists, research scholars, librarians and users interested in bibliographies and tutorial information on South Asia. It allows them to search the DELNET union catalogues through E-mail and is a great tool for research scholars. The software is developed on UNIX platform and allows the users to send their search requests through E-mail. As soon as the query is received by the system in the form of an E-mail, the respective databases are searched for the query word and the results are returned to the addressee immediately. The searching of the database does not require any human intervention and the searches are done by the system automatically.

### The Future of DELNET

The future of DELNET is very promising. Its membership with India and outside India is going to take a quantum jump. The DELNET databases are growing in number and size and as a variety of information on South Asia is becoming available through DELNET, it is expected that all institutions outside India specializing in South Asian studies to take DELNET membership. DELNET databases are going to be accessible through INTERNET which will made accessibility very fast. INTERNET users in India are increasing and it will increase DELNET presence in different parts of India. DELNET has already created software, viz. DELDOS and DEL-WINDOWS for creating MARC records.

These software will so on be developed to perform library operations as well. There developments are likely to give more revenue to DELNET and provide justification for more and more libraries to join DELNET. As a resource, it is hoped the DELNET will grow faster as a service based resource sharing model in India.

## 4. CALCUTTA LIBRARY NETWORK (CALIBNET)

It was the first library network visualized and started by NISSAT. At a meeting in 1986 in Calcutta, DSIR initiated action for preparation of a feasibility study for networking about 40 libraries in Calcutta. CALIBNET now is a society under West Bengal Societies Registration Act 1961 and responsible for Calcutta Library Network, a project sponsored and supported by NISSAT. NISSAT also contributed to the development of MAITRAYEE software package based on INGRESS 5.2 for CALIBNET. This package was developed through CMC Ltd. And given to CALIBNET. So far, no data has been created in machine readable from using MAITRAYEE. At present, CALIBNET has become a centre for CD-ROM databases.

**Objective s**

CALIBNET has made significant studies towards fulfilling its dual objectives:

Launching its library network programs, facilitating remote online access to the holding data of Calcutta libraries and other specialized databases as well – a significant step towards bibliographic resource sharing amongst Calcutta libraries; and

Providing electronic access to globally available information, imbibing its information centre approach.

Both are essential for advanced learning and scholarship. In the process, CALIBNET aims at covering a wide panorama of information end-user interests, with diffusion of new electronic information technology as the primary concern.

Software Developed and Library Network Launched:

Intense in-house research and development efforts have now achieved the Library Network capability by three significant studies:

A multi-user storage and retrieval software **'SANJUKTA'** to support CALIBNET's centralized Database (CDB) and to provide online access to its from remote locations.

A conversion software package 'PARAPAR' to support interchange of bibliographic data between USMARC, UNIMARC and CCF files and also from non-standard formats to standard ones.

Evaluation of a centralized Database (CDB) of holdings data of Calcutta libraries, and specialized databases as well.

These apart, CALIBNET'S pioneering study and research led to its publication of the "Guidelines for

Implementation of UNIMARC in Indian Libraries". This will be an invaluable aid for the national database development programme under consideration, that favors adoption of UNIMARC format.

With the support of SANJUKTA, the centralized database hosted on CALIBNET server and located at the Network Service Centre, can be accessed and searched online by any one from a remote location, provided one is equipped with a computer, a telephone, a modem and a password from CALIBNET. The efficacy of SANJUKTA has been tested by successful remote logging of the CALIBNET server at Jadavpur, hosting the CDB from a workshop venue at Great Eastern Hotel, Calcutta. Online access to the locational information of bibliographic resources via the CDB and sharing up such resources amongst the libraries of this metropolis is now a reality.

The capability of PARAPAR was established through exercises and tests on sample records furnished by a major library in New Delhi and conducted in-house at Calcutta at their instance and eventually demonstrated at a workshop-cum-meeting in New Delhi.

## The Centralized Database

Since library network capability has been established, the most crucial and indispensable activity is to develop the basic resource – the Centralized Database (CDB), that constitute the very backbone of any library network – by inputting the holding data of Calcutta libraries. The centralized database, launched only recently, currently held around 30,000 record covering:-

* conference documents held by Calcutta and contiguous libraries.
* social science management and economics, behavioral sciences, quantitative methods, computer science, etc.

including predominantly journals held by management libraries in South Asia libraries of Indian Statistical Institute and the Indian Institute of management, Calcutta and

★ Index to contents of serials published by Asiatic Society in previous two centuries.

**Library Network**

The Centralized Database (CDB) is the bedrock of CALIBNET and its development essentially calls for a cooperative movement, whereby each library par rakes in the movement by contributing its own holdings data to be incorporated in the CDB and thereby enrich it. The CDB needs to be now augmented by inputting holdings data of as many libraries as possible and getting the data continuously updated. Optimum coverage of libraries, which alone will progressively transform the CDB into a truly resourceful online searchable central pool of Calcutta's bibliographic holding data, is now on with the cooperation of libraries.

**The participating libraries**

The responses from institutional libraries are very encouraging. The libraries of following institutions have extended co-operation by way of furnishing their respective machine-readable database and current journal subscription lists:

Calcutta University
Jadavpur University
Indian Statistical Institute
Indian Institute of Management
Central Research Institute for Jute and Allied Fibres
Anthropological Survey of India
Botanical Survey of India

Geological Survey of India

Zoological Survey of India

Bengal Engineering College ( a deemed university)

National Atlas and Thematic Mapping Organization

Bose Institute

University College of Medicine (Calcutta University)

These are being now inputted into the CDB. In coming years, holding data of many more libraries are expected to go into the CDB. Priority is being accorded to holding data relating to current journals subscribed and new additions from January 1, 1999.

## Electronic Access to Global Information

In addition with its library network programme, CALIBNET has added to itself under to information centre approach, a new dimension that of a purveyor of global information, a phenomenon that now pervades international information market.

With online access to Internet and in-house CD-ROM resources, CALIBNET can explore a wide spectrum of the knowledge base and cooperate and professional enterprises, and meet the information requirements of researchers, academics and other scholars, professional and any other practitioners engaged in a wide gamut of subject interest.

## CALIBNET

### *Services Activities*

(i) *On-demand Information services*

CALIBNET has several attractive information packages:

**Confile Service** : CALIBNET's Confile service reaches at one's desk contents of any journal of one's choice out of over 20,000 high-impact journals. Libraries can now prune their journal subscription list or even forego subscribing to new ones, when budgetary constraints so demand, and still get expressed to their contents from ConFile. ConFile helps libraries in economizing on journal subscription and reducing the drain on precious foreign exchange resources.

*Caliborder* : On demand, caliborder offers the requisite back-up service by way of delivery of full text of any article and even patents.

*ConAlert* : Through ConAlert service CALIBNET gives current and tailored bibliographic information. One can leave with CALIBNET just keywords defining his subject interest and get at regular intervals, the current information related to his interest at his desk.

*RetroFile* : This service offers latest status and trend of research on any specific topic.

ConFile, ConAlert and RetroFile, in combination, offers the latest information and advances in the entire spectrum of the subject interest.

(ii) *CALIBLINK*

A special feature of CALIBNET is the Caliblink, a email connectivity (from its ERNET hub) installed and working fine at four institutions.

(iii) *Institutional Resources Development Services*

Some of the key institutional resources development services offered are:

(a) Retrospective conversion of existing card catalogue in libraries into computerized local databases via electronic mode by down loading from international databases;
(b) Consultative services on LIS automation
(c) Manpower development for operating and manning automated LIS environment through a wide range of graded training programmes, and customized courses for individuals or group at client's site.

(iv) *SANJUKTA & PARAPAR Software*

**SANJUKTA :** A multi-user storage and retrieval software has been developed in-house to support CALIBNET's Centralized Database and to provide online access from remote locations. SANJUKTA has been designed and implemented by A Mukhopadhyay, Technical Consultant, CALIBNET and his associates based on MOD+, a software he developed earlier to support management of small/medium-size libraries. The software has been developed, using 4 GL Code and designed to provide the user with options and flexibility in generating records, organizing and searching information viewing the search outputs, and interchanging data files with external databases with least manual interference.

**PARAPAR :** A conversion software package, PARAPAR has been developed in CALIBNET to support interchange of bibliographic data between USMARC, UNIMARC and CCF Files and also from non-standard formats to standard ones. Its primary objective is to convert data files, received from the participating libraries in variant formats, into a ISO-2709 compliant implementation through which the files are merged into the centralized Database of CALIBNET.

(v) *Guidelines for Implementation of UNIMARC*

It has been brought out by CALIBNET to provide the library professionals in India with a working tool for developing their databases in a mutually exchangeable format. The document has been prepared in 1994, based on UNIMARC Manual (1987), by A Mukhopadhyay, Technical Consultant, under a project sponsored by the National Information System for Science and Technology (NISSAT), Department of Scientific and Industrial Research, Government of India. The guidelines have made an attempt to take care of the special requirements of the Indian libraries. They are expected to serve the Indian libraries in upgrading their databases to the international standard.

## Immediate Focus

### *(i) Indian Resources Database*

Development of Indian Resources Database on historical value covering manuscripts and rare books, and personal collections, has already been initiated with porting on the CDB and index to serials published by Asiatic Society during the last two countries.

### *(ii) CALIBNET on INTERNET*

The design of CALIBNET web page is complete and is available on the Net . The web page(http://www.calibnet.org/) facilitates access to bibliographic information resources available through hosting of CALIBNET's centralized database. The CALIBNET web site provides:

Active link to access

Indian Library and Network Resources

Overseas Library Resources on India, including rare documents, printed and manuscripts.

Worldwide Library Catalogues

National Libraries of the world

Newspapers and journals

Electronic Reference tools

Factual Information sources

Book Trade Databases

## Varied CALIBNET programs for

On-demand Information services

Electronic-mail connections

Consultative services for Library Automation

Manpower Development

R&D in IT Application

## 5. AGRICULTURAL RESOURCES INFORMATION SYSTEM (AGRIS)

The Agricultural Resources Information System (AgRIS) is the Central Sector Scheme for promoting Agricultural Information System in India. It is an e-Government Programme for fostering agricultural growth, poverty reduction and sustainable resource use in the country at grassroots level and also a step towards establishing a location-specific e-Government model for the Poor. AgRIS is aimed to facilitate development of typology specific agriculture development plan in the country. This Project is being executed by Agricultural Informatics Division of National Informatics Centre.

Agriculture is very crucial to the country's economy. The economic and industrial growths are dependent on production and productivity in agriculture. Agriculture has undergone several fundamental changes during the 20th century. Agriculture has become competitive under the new economic order with decreasing subsidies. Existing knowledge on socio-economic, geomorphologic (farm location, drainage and slope) and biophysical (soil samples) determinants to agricultural productivity needs to be enhanced. The locus of agricultural growth has since been shifted from "production" front to "processing and marketing" front.

India is a vast country with a variety of landforms, climate, geology, physiography, and vegetation. It is endowed with regional diversities for its uneven "economic and agricultural" development. The existence or absence of favourable natural resources can facilitate or retard the process of economic development. Developing countries, embarking on programmes of economic development, usually have to begin with and concentrate on the development of locally available natural resources as an initial condition, for lifting local levels of living and purchasing power, for obtaining foreign exchange with which to purchase capital equipment, and for setting in motion the development process.

Land is an indispensable resource for the most essential human activities: it provides the basis for agriculture and forest production, water catchments, recreation, and settlement. The characterization of land resources includes components of climate, soils, landform, and present land cover. Adequate agricultural exploitation of the climatic potentials and maintenance of land productivity largely depend on soil fertility and the management of soils on an ecologically sustained basis. The composition of soil associations is described in terms of percentage occurrence of soil units, soil phases and textures. The digital soil information constitutes part of the land resources database and is kept together with other geographic information (i.e., elevation, terrain slopes, distance to coast, protected areas, land cover, and administrative divisions).

The search for socially desirable, technologically appropriate, economically viable, and ecologically sound pattern of resource use and ways of life, to promote sustainable development, has been going on, ever since its most popular exposition in the well-known Brundtland Report entitled "Our Common Future" in 1987. Sustainable Development is the management and conservation of the Natural Resources Base and the orientation of technological and institutional change in such a manner as to ensure the attainment and continued satisfaction of human needs for the present and future generations.

According to Food & Agriculture Organisation (FAO)'s definition, such sustainable development (in the agriculture, forestry and fisheries sectors) conserves Land, Water, Genetic (plant, fish & animal) Resources, and is environmentally non-degrading, technologically appropriate, economically viable and socially acceptable. The Agenda-21 recommends major adjustments in agricultural, environmental and macro-economic policy to create conditions for Sustainable Agriculture and Rural Development, and its recommendations on "Information for decision making" were as follows: -

- Development of indicators for sustainable development,
- Promotion of global use of indicators for sustainable development,
- Improvement of data collection and use,
- Improvement of methods of data assessment and analysis,
- Establishment of comprehensive information framework,
- Strengthening of capacity for traditional information,
- Production of information usable for decision making,
- Development of documentation about information,
- Establishment of standards and methods for handling information,
- Establishment and strengthening of electronics networking capabilities, and
- Making use of commercial information sources.

Agricultural Resources, inter alia, includes Soil resources, Water resources, Livestock resources, Plant resources, Fisheries resources, Forest resources, Climate, Rainfall, Human resources, Capital resources, Fodder resources, Institutional resources, Land owners data, Environment data, Socio-economic and Infrastructure data, and Production inputs resources. Agricultural resources are assessed on the basis of existing agricultural resources and the existing policies. The agricultural sector workforce is large and diverse. Agricultural resources, governance and ecology are inseparable.

The scientific management of Agricultural Resources thus becomes a very important part of modern agricultural production in the 21st Century and is a new direction in the domain of agricultural engineering. Agriculture is highly dynamic in nature, because of the changing phenomenon of agricultural crops, which is further complicated by the interaction of crops with environment. Precision farming is one of the most scientific and modern approaches to sustainable agriculture that is gaining momentum in the new millenium. This approach serves the dual purpose of enhancing productivity and reducing ecological degradation, as it deals with the question of where and when. Farmers, Land and Natural Resources have intrinsic and dynamic relationship. Resources Application and Agronomic Practices are to match with soil attributes and crop requirements, as they vary across a site.

The Report of the Committee on "Natural Resources Information System (NRIS) - Linkage and Networking Project", constituted by the Department of Space in early 1990s, envisaged about 435 district level NRIS nodes in conjunction with DISNIC nodes of NIC, 26 state level NRIS nodes, 182 NRIS Project nodes (7 Themes and 26 States), and 42 NRIS Regional nodes (7 themes and 6 regions). Development of "Natural Resources Information System (NRIS) - Linkage and Networking Project" was initiated by NIC in its pilot project districts (Aligarh and Bhulandshar Districts in the State of Uttar Pradesh) in early 1990s.

The Department of Land Resources (DLR) of the Ministry of Rural Development, through its land resources development programmes, and the Department of Agriculture & Cooperation (DAC) of the Ministry of Agriculture, through its NWDPRA Projects, have been involved in the implementation / development of Natural Resources Information System (NRIS) to strengthen their schemes through their various implementing agencies. The existing data available from surveys / reports: Soil survey, Geological survey, Forest inventories, Hydro-meteorological studies, Aerial photographs and Contour maps, Ownership data and infrastructure information, Rainfall and stream flow data, Land use details, and Development plans, facilitate strengthening the necessary natural resources databases.

The Nagpur Declaration of the 21st Indian Geography Congress (2000) on "Natural Resources Planning and Management for Sustainable Development" suggested "systems approach to development" and also recommended that developing natural resources database in each state should be the first and foremost requirement for scientific land and water use planning and management and the National Informatics Centre (NIC) can be the nodal point for disseminating credible databases on natural resources down to the district level. In doing so, NIC should collaborate and network with academic institutions, agricultural universities, research institutes of ICAR, Central and State Government Agencies. According to Professor G.B.Singh (2000) , the future agricultural growth might come from:

- ★ New technologies which are not only "cost effective" but also "in conformity" with natural climatic regime of the country;
- ★ Technologies relevant to rain-fed areas specifically;
- ★ Continued genetic improvements for better seeds and yields;
- ★ Data improvements for better research, better results, and sustainable planning;
- ★ Bridging the gap between knowledge and practice; and

★ Judicious land use resource surveys, efficient management practices and sustainable use of natural resources.

A farmer is a born-GIS specialist with so many layers of information. He sees his field, as a "spatial entity", plans according to land capability and crop suitability to the extent possible, understands the weather situation, networks with financial institutions etc. But he does have "Information Access" problem to his disadvantage. The need of the hour is to use the "Digital Opportunities" which has emerged as a powerful force for fostering Agricultural Growth, Poverty Reduction and Sustainable Resources use. Such environment can be created through the following ways: -

(a) Utilise Information and Communications Technologies (ICTs) to advance the needs of Agricultural Planning and Management.

(b) Increase farmer's production through enhanced yields and more hectares planted.

(c) Help farmers maximize profits by buying inputs cheaply and efficiently and then marketing product at best prices.

(d) Focus on ICTs for farmers but with support needs of Researchers, Industry, Students and Extension.

(e) Develop digitized interactive "Commodity Handbook" (i.e. a web site) for farmers, to provide value-added features (in the form of digital library, decision aids and databases) such as:

★ Expert FAQ's / Ask the Expert

★ Recent research findings

★ Market prices and projections

★ Present and projected conditions for climate and pests

★ Sources of inputs such as fertilizer, micro-nutrients & seed

- ⋆ DSS on variety selection, timely planting, optimum plant stand, and financial management
- ⋆ Databases on soil types, seed varieties, climate history, key pests and diseases
- ⋆ Practical decision trees guiding planting, crop rotation, soil treatments. Pest identification and management, harvesting, marketing
- ⋆ Guidelines for harvesting and threshing of seeds and on-farm drying facilities for storage of seed grain
- ⋆ Fact sheets on integrated nutrient management (organic residues, balanced nutrition, sulphur, bio-fertilisers, native soil nutrients, fertilisers, micronutrients)
- ⋆ Fact sheets on herbicide selection and tolerance
- ⋆ Fact sheets on land treatment (Furrow, ridges, beds)
- ⋆ Fact sheets on low cost farm machinery and proper use

(f) Utilize e-mail and other electronic messaging options to deliver timely information during the growing season:

- ⋆ Scouting reports to warn of probable climate conditions (especially monsoons), diseases and pests
- ⋆ Success and failure stories from previous season
- ⋆ Information and mechanics of provincial and government subsidies

(g) Develop a special web site for researchers providing "knowledge-base": -

- ⋆ Digital library of research abstracts, full text articles when possible, bibliographies
- ⋆ Database of hybrid varieties suitable for local conditions and with desired qualities such as amino acids and iso-flaviones

- ★ Quality seed issues - Other Distinguishable Varieties (ODV), undersize, rapid loss of germination and loss of vigour, Seed replacement, Alternative seed supply systems, seed production and storage, good germination,

(h) Develop a "researcher communication system" allowing exchange on all facets of research: -

- ★ Seed Exchange
- ★ Timely communications on research developments and seasonal pest, disease and climate conditions (ideally functions as a rapid response network)
- ★ Support researchers interaction with farmers on participatory on-farm trials

(i) Develop a special web site addressing needs of the Agro Industry and Agri industry.

(j) Utilize web sites, e-mail and other technologies to help market agricultural produces and products to the general public: -

- ★ Work with marketing experts to develop prototype marketing campaign targeting likely demographic groups
- ★ Develop liaisons with food distributors and supermarkets to carry and promote products

(k) Utilize web sites, e-mail and other technologies to help train Govt. Extension staff to help farmers run profitable operations.

(l) Work with Government to make available data on Climate, Weather, Soil and other kinds of existing public domain information.

(m) Train the trainers for effective management of weeds, insects and diseases.

As an enabling technology, Information Technology (IT) plays an important role in the rapid economic growth and social transformation in rural areas. It is therefore to establish an effective channel of communication between policy makers, government agencies, academic and research institutions and persons concerned with the complex role of agriculture in society, particularly developments in the field of agricultural resources.

Despite 50 years of development planning, rainfed agriculture continues to be the largest and the most important segment of crop production in India. The Department of Agriculture and Cooperation (DAC) is responsible for formulation and implementation of national policies and programmes to achieve sustainable agricultural growth through "optimum utilisation" of agricultural resources. The efficient use of available resources to maximise production and productivity requires comprehensive and reliable information on various facets of agriculture (Figure-1 & Figure-2). Issues depicted in these two figures will certainly be addressed and be the guiding spirit of the Project.

During the Tenth Plan, the Department has planned to (i) initiate pilot projects on "Agricultural Resources information System (AgRIS) in districts in order to work out the cost and efficiency of this project and then expand to the entire country; (ii) develop a comprehensive database on various parameters related to land use, inputs (seeds, fertiliser, agricultural technology, agricultural credit) use, and water use; (iii) development of decision support systems (DSSs) packages for strengthening advisory services to farmers, and (iv) capacity building through Human Resources Development.

In view of this, the AgRIS Project aims at, among the others, mainly the development and deployment of the following DSSs and customised to the chosen district typology for pilot project: -

* Crop Suitability based on factor endowment;
* Land Suitability Assessment;
* Land Productivity Assessment;
* Population Supporting Capacity;
* Land Evaluation and Land Use Planning;
* Land Degradation Risk Assessment;
* Quantification of Land Resources Constraints;
* Land Management;
* Agro-ecological Characterization for Research and Planning;
* Agricultural Technology Transfer;
* Agricultural Inputs Recommendations;
* Farming Systems Analysis and Development;
* Environmental Impact Assessment;
* Monitoring of Land Resources Development.
* Livestock (cattle, buffalo, goat, & sheep) Farming Systems
* Water allocation in an irrigation system
* Fodder Resources Development
* Water Bodies (Basin) planning systems using Watershed and Agro-Eco Region Planning Concepts

In the Pilot districts, the AgRIS Project is expected to emerge as the richest "agricultural resources information system" covering all aspects of agricultural, natural resource, and food systems, to:

* Enable farmers to locate needed information to improve yields,
* Plan for weather contingencies,
* Access research,

- ⋆ Calculate treatments and runoff,
- ⋆ Simulate the growing season,
- ⋆ Visualize precision data,
- ⋆ Manage finances,
- ⋆ Buy inputs and sell outputs, and
- ⋆ Monitor prices in local as well as world markets.

Agricultural planning and development require (a) knowledge about recent progress in agriculture, (b) the existing situation (especially the main problems impeding development), and (c) the potentialities for achieving agricultural objectives. This information is needed for re-assessing current investment and other development activities as well as for planning new measures, setting benchmarks against which to monitor progress. Proper analysis of the agricultural sector requires that it be seen as a system of functionality inter-related and inter-dependent elements, each of which contributes to the existing and potential level of performance of the sector.

The design and development of "AgRIS" will be based on the improved version of the seven-layered architectural model, proposed by Zhu Zesheng and Sun Ling (1996), for agricultural resources management:

- ⋆ Application layer,
- ⋆ Management layer,
- ⋆ Decision models layer,
- ⋆ Decision data layer,
- ⋆ Production data layer,
- ⋆ Weather data layer, and
- ⋆ Environmental data layer.

This project has envisaged creation of metadata, and application of OpenGIS model for optimal utilisation of agricultural resources.

The content of the AgRIS will be based on Mollet (1984), who recommends data and information on basic resources such as (i) soil resources, (ii) water resources, (iii) climate resources, and other data sets (collated from Remote Sensing as well as conventional means) such as (iv) basic data on crops, (v) animal husbandry and fisheries, (vi) genetic (plant, animal & fisheries) materials, (vii) land ownership, (viii) Socio-economic data, (viii) infrastructure for agricultural development.

A stocktaking and diagnostic survey is needed early in the planning process to provide information about the wide range of factors, among the others, influencing agricultural performance:

- ★ Agro-climatic data
- ★ Agro-economic data
- ★ Agro-forestry Resources
- ★ Animal Resources
- ★ Capital Resources
- ★ Climate Resources
- ★ Crops and Cropping Systems
- ★ Environment data
- ★ Fisheries Resources
- ★ Forestry Resources
- ★ Institutional Resources
- ★ Land owners data
- ★ Plant Resources
- ★ Socio-economic & Infra-structure data
- ★ Soil Resources
- ★ Spices Resources
- ★ Water Resources.

The proposed AgRIS includes:

* Raw data at different spatial levels (Farm, Village, Block & District);
* Raw data translated into indicators, which add value to the data and link it to a specific purpose; and
* A number of indicators aggregated into an "index", which gives information, a meaning beyond its face value ["An index seeks to reduce a large quantity of data down to its simplest form, retaining the essential meaning for the questions that are being asked of the data"].

All the above three types of information should be rendered sensitive and relevant to suit the needs of diagnostic research in the five different ecosystems, recognized in the NATP project viz. Arid, Coastal, Hill & Mountain, Irrigated and Rainfed.

Different physical, social or cultural perspectives do not only cause the differences in different regions, but also by the stage of development and management of environmental problems. Thus the varied types of information required for the pilot project studies must be tuned to the needs of the different geographical regions of the country. Evolving a Geospatial perspective of agricultural resources for a viable society in a rural space will, thus, mean "actions for facilitating the productivity per unit of available land and water resources and for monitoring the impact of technology inputs on the viability of physical environment of the rural society:

a. "Resource Degradation" does not exceed "Resource Productivity"
b. "System Production" does not exceed "Resource Productivity"
c. "Purchased Inputs" do not degrade "Resource Base"
d. "Value of System Production" exceeds "Value of Inputs"

For successful implementation of this project, all the respective State and UT Agricultural Departments will be both shareholders and stakeholders of the Project. Inputs from the already ongoing CAPE and FASAL projects of the DAC (being undertaken in collaboration with the Department of Space) are envisaged for integration appropriately. The Department of Science & Technology (DST) has assisted the State of Punjab, under its NRDMS Programme, through a UNDP supported project on "Information Technology for Agriculture". Best practices adopted and methodologies developed for this project will be taken into consideration. The project will benefit from the works already done in the districts, if any. Agricultural Resources information System (AgRIS) will eventually become the "National Spatial Data Infrastructure (NSDI) for Agriculture".

## Implementation Methodology

For developing Agricultural Resources Information System (AgRIS), as a decision-support system and demonstrating its value as guide to policy formulation and planning, focusing on a number of key issues relevant to agricultural planning, it is necessary to conduct some unique experimental pilot project studies, in different geographical regions of the country, with markedly different requirements of spatial and non-spatial database for policy formulation and planning.

National Informatics Centre (NIC) will be the nodal agency to implement this programme, through institutional linkages with both the State and National Institutions, and Government/ Non-Governmental Organisations, who have specialised expertise on dealing with the problems identified for the pilot districts of different typologies.

These Institutions will have specialisation in quantitative spatial planning techniques as well as GIS applications. In addition, various other institutions (government and non-government) will be utilised for data collection, digitalisation and analysis. NIC will undertake system integration with the involvement of district functionaries dealing with agricultural development. The selected institutions will keep the following objectives in mind: -

- ★ To prepare a comprehensive database on production practices and production systems for a diversified agricultural development of the selected district, including animal husbandry, crop husbandry, dairying, fishery, floriculture, horticulture, poultry, agro-processing and agri-markets;
- ★ To compile the data on the above mentioned areas from farm, village, block, and the district levels;
- ★ To study the farming systems, farming practices, access to market and problems facing the small farmer;
- ★ Through intensive village surveys, using participatory approaches, collect data on agricultural production and production practices, technologies in use, and the physical, biophysical and socio-economic problems relating to development, and the priority needs of the villagers.
- ★ To prepare prototype development plans for village, block and district development;
- ★ To foresee, in the light of changing local consumption practices, the new market demands that will arise during the period upto 2020 and coping with such challenges;
- ★ To access the export opportunities in the light of technological empowerment of the farmer and his entrepreneurial abilities;
- ★ To understand the problems in achieving food and nutrition security and alleviation of poverty and hunger during the period upto 2020;

★ To visualize the off-farm and non-farm opportunities that could be created during the period upto 2020.

## Participating Institutions

About all the Institutions of the Central Government and State Governments involved in various aspects of agricultural development will be consulted, in the process, for the development of Agricultural Resources Information System (AgRIS) in the Country.

## Organisational structure

The AgRIS project as envisaged above, involves an intensive study of the selected district and its problems. In order to ensure the successful development of the selected pilot projects, special institutional mechanisms have to be created. Throughout the duration of the project, technical guidance has to be imparted, with detailed technical guidelines for the necessary surveys and studies.

The project will be closely monitored and its progress evaluated from time-to-time, to enable corrective measures to be taken in due time. It is visualized that such technical guidance, monitoring and evaluation tasks are done by a third party "Planning-Oriented Organisation", in the nature of a technical NGO (such as the "Bhoovigyan Vikas Foundation" at New Delhi).

## Implementing Agency

National Informatics Centre (NIC) will be the Project Implementing Agency through institutional participatory approach. The Agricultural Informatics Division of NIC will be the Project Directorate.

## Budget Estimates

The AgRIS project will get implemented, through Institutional Participatory Mode, in a distributed collaborative manner. As this project implementation will be on pilot scale in eight identified typology, the project components, given below, are essential to make the pilot projects successful and get transferred to the respective district authorities for enriching as "model centres".

The development of Agricultural Resources Information System (AgRIS) will become an effective channel of communication between policy makers, government agencies, academic and research institutions and persons concerned with the complex role of agriculture in society. Agriculture Resources Information System (AgRIS) provides a new approach to agricultural input applications. This approach involves development of tools that will regulate the amount of crop input applied to a field based on the actual need. A key component to this approach is the utilisation of Geomatics technology, which provides the visual integration of all the data sources tied to an agricultural field and allows farmers to identify the within-field variability of their systems. It also aims to promote and coordinate developments in the field of agricultural resources. The AgRIS is thus envisaged ushering in "informatics led agriculture" to foster agricultural growth, reduce poverty, and sustainable use of resources. Deliverables will be "DSSs on Production Practices and Systems" and "creation of metadata" to become the Country's initiative of "NSDI on Agriculture"

# Bibliography


1. Arms, W. Y. (2000). Digital Libraries. Cambridge, MA: MIT Press.
2. Bhattacharya, Partha. "Advances in Digital Library Initiatives: A Developing Country Perspective." The International Information & Library Review 36.3 (2004): 165-175. Library & Information Science. WilsonWeb. U of British Columbia Library. 9 Mar. 2006 <http://tinyurl.com/fwfbf>.
3. Birmingham, W. (1995). University of Michigan Digital Library Project. [Homepage online at]: http://http2.sils.umich.edu/UMDL/
4. Borgman, C. (1996). Social Aspects of Digital Libraries (NSF Workshop Report). Los Angeles: UCLA. Feb. 16-17, 1996. [Online at]: http://www-lis.gseis.ucla.edu/DL/
5. Borgman, C. L. (1999). What are digital libraries? Competing visions. Information Processing and Management, 35(3), 227-243.
6. Borgman, C., & Fox, E. A. (2001). Proceedings of the First Joint Conference on Digital Libraries. June 24-28, 2001. New York: ACM Press.[Online at]: http://www.jcdl.org

7. Brundtland, G. H: Global change and our common future, Environment. 13 (1989).

8. Bush, V. (1945). As We May Think. Atlantic Monthly, 176, 101-108.

9. Cassel, L., & Fox, E. A. (2000). ACM Journal of Education Resources in Computing. [Online at]: http://purl.org/net/JERIC/

10. Chandler, W. Worldwatch paper, n.72. Worldwatch Institute, Washington.

11. Chen, S., & Fox, E. A. (1996). Guest Editors' Introduction to Special Issue on Digital Libraries. Journal of Visual Communication and Image Representation, 7, 1.

12. Chowdhury, Gobinda G. "Digital Divide: How Can Digital Libraries Bridge the Gap?" Online. Lecture Notes in Computer Science 2555 (2002): 379-391. 7 Mar. 2006 <http://www.cis.strath.ac.uk/research/publications/papers/strath_cis_publication_334.pdf>

13. Cronin B. (1998) "Social dimensions of the digital revolution". Journal of Information, Communication and Library Science, 4 (4)

14. CSCS Media and Culture Archive http://www.cscsban.org/html/media_archive.htm

15. Daly, H. E. and Cobb, J. B. For the common good: Redirecting the economy toward community, the environment and a sustainable future (Boston: Beacon Press. 1989).

16. Das Neves, F. A., & Fox, E. A. (2000). A study of user behavior in an immersive Virtual Environment for digital libraries, Proceedings of the Fifth ACM Conference on Digital Libraries: DL '00, June 2-7, 2000, San Antonio, TX (pp. 103-111). New York: ACM Press.

17. DeSolla Price, D. J. Little science, big science. Columbia University Press, New York, 1963.
18. Digital Library Initiative, FY 1994, A joint initiative of the National Science Foundation, the Advanced Research Projects Agency, and the National
19. Digital Library of India: www.new.dli.ernet.in
20. Digital Library of Georgea : http://www.public.lib.ga.us/homeplace/
21. Digital South Asia Library: http://dsal.uchicago.edu
22. Dougherty, W. C., & Fox, E. A. (1995). TULIP at Virginia Tech. Library Hi Tech, 13(4), 54-60.
23. Dublin Core Community. (1999). Dublin Core Metadata Initiative. [Online at]: http://purl.org/dc
24. Dumais, S. T. (1998). References to LSI Papers. [Online at]: http://superbook.bellcore.com/~std/lsiPapers.html
25. eGranary Digital Library. 2006. The WiderNet Project at the University of Iowa. 6 Mar. 2006 <http://www.widernet.org/digitallibrary/>.
26. Elder, K. I. The rise of counter-culture movements against modernity: Nature as a new field of class struggle, Theory, Culture and Society. 7 (1990), 21-47.
27. Emmerij, L. High tech and responsible growth, Development. 2 (1987).
28. ERNET, India New Delhi, Digital Library - http://www.digitallibrary.ernet.in
29. Eyerman, R. and Jamison, A. Social movements: A cognitive approach. The Pennsylvania State University Press, Philadelphia, PA. 1991.
30. Fahmi, Ismail. "The Indonesian Digital Library Network is Born to Struggle with the Digital Divide." The International Information & Library Review 34.2 (2002):

153-174. Library & Information Science. WilsonWeb. U of British Columbia Library. 9 Mar. 2006 <http://tinyurl.com/lyaqu>.

31. Fosmire, M. and Young, E. (2000) "Free Scholarly Electronic Journals: An Annotated Webliography". Issues in Science and Technology Librarianship, No. 28 http://www.istl.org/00-fall/internet.html

32. Fox, E and Lunin, L. Introduction and Overview to Perspectives onDigital Libraries, Journal of the American Society for Information Science (JASIS) 44(8), 441-443, (Sept. 1993).

33. Fox, E. (1997). Networked Digital Library of Theses and Dissertations: An International Collaboration Promoting Scholarship. ICSTI Forum, Quarterly Newsletter of the International Council for Scientific and Technical Information, 26, 8-9. [Online at]: http://www.icsti.org/icsti/forum/fo9711.html#ndltd

34. Fox, E. (1999). The Digital Libraries Initiative: Update and Discussion: Guest editor's introduction to Special Section. Bulletin of the American Society of Information Science, 26(1), 7-11.

35. Fox, E. A. (1983). Some Considerations for Implementing the SMART Information Retrieval System under UNIX (Technical report TR 83-560). Ithaca, NY: Cornell University, Computer Science Department.

36. Fox, E. A. (1993). Sourcebook on Digital Libraries: Report for the National Science Foundation. (Technical Report TR-93-35). Blacksburg, VA: Dept. of Computer Science, Virginia Tech. [Online at]: fox.cs.vt.edu

37. Fox, E. A. (1998). Digital Libraries: Preparing the Next Generation of Scholars. Paper presented at the NFAIS'98, Philadelphia, PA. Feb. 24, 1998. [Online at]: http://

www.ndltd.org/talks/NFAIS98.ppt

38. Fox, E. A. (1998). Digital Library Courseware. Virginia Tech, Department of Computer Science: Blacksburg, VA. [Online at]: http://ei.cs.vt.edu/~dlib/

39. Fox, E. A. (1999b). The 5S Framework for Digital Libraries and Two Case Studies: NDLTD and CSTC, Proceedings NIT'99. Taipei, Taiwan. [Online at]: http://www.ndltd.org/pubs/nit99fox.doc

40. Fox, E. A., & Lunin, L. (1993). Introduction and Overview to Perspectives on Digital Libraries; guest editor's introduction to special issue. Journal of the American Society Information Science, 44, 441-443.

41. Fox, E. A., & Marchionini, G. (1996). Proceedings of the First ACM International Conference on Digital Libraries, DL '96. Bethesda, MD; New York: ACM.

42. Fox, E. A., Hall, R., & Kipp, N. (1997). NDLTD: Preparing the Next Generation of Scholars for the Information Age. The New Review of Information Networking (NRIN), 3, 59-76. [Online at]: http://www.ndltd.org/pubs/nrin.pdf

43. Fox, E. A., Hall, R., Kipp, N. A., Eaton, J. L., McMillan, G., & Mather, P. (1997b). NDLTD: Encouraging International Collaboration in the Academy. Special Issue on Digital Libraries of DESIDOC Bulletin of Information Technology (DBIT), 17(6), 45-56. [Online at]: http://www.ndltd.org/pubs/dbit.pdf

44. Fox, E. A., Hix, D., Nowell, L., Bruen, D., Wake, W., Heath, L., & Rao, D. (1993). Users, User Interfaces, and Objects: Envision, a Digital Library. Journal of the American Society Information Science, 44, 480-491.

45. Fox, E. Digital Libraries, IEEE Computer 26(11), 79-81, (Nov. 1993).

46. Fox, E., France, R., Sahle, E., Daoud, A., & Cline, B. (1993a). Development of a Modern OPAC: From REVTOLC to MARIAN, Proceedinds 16th Annual International ACM SIGIR Conference on R&D in Information Retrieval, SIGIR '93 (pp. 248-259). Pittsburgh: ACM Press.

47. Fox, E.A. (ed.), Source Book on Digital Libraries, TR 93-35, Dept. of Computer Science, Virginia Tech, (1993); available using anonymous FTP to fox.cs.vt.edu

48. France, R. K. (2000). MARIAN Digital Library Information System. [Online at]: http://www.dlib.vt.edu/products/marian.html

49. Fritz, Mark. Food For Thought: Localized Content Aids Disconnected Africa. EContent 28.7/8 (2005): 10-11. Academic Premier. EBSCO. U of British Columbia. 7 Mar. 2006 <http://tinyurl.com/ez32j>.

50. Fromholz,Ingo, Knezevic, Predrag et al., Supporting Information Access in Next Generation Digital Library Architectures. In Proceedings of the Sixth Thematic Workshop of the EU Network of Excellence DELOS(2004).

51. Fumento, M. Science under siege: Balancing technology and the environment. William Morrow and Company, Inc, New York, 1993.

52. Gladney, H. M. (1998). Safeguarding Digital Library Contents and Users: Interim Retrospect and Prospects. D-Lib Magazine, 4(7). [Online at]: http://www.dlib.org/dlib/july98/gladney/07gladney.html

53. Gladney, H. M., Mintzer, F., Schiattarella, F., Bescos, J., & Treu, M. (1998). Digital Access to Antiquities. Communications of the ACM, 41, 49-57.

54. Goldsmith, E. The World Bank: Global financing or

impoverishment and famine. Ecologist. 15 (1985).

55. Heath, L., Hix, D., Nowell, L., Wake, W., Averbock, G., & Fox, E. A. (1995). Envision: A User-Centered Database from the Computer Science Literature. Communications of the ACM, 38, 52-53.

56. Hettne, B. Three worlds of crisis for the nation-state. Development. 2/3 (1982).

57. Hirsch, F. Social limits to growth. The Twentieth Century Fund, New York, 1976.

58. Hirschmann, A. Essays in trespassing. Cambridge University Press, London, 1981.

59. Hong, J.-S., Chen, H.-Y., & Hsiang, J. (2000). A Digital Museum of Taiwanese Butterflies, Proceedings of the Fifth ACM Conference on Digital Libraries: DL '00, June 2-7, 2000, San Antonio, TX (pp. 260-261). New York: ACM Press. [Online at]: http://digimuse.nmns.edu.tw

60. IGNCA Digital Library: www.ignca.nic.in/dgt_0001.htm

61. Indian National Library in Engineering Science and Technology Consortium (INDEST), IIT-Delhi-http://www.indest.iitd.ac.in

62. Indira Gandhi National Center for Arts (IGNCA), New Delhi - www.ignca.gov.in

63. INFLIBNET: Information and Library Network Centre: www.inflibnet.ac.in

64. International Standard Maintenance Agency Z39.50. (2000). International Standard Maintenance Agency Z39.50. The Library of Congress Network Development and MARC Standards Office, Washington, DC. [Online at]: http://lcweb.loc.gov/z3950/agency/, September 9, 2000

65. International Telecommunication Union. "The Digital Divide at a Glance." 2005. Executive Secretariat, World Summit on the Information Society (WSIS). 17 Mar. 2006 <http://www.itu.int/wsis/tunis/newsroom/stats/>.

66. Johnson, J. S. Computerizing information systems in developing countries: Keys to sustainable development, PBL XXII (3) (1991), 22-30.

67. Kates, Robert W. Sustaining life on earth, Scientific American. October (1994), 114-122.

68. Kilker, J., & Gay, G. (1998). The Social Construction of a Digital Library: A Case Study Examining Implications for Evaluation. Information Technology and Libraries, 17, 60-70. [Online at]: http://www.lita.org/ital/ital1702.htm

69. Lagoze, C., & Davis, J. R. (1995). Dienst: An Architecture for Distributed Document Libraries. Communications of the ACM, 38, 47.

70. Lagoze, C., & Payette, S. (1998). An Infrastructure for Open-Architecture Digital Libraries (TR98-1690): Cornell University, Computer Science.

71. Lavoie, B. (2003) "The Incentives to Preserve Digital Materials: Roles, Scenarios, and Economic Decision-Making". White paper, OCLC Research http://www.oclc.org/research/projects/digipres/incentives-dp.pdf (747K/51pp)

72. Lesk, M. (1997). Practical Digital Libraries: Books, Bytes and Bucks. San Francisco: Morgan Kaufmann Publishers.

73. Lesk, M. (1999). Perspectives on DLI-2 - Growing the Field. D-Lib Magazine, 5(7/8). [Online at]: http://www.dlib.org/dlib/july99/07lesk.html

74. Levi-Strauss, C. Antropologia Enciclopedia del Novecento, 1. Treccani, Roma, 1975.

75. Licklider, J. C. R. (1965). Libraries of the Future. Cambridge, MA: MIT Press.

76. Lor, Peter Johan. "National Libraries and the Digital Divide." Mousaion 21.2 (2003): 62-78. Library and Information Science Abstracts. CSA Illumina. Online. 7 Mar. 2006 <http://www.nla.gov.au/initiatives/meetings/cdnl/2003/09digdiv.pdf>.

77. Lutz, M. Toward humanistic development economics, Development, 3 (1986).

78. Marchionini, G., & Fox, E. A. (1999). Progress toward digital libraries: Augmentation through integration; Guest Editor's Introduction to Special Issue on Digital Libraries. Information Processing and Management, 35, 219-225.

79. Marsden, Gary, Robert Cherry & Alan Haefele. "Small Screen Access to Digital Libraries." CHI (2002). Online. 7 Mar. 2006 <http://www.chi-sa.org.za/CHI-SA2001/smallscreens.pdf>.

80. Mathur, Akshay, and Dhirubhai Ambani. "ICT and Rural Societies: Opportunities for Growth." The International Information & Library Review 37.4 (2005): 345-351. Library, Information Science & Technology Abstracts. EBSCO. U of British Columbia. 7 Mar. 2006 <http://tinyurl.com/gwzh5>.

81. Melnik, S., Garcia-Molina, H., & Paepcke, A. (2000). A Mediation Infrastructure for Digital Library Services. Paper presented at the Proceedings of the Fifth ACM Conference on Digital Libraries, San Antonio, Texas.

82. Melucci, A. Liberation or meaning? Social movements, culture and democracy, Development and Change. 23, 3 (1992).

83. Melucci, A. The nomads of present. Temple University Press, Philadelphia, 1989.

84. Menou, Michel ed. Measuring the impact of information on development. International Development Research Centre, Ottawa, Canada, 1994.

85. Menou, Michel. The impact of information on development: Results of a preliminary investigation, Paper presented at the 3rd Int. Information Research Conf. at Poigny - la Foret, France, 11-13th July, 1993.

86. Miner, Edward A. and Cliff Missen. "Internet in a Box: Augmenting Bandwidth with the eGranary Digital Library." Africa Today 52.2 (2005): 21-37. Project Muse. U. of British Columbia. 6 Mar. 2006 <http://muse.jhu.edu/journals/africa_today/v052/52.2miner.html>.

87. Mintzer, F., Boyle, L., Cazes, A., Christian, B., Cox, S., Giordano, F., Gladney, H., Lee, J., Kelmanson, M., Lirani, A., Magerlein, K., Pavani, A., & Schiattarella, F. (1996). Towards online worldwide access to Vatican Library materials. IBM Journal of Research and Development, 40, 139-162.

88. Moen, W. E. (1998). Accessing Distributed Cultural Heritage Information. Communications of the ACM, 41, 45-48.

89. Morris, Expert systems for library and information services - a review, Information Processing and Management 27(3), 713-724, (1991).

90. Mydral, G. Development and underdevelopment. National Bank of Egypt Press, Cairo, 1973.

91. Nadler, I. A. Ignoring the limits to growth. IEEE Technology and Society Magazine. Summer (1993), 24-28.

92. Niang, T. For a sustainable agricultural information system in French speaking Africa, Bulletin of the American Society for Information Science. Dec/Jan (1993), 19-20.

93. Nicholas, C., Crowder, G., & Soboroff, I. (2000). CARROT: An Agent-Based Architecture for Large-Scale Document Information Systems (TR CS-2000-01). Baltimore: UMBC.

94. Noerr, P. (Ed.). (2000). The Digital Library Toolkit (2nd ed.). Palo Alto, CA: Sun Microsystems, Inc.

95. Nowell, L., & Hix, D. (1992). User interface design for the project Envision database of computer science literature. Twenty-second Annual Virginia Computer Users Conference (pp. 29-33). Blacksburg, VA.

96. Nowell, L., & Hix, D. (1993). Visualizing search results: User interface development for the project Envision database of computer science literature. Advances in Human Factors/Ergonomics, Proceedings of HCI International '93, 5th International Conference on Human Computer Interaction (Vol. 19B, Human-Computer Interaction: Software and Hardware Interfaces, pp. 56-61). Elsevier.

97. Ogunsola, L.A. "Information and Communication Technologies and the Effects of Globalization: Twenty-First Century "Digital Slavery" for Developing

98. Paepcke, A. (1999). Using the InfoBus. Palo Alto: Stanford University Digital Libraries Project. [Online at]: http://www-diglib.stanford.edu/diglib/pub/userinfo.html

99. Paepcke, A., Chang, C.-C. K., Garcia-Molina, H., & Winograd, T. (1998). Interoperability for Digital Libraries Worldwide. Communications of the ACM, 41, 33-43.

100. Payette, S., Blanchi, C., Lagoze, C., & Overly, E. A. (1999).

Interoperability for Digital Objects and Repositories: The Cornell/CNRI Experiments. D-Lib Magazine, 5(5). [Online at]: http://www.dlib.org/dlib/may99/payette/05payette.html

101. Pearce, D. Blueprint for a green economy. Routledge, London, 1989.

102. Poitevein, G. AIBD: A valuable endeavor in agricultural in agricultural libraries and information services for Latin America and the Caribbean, International Journal of Information and Library Research. 4, 2 (1992), 149-152.

103. Powell, J., & Fox, E. (1998). Multilingual Federated Searching Across Heterogeneous Collections. D-Lib Magazine, 4(8). [Online at]: http://www.dlib.org/dlib/september98/powell/09powell.html

104. Rao, R., Pedersen, J. O., Hearst, M. A., Mackinlay, J. D., Card, S. K., Masinter, L., Halvorsen, P.-K., & Robertson, G. G. (1995). Rich Interaction in the Digital Library. Communications of the ACM, 38, 29-39.

105. Resnick, T. Turtles, termites and traffic jams: Explorations in massively parallel micro world. The MIT Press, The MIT Press, 1994.

106. Rodriguez, A. (2001) "The digital divide: the view from Latin America and the Caribbean". In 67th IFLA Council and General Conference, Boston, USA, August www.ifla.org/IV/ifla67/papers/111-114e.pdf

107. Rothenberg, J. Avoiding Technological Quicksand: Finding a Viable Technical Foundation for Digital Preservation. Rep. to Council on Library and Information Resources, January 1999.

108. Salton, G. (1968). Automatic Information Organization and Retrieval. New York: McGraw-Hill.

109. Sánchez, J. A., & Leggett, J. L. (1997). Agent services for users of digital libraries. Journal of Network and Computer Applications, 20, 45-58.

110. Sánchez, J. A., Leggett, J. J., & Schnase, J. L. (1997). AGS: Introducing agents as services provided by digital libraries, Proceedings of the Second ACM International Conference on Digital Libraries (DL'97) (pp. 75-82). Philadelphia: ACM.

111. Sánchez, J. A., Lopez, C. A., & Schnase, J. L. (1998). An agent-based approach to the construction of floristic digital libraries, Proceedings of the Third ACM International Conference in Digital Libraries (DL´98) (pp. 210-216). Pittsburgh: ACM.

112. Saracevic, Tefko. Information science: Origin, evolution and relation, in Proc. Int. Conf. on Conceptions of Library and Information Science: Historical, Empirical and Theoretical Perspectives held at the University of Tampere, Finland, August 26-28, 1991.

113. Saracevic, Tefko. Perception of the needs for scientific and technical information in less developed countries, Journal of Documentation. 36, 3 (1980), 213-237.

114. Sen, A. The basic needs approach to development vs. NIEO, World Development. 7 (1979).

115. Shibanda, G. G. (2001) "Skills and competencies for digital information management in Africa". In 67th IFLA Council and General Conference, Boston, USA, August www.ifla.org/IV/ifla67/papers/009-143e.pdf

116. Shiva, V. Receiving the real meaning of sustainability. In The environment in question. eds. D.Cooper., J. Palmer. Routledge, London, 1992.

117. Sornil, O. (2000). A Distributed Inverted Index for a Large-Scale, Dynamic Digital Library. Unpublished Ph.

D. Dissertation Draft. Virginia Tech., Blacksburg: Department of Computer Science.

118. Springer-Verlag. (2000). International Journal on Digital Libraries, Springer-Verlag. [Online at]: http://link.springer-ny.com/link/service/journals/00799/

119. Tolba, M. K. Sustainable development: Constraints and opportunities. Butterworths, London, 1987.

120. Tolba, M. K. Sustainable development: Differing perspectives of ecologist and economist, and the relevance to LDCs, World Development. 16, 3 (1988).

121. Universal Library Project (www.ulib.org)

122. Van de Sompel, H. (2000). Open Archives Initiative. WWW site: Universteit van Ghent: OAI Group. [Online at]: http://www.openarchives.org

123. Van de Sompel, H., & Lagoze, C. (2000). The Santa Fe Convention of the Open Archives Initiative. D-Lib Magazine, 6(2). [Online at]: http://www.dlib.org/dlib/february02vandesompel-oai/02vandesompel-oai.html

124. Vidyanidhi Digital Library, University of Mysore. - www.vidyanidhi.org.in

125. Weerasinghe, Shivanthi. "Revolution Within the Revolution: The Sri Lankan Attempt to Bridge the Digital Divide through E-governance." The International Information & Library Review 36.4 (2004): 319-327. Library & Information Science. WilsonWeb. U of British Columbia Library. 9 Mar. 2006 <http://tinyurl.com/zz8nl>.

126. Witten, I.H., Loots, M., Trujillo, M.F. and Bainbridge, D. (2001) "The promise of digital libraries in developing countries". Communications of the ACM, 44(5) May, 82-85

127. Witten, Ian H. "Digital Libraries and Society: New Perspectives on Information Dissemination." In Design and Usability of Digital Libraries: Case Studies in the Asia Pacific, edited by Y.L. Theng, et al. Information Science Publishing, 2005. 191-215. Online. 7 Mar. 2006 <http://www.cs.waikato.ac.nz/~ihw/DLs.and.society.pdf>.

128. World Commission on Environment and Development. Our common future. Oxford University Press, New York, 1987.

129. Zhao, J. (1999). Making Digital Libraries Flexible, Scalable, and Reliable: Reengineering the MARIAN System in JAVA. Unpublished Master of Science Thesis, Virginia Tech, Blacksburg, VA: Department of Computer Science. [Online at]: http://scholar.lib.vt.edu/theses/available/etd-070499-204531/unrestricted/SGML-etd

# Index


**A**

AAAS, 121

Acquisition of Digital Resources, 81-2

Agricultural Resources, 380

AGRIS, 378-94

AICTE, 189

Anthropology Plus, 240

Arabic cataloging, 212

Archives Hub, 227

Art History Bibliography, 241

Association of Women in Science, 121

Atoms for Peace, 243-4

**B**

Batch Processing, 211

Best Book Approach, 40-41

Book Reviews from Internet, 365

Britain in Print, 228

Broadband VSAT, 356

Bush, Vannevar, 5

**C**

CALIBER, 345

CALIBNET, 370-8

Campus LANs CatExpress, 211

CatMe, 212

Central Council for Industrial Research, 184

Centre for Study of Culture and Media Society, 177

CIL, 191

CJK Cataloging, 212

Collaborative Resource Management, 326

Collection analysis, 214

Confile Service, 374-6

Content Building, 166

Content Selection, 13, 149

CONTENTdm, 215

Controlling access, 80

Copyright laws, 30-31

Copyrighted materials, 39-40

CovDoc, 212

CSCS Media Archives, 178-9

CSIR, 184

Cultural Information Laboratory, 191

CURL Databases, 223

CURL, 220-32

CURL-CoFoR, 228
Cushman Collection, 109
Custom Cataloging, 211

**D**

Data Centre, 354
DEL-LISTSERV, 365-6
DELNET Products, 368-70
DELNET, 359-67
DELSEARCH, 369-70
DELSIS, 368
DEL-WINDOWS, 369
DIDO,106-7
Digital Archive, 215
    eContent, 216
Digital Image Online, 106-7
Digital Leased Lines, 355-6
Digital Media and Image Centre, 107-8
Digital Music Library, 110
Digital preservation, 62-4
Document Transfer, 366
Dublin Core, 139

**E**

Education Development Centre, 123
Eduprise, 123
E-education, 342-3
Electronic Atlas of Central Indiana, 111-2
Electronic Collection Online, 214
Electronic Mail, 367
Electronic subscription of Journals, 355
Electronic Theses and Dissertations, 159-60
Energy Technology Data Exchange, 249-50
ERD List serv, 167
ERNET, 351
Errata, 324-5
eScholarship Editions, 62
eScholarship Publications, 62
eScholarship Repository, 62
E-scholarship, 61-2

**F**

Federated Search, 129
FirstSearch, 217
Food and Agriculture Organization, 379-80

**G**

GALILIO, 90-1
Geographic Information system, 112
Georgia HomePLACE, 100-1
Grantha, 173
Greenstone, 171

**H**

Historical Aerial Archive, 112
Hosting Services, 130
Humanities and Social Sciences Index, 241-2

**I**

IAEA, 243-5
IFAP, 287-94
IFIP World Computer Congress, 262
IFIP, 260-6
IGNCA, 190-3
ILL Manager, 238
ILL Online, 364
ILLiad,218
ILumina, 124
Index to Hindu, 365-6
Index to Periodical Literature, 254
Indian Doctoral Research, 162

Indian National Institute for Science Communication and Information Resources, 184
Indiana Geographical Information Catalog, 112-3
Indira Gandhi National Centre for the Arts, 190-3
INDSET, 188-90
INDSET-AICTE Consortium, 189
INIS Reference Series, 253
IN1S Database, 245-6, 250
INIS Non-conventional literature, 251-2
INIS Secretariat, 246-7
INIS, 243-60
Inspec Archive, 281-3
Instructional Architect, 124
Interactive University, 124
Interface, 81
Interim Database, 224
International Atomic Energy Agency, 243-5
International Development Research Centre, 268
Internet Scout, 124
Intranet for Universities, 352
IPL,9
IPL, Role of, 12
ISC11, 138,

**K**

KidSpace, 22
Knowledge Conservancy, 49-53

**L**

Learning Matrix, 124
Library Bill of Right, 11
Library of Congress, 46 7
Licklier, 5
Lilavati, 174
Literature Selection Technical Review Committee, Loansome Doc, 314
Local Area Network, 342

**M**

Marcadia@cataloging, 239-40
Maths Forum, 125
Medical Literature Analysis and Retrieval System Online, 304-33
MEDLARS, 326
Medline Plus, 314-6
Melvyl@catalog, 56
Merit Network, 125
MeSH, 316-8, 329-30
Michigan Teacher Network, 126

**N**

Nagpur Declaration, 382
National Centre for Biotechnology Information, 305
National Information System for Science and Technology, 359
National Institute of Health, 304
National Library of Medicine, 304
Natural Resources Information System 381
NCBI, 305
NetLibrary, 214
NetLibrary, 216
Network Access Centre, 357
Network, Architecture, 354
Network-Trained Manpower, 357-8
Newspaper, 20NIH, 304
NISCAIR, 184
NISSAT, 359
NLM Gateway, 321-4
NLM, 304

Non-copyrighted materials, 37-9
NRIS, 381

**O**

OCLC Databases, 217
OCLC, 209-220
OCR, 33-4
OECD/NEA, 249
OLDMEDLINE Data, 326
Olive, 215
Online Databases, 363-4
Online newspaper, 20-21
Optical Character Recognition, 33-4

**P**

PADIS, 266-73
PADISNET, 271-2
PAIS International, 216
PARAPAR, 376
Philanthropic Studies Index, 113-4
PMC Overview, 331, 3
PRL, 202-4
Project Brief, 229-30
Project Kaleidoscope, 127
PrompCat, 211
PubMed, 318-9
Puranas, 173
PURL, 139

**Q**

QuestionPoint,217

**R**

Referral Services, 366
Resource Discovery, 226
Resource Sharing, 362
Retro-Conversion, 366
RLG Cultural Materials, 242-3
RLG Online Databases, 237-8
RLG Serial File, 243
RLG, 232-43
RLG's Archival Resources, 240-1

**S**

SAARC, 183
SANJUKTA, 371
Satellite based Wide Area Network, 356
Scanning, 32-3
SCPC VSATs, 357
SHARES, 238
SOUL, 347
South Asian Association for Regional Cooperation, 183
Sri Sarda Pitham, 172-3
Storage, 82

**T**

TeacherLIB, 127
Technology Partnership
Test Database, 224
Transactional Interoperability, 130

**U**

UGC-Infonet, 199
UNECA, 266
Unicode, 137-8
United Nations Economic Commission for Africa, 266
University Grants Commission, 358
US Steel Photograph Collection, 109

**V**

V. V. Giri National Labour Inatitutre, 170
Victorian Women Writers Projects, 108
Vidyanidhi Database, 168
Vidyanidhi Promotional Activities, 169

Vidyanidhi Strategies, 163-6

**W**

Watch WorldCat, 213
Web Accessibility Initiative, 140-1
Wide Area Network, 342
WIPO, 183
WorlCat Collection Sets, 212
World Intellectual Property Organization, 183
WorldCat, 212-3, 218
Wright American Fiction Project, 108-9

**Z**

Z39.50 Cataloging Archive, 212